Electronic Funds Transfer Systems

Electronic Funds Transfer Systems

The Revolution in Cashless Banking and Payment Methods

PATRICK KIRKMAN

Basil Blackwell
in association with The Institute of
Chartered Accountants in England and Wales

Copyright © Patrick Kirkman 1987

First published 1987
First published in USA 1987

Basil Blackwell Ltd
108 Cowley Road, Oxford, OX4 1JF, UK

Basil Blackwell Inc.
432 Park Avenue South, Suite 1503
New York, NY 10016, USA

British Library Cataloguing in Publication Data
Kirkman, P.R.A.
Electronic funds transfer systems: the
revolution in cashless banking and
payment methods.
1. Electronic funds transfer—Great
Britain
I. Title
322.1'7   HG1710
ISBN 0–631–15317–9

Library of Congress Cataloging in Publication Data
Kirkman, Patrick R. A.
Electronic funds transfer systems.

Includes index.
1. Electronic funds transfers.   I. Title.
HG1710.K57 1987   332.1'028   86-26410
ISBN 0-631-15317-9

Typeset in 10 on 12 pt Plantin Light
by Oxford Publishing Services
Printed in Great Britain

Contents

	Preface	ix
1	Traditional Payment Systems	1
	International Payment Methods	1
	UK Payment Methods	3
	Reasons for Change	5
	Summary and Conclusions	7
2	Cash – Essential or Dispensable?	8
	Cash as a Payment Method	8
	User Viewpoints	10
	Cash Dispensing Machines	14
	Summary and Conclusions	15
3	The Cheque Business	17
	Bank Clearing Systems	18
	General Clearing	19
	Town Clearing	22
	User Viewpoints	24
	Bank Charges	26
	Cheque Guarantee Cards	29
	Future Developments	31
	Summary and Conclusions	33
4	Credit Transfers and Bank Giro Services	34
	Historical Developments	34
	Credit Clearing	36
	Business Considerations	38
	Customer Viewpoints	41
	Summary and Conclusions	42
5	The Credit Card Business	43
	Types of Cards	44
	Potential Retail Benefits	47
	Retail Costs and Problems	51
	Customer Viewpoints	54
	Card Issuer Viewpoints	57
	Future Developments	61
	Summary and Conclusions	63

6 Electronic Payment Systems 65
  Electronic Funds Transfers 66
  Current Operational Systems 68
  Future Developments 69
  Summary and Conclusions 70

7 Funds Transfer Agencies 72
  Bankers' Automated Clearing Services 73
  Clearing House Automated Payments System 79
  National Girobank 82
  Society for Worldwide Interbank Financial Telecommunication 84
  Summary and Conclusions 86

8 Direct Debit Agreements 88
  Organization and Systems 89
  Payer Viewpoints 90
  Payee Viewpoints 93
  Current Users and Applications 95
  Comparison with Standing Orders 98
  Future Developments 100
  Summary and Conclusions 102

9 Purchase Ledger Payments 104
  Traditional UK Practices 105
  Potential Benefits 105
  Costs and Problems 107
  Summary and Conclusions 110

10 Wages and Salaries 112
  Background Situation 112
  Legal Framework 114
  Employer Viewpoints 115
  Employee Viewpoints 117
  Other Interested Parties 119
  Alternatives to Cash Payment 120
  Payment Frequency and Incentives 123
  Future Developments 125
  Summary and Conclusions 126

11 Government Benefits 128
  UK Social Security Payments 129
  Government Initiatives 131
  Implementation Policies and Problems 132
  Future Developments 134
  Summary and Conclusions 137

12 Automated Cash Dispensing   138
    International Developments   139
    UK Installations   141
    Bank Viewpoints   143
    Customer Viewpoints   145
    Future Developments   146
    Summary and Conclusions   148

13 Point-of-Sale Transactions   149
    Scope and Operation   150
    Retail Viewpoints   152
    Customer Viewpoints   156
    International Developments   159
    UK Installations   162
    Future Developments   165
    Summary and Conclusions   167

14 Plastic Card Developments   168
    Magnetic Stripe Card Systems   169
    Memory Cards   172
    Future Developments   177
    Summary and Conclusions   178

15 Home and Office Banking   181
    Communication Systems   182
    International Developments   184
    UK Installations   187
    Business Considerations   190
    Summary and Conclusions   191

16 Electronic Cash Management Services   193
    Systems and Applications   194
    Benefits and Problems   197
    Bank Viewpoints   200
    Summary and Conclusions   202

17 Major Effects and Implications   204
    Consumer Interests   204
    Legal Regulations   206
    Computer Fraud and Security   209
    Employment Opportunities   212
    Government Involvement   215
    Summary and Conclusions   216

18 Payment Systems in the 1990s   218
    The Banking Sector   219
    UK Developments   220
    Hardware and Software Problems   223
    Preparation for Change   224
    Summary and Conclusions   226

    Index   229

Preface

In the last ten years changing technology has affected the lives of many individuals. For some people – especially the young – the effects have been exciting, particularly for those who enjoy using computers or electronic equipment. For others, the results have been frightening, perhaps because the end-result of the use of new technology has been an unfamiliar work situation or even the loss of a job.

Few aspects of employment have been unaffected by new technology. For some time it seemed that payment practices would be relatively unaffected as the amount of paperwork generated by till rolls and receipts, cheques, credit transfers and credit cards relentlessly increased. In retrospect it was inevitable that steps would have to be taken to reduce this flow of paper, although the small but increasing use of electronic systems has done little more than slow down the rate of increase.

The technology now exists, however, for dramatic changes to take place in payment systems, and there seems little doubt that in the 1990s there will be a rapid changeover to electronic systems. This will not lead to a cashless society by the end of the century, but it could lead to a situation in which well over 10 per cent of UK payments are arranged with the aid of electronic funds transfer (EFT) systems as opposed to about 2 per cent today.

The primary objective of this book is therefore to prepare users of payment services for the electronic systems that will undoubtedly be increasingly used over the next decade. There are, however, many different users of payment services, such as central and local government, nationalized industries, financial institutions, commercial and industrial organizations, trade unions, charities, professional organizations and private individuals, and their viewpoints may be very different depending on the type and range of payment services that is used. It may therefore be found that a few of the chapters in this book will not be of interest to very specialized users, although it is hoped that the vast majority will be helpful.

It is also hoped that the book will be read by the providers of payment services such as bankers, building society personnel and credit card employees, although they may find that the book is not written in the jargon to which they are accustomed! Communication has, however, always been one of the problems of the specialist professions, and I hope that my attempt to explain complex subject matter in readily understandable terms will be reasonably successful, although it has been assumed that the reader will have at least a superficial knowledge of computer terminology and equipment.

The book is divided into three major sections. The first section – chapters 1 to 5 – deals with traditional payment systems with particular emphasis on their advantages and problems. This is followed by the section on existing electronic systems – chapters 6 to 13 – which are now responsible for about 1¼ billion of the UK's 65 billion payments. The final section – chapters 14 to 18 – peers into the future, and examines developments of the late 1980s and 1990s, with particular emphasis on point-of-sale systems, home and office banking, and plastic card developments.

In the production of this book I have received help and advice from many different sources, such as academic colleagues, computer specialists, bankers, credit card personnel, accountants, treasurers and civil servants. Some of these advisers have read numerous chapters and I am particularly grateful for the help I have received from Derek Balmforth, Paul Collier, Alfred Kenyon, Michael Ludmon, Bill Partington, Roger Ward and Roger Williams. Any errors that are present in the final version of the book are, of course, my responsibility, and cannot be blamed in any way on those who have helped me in so many different ways.

I am also grateful to my publishers, Basil Blackwell, for the encouragement they have provided in the preparation of this book, and to the Institute of Chartered Accountants in England and Wales for their financial support and sponsorship. The views expressed in the book are, of course, my own views, and do not in any way represent the views of the Institute.

Finally I would like to thank the typists who have toiled for many hours over my handwriting and frequent alterations. Janet Woodcock has borne most of this burden, and I would like to thank her for her unfailing good humour and efficient word processing. I hope that the end-result of our efforts will be of assistance in bringing about a more widespread understanding of EFT systems.

Patrick Kirkman

To my wife and children for their support and encouragement during the many hours I have spent in the writing of this book. I hope that this book will convince my children that I am not quite as 'computer-illiterate' as they imagined!

1 Traditional Payment Systems

The first section of this book – chapters 1 to 5 – will be concerned with traditional payment systems. It is difficult to define 'traditional' systems, although in the context of this book the term is used to cover all cash and paper-based payments such as cheques and credit transfers. These methods of payment are examined in some detail because of the importance of establishing the benefits and problems attached to these popular forms of settlement.

Electronic aids are now being used to improve the processing of some of these methods of payment; for example, most cheques are now magnetically encoded to speed up bank clearing processes. In addition, some payments are processed by electronic methods with little or no paper input or output; these methods of payment, which are usually described as 'electronic funds transfer systems', will be considered from chapter 6 onwards, with both current and possible future developments being covered. An attempt will also be made to assess the effects and implications of these 'new' methods of payment, which could have a significant future influence on business and government organizations and private individuals.

INTERNATIONAL PAYMENT METHODS

Cash is still the most important method of payment in the world, although in some highly developed countries, e.g. the USA, cash payment is sometimes discouraged because of the costs involved in storage, theft, transport, etc. Nevertheless, cash is still regarded as essential in the economies of all countries, especially in the less-developed parts of the world where other payment methods are not widely used.

In many countries the postal authorities have traditionally provided an important part of the payment system. Cash registration processes, postal orders and other similar money transfer methods are extensively used, although the importance of these forms of payment has tended to decline as an increasing number of private individuals have opened bank accounts. In some parts of Europe, e.g. Germany, the Netherlands, Sweden and Switzerland, the postal giro account is extremely popular, and postal cheques and transfers from one giro bank account to another are frequently used for payment purposes. The importance of the credit transfer in these countries can be seen from an examination of table 1.1, although the compilers of this table were not able to provide a split between postal and other bank transfers.

Commercial banks dominate the payment system in most developed countries, although postal and savings banks sometimes make an important contribution. In most countries in Western Europe and North America, business payments have traditionally been made by cheque, and extensive use is still made of this method of payment, especially in countries such as the UK, France, Italy, USA and Canada (see table 1.1). Bills of exchange may also be extensively used, e.g. in Spain, but they are now mainly used for international transactions. Direct transfers from one commercial bank account to another are used for many domestic transactions; for example, the direct debit system is very popular in Japan and West Germany, although there is little usage in the USA. Paper-based

Table 1.1   Non-cash methods of payment in ten major developed countries (percentage of total volume of transactions)

	Cheques	Credit transfers	Direct debits	Credit cards
UK	61.0	23.0	6.0	8.0
France	82.5	9.2	6.2	2.1
Germany	11.0	57.0	32.0	I/S[a]
Italy	85.3	12.7	1.5	0.5
Netherlands	22.3	62.0	15.6	I/S
Sweden	20.0	72.0	1.0	7.0
Switzerland	10.6	88.0	0.8	0.5
USA	91.4	0.9	I/S	7.2
Canada	91.0	I/S	2.0	7.0
Japan	18.7	14.8	56.3	10.2

[a] I/S = insignificant.
Source: Bank for International Settlements, *Payment Systems in Eleven Developed Countries*, Bank Administration Institute, USA, 1985, p. 12. No attempt has been made to separate credit transfers and direct debits into paper-based and electronic systems as in table 1.2.

bank transfer methods are gradually being replaced by electronic transfer systems, although this will inevitably be a long-term process.

The growth in worldwide travel has produced a substantial demand for travellers cheques. These cheques are also used for domestic transactions, especially in the USA where it is often difficult to cash personal cheques when the account-holder is visiting another state. These problems are not so great in Western Europe because of the widespread acceptance of cheque guarantee cards which can be used in many different countries, e.g. the Eurocheque card. Travellers cheques are not normally included in national payment statistics. It is difficult, therefore, to estimate the scale of their use, although it is believed that worldwide turnover is in the region of £30 billion per annum.

Credit cards have become an important part of the international payment system over the last decade. These cards are not strictly speaking a method of payment by the purchaser, as the account has to be paid at a later date, although they are often the equivalent of a form of settlement as far as the retailer is concerned. The USA is the major user of the credit card in terms of the number of cards issued, but use in Europe has increased substantially in the 1980s. There are, however, reservations about them in some major countries, e.g. Germany and the Netherlands, mainly because of bank reluctance to become involved in credit card transactions.

Efforts are now being made in nearly all the major developed countries to increase the use of electronic funds transfer systems. The development of these systems is, however, in its early stages, and many experiments are currently taking place. The Americans are in some respects handicapped by their large number of banks – there are currently over 14,000 commercial banks – and there are indications that some of the more advanced schemes may be developed in Western Europe, where most countries have a small but powerful number of banks.

UK PAYMENT METHODS

Payments by private individuals are still largely in the form of cash. In most situations cash provides a quick and convenient method of settlement, especially for the substantial number of small retail transactions in which most individuals are involved. Larger transactions obviously create more problems, and non-cash methods of payment are now believed to make up the majority of consumer payments over £25.[1]

1 P. Frazer, *Plastic and Electronic Money* (Woodhead-Faulkner, 1985), p 65.

If settlement is made through the postal system, difficulties may arise in the use of cash. At one time, post office services were heavily used for this purpose with the registration of cash and the provision of postal orders. Postal orders are, however, available only for amounts up to £10, and their use has fallen from 400 million in 1970/1 to fewer than 60 million in 1984/5. One of the reasons for this change has been the substantial increase in the number of bank accounts, which has naturally produced more cheques and credit transfers. The National Girobank has also shown significant growth in the last decade and the recent decision that this organization should become a member of the Bankers Clearing House probably indicates that in the future a much more extensive range of banking services will be provided.

Credit cards have also been increasingly used in the last decade in the UK, mainly by private individuals in their transactions with business organizations. These cards are growing very rapidly in popularity, and there seems little doubt that many consumers are using this form of settlement in preference to cash and cheques, largely because payment can be spread over several weeks or months. Interest will normally have to be paid if the stipulated period of credit is exceeded.

Payments by business organizations are in most cases made by cheque, as settlement is usually made through the postal system. Central and local government bodies also make many of their payments in this form, although central government does, of course, have the responsibility for the payment of government benefits. Most of these benefits are paid in cash through the post office system, although attempts are currently being made to persuade recipients to accept non-cash methods of settlement such as payment directly into a bank account.

UK payment methods are therefore dominated by cash transactions, as can be seen from an examination of table 1.2. The number of cash payments is inevitably a very rough estimate, although most recent government and bank estimates have suggested figures in the range of 50 to 60 billion transactions.[2] In the table the figure of 60 billion is used, as this appears to be the most recent estimate of the clearing banks.[3] Cheques are obviously the second most popular method of payment with over 2.4 billion cheques being handled by the London clearing banks in 1985. Cheques cleared in Scotland and Northern Ireland and at local branch level probably increase this figure to about 3 billion. In addition, there are in the region of 0.4 billion transactions settled by means of paper-based credit transfers. Precise figures for credit card transactions are not

2 The term 'billion' is used as the equivalent of 1,000 million throughout this book.
3 *Payment Clearing Systems* (Banking Information Service, 1984), appendix 3, p. 1.

available, although most informed estimates suggest that the total number of transactions is in the region of 0.5 billion (this figure includes store cards, which were not taken into account in table 1.1).

Table 1.2 Methods of payment within the UK

Method of payment	billions of transactions per annum	%
Cash	60.0	91.9
Cheques	3.0	4.6
Paper-based credit transfers	0.4	0.6
Credit card transactions	0.5	0.8
Other paper-based transactions, e.g. postal orders	0.1	0.1
Electronic funds transfers, e.g. automated credit transfers, direct debits and cash dispensing transactions	1.3	2.0
Total	65.3	100.0

Source: Bank and credit card company estimates for 1985.

The UK is therefore a considerable distance away from a cashless society, despite all the progress that has been made in the introduction of automated methods in the last decade. Electronic funds transfer methods are now being used for over 20 per cent of non-cash payments, but these techniques have so far had little effect on the number of cash transactions. Predictions of a cashless society by the year 2000 are therefore unlikely to be fulfilled, although there will probably be a considerable increase in the number of electronic transfers over the next decade.

REASONS FOR CHANGE

There are many interested parties in the process of change in payment systems, among them central and local government, banks and other financial institutions, credit card companies, computer hardware and software organizations, telecommunication agencies, retailers and other businesses, consumers, employees and trades unions. Most of these organizations and individuals are likely to have vested interests, although this is by no means unusual when substantial changes are being considered in long-established practices.

The reasons for change must, however, be carefully examined before plans for new systems are accepted. The technology for electronic funds transfer systems is now available, but this does not mean that the proposed new systems will automatically be advantageous to all parties. Detailed examinations of existing systems will therefore be highly desirable, as little information appears to have been collected by government and businesses regarding the internal and external costs of traditional payment systems. Non-quantifiable elements will make this a difficult task, but they should not be used as an excuse for avoiding this important exercise.

In the midst of all these decision-making processes, the banks will have some difficult capital expenditure and pricing decisions to make, especially if it is decided that a national electronic funds transfer system should be made available for retail transactions. The sharing of costs between banks, retailers and consumers will be an extremely difficult task, particularly if one considers the long-term implications of some of these decisions. Banks, credit card companies and retailers naturally want to reduce the heavy handling costs associated with cash, cheques and credit card transactions, but the responses of consumers cannot be ignored, especially in those countries where it is normal for consumers to be allowed a choice of payment methods.

The interests of employees and their trades unions (if any) will also have to be carefully studied. The banking and retail sectors have traditionally been very labour-intensive, and there are obviously great dangers that one of the results of the widespread use of electronic payment systems could be severely reduced employment opportunities. Some employees and trade unions would therefore prefer that electronic payment systems were not introduced in their particular sector, although this attitude is unlikely to be accepted in the present state of technological development.

In the computer and telecommunications sectors there will obviously be many marketing opportunities in the banking and retail sectors. These opportunities will not be restricted to the UK, and it may therefore be found that companies with extensive international interests obtain most of the new business, especially in large organizations. New electronic developments should produce more employment opportunities in manufacturing, distribution and servicing, and this could be of assistance in offsetting the probable long-term reduction of jobs in banking and retailing. It is virtually certain, however, that most of the new jobs will be very different from the jobs that are no longer necessary.

The role of government in the process of change will be interesting to observe. In France there has been heavy government involvement in technological change, and financial support has been provided on a fairly generous scale. In the UK and the USA there is unlikely to be substantial government support, although decisions will have to be made as to whether government should stimulate or encourage change and, if so, what action should be taken in respect of new legislation, education and training, fraud prevention, control systems, etc.

The next decade should therefore see some very detailed examinations of traditional payment systems. The results of these processes will not necessarily mean that electronic payment methods will be adopted on a widespread basis. The long-established systems carry with them many advantages of cost and familiarity, and all the major participants will have to be convinced that changes are desirable. When electronic systems are installed, significant benefits may be obtained, although it is possible that these benefits will have to be shared out amongst interested parties more generously than some participants would like. Marketing of these systems will also be extremely important, although it is difficult to predict to what lengths the banks and other innovators will go in order to get the new systems 'off the ground'.

SUMMARY AND CONCLUSIONS

Payment systems in the UK and most other countries have traditionally been dominated by cash transactions. In addition, cheques, credit transfers and credit cards are frequently used for initial or final settlement purposes, although the scale of this can vary significantly, depending on factors such as the national state of development and local banking practices.

In the last two decades most developed countries have entered into a situation in which it has become possible for the banks and other interested organizations to introduce electronic transfers in place of paper-based methods. Developments were slow initially, but there is now a wide range of technology available to assist in the introduction of electronic systems.

In these circumstances it is essential that traditional payment methods should be carefully examined to assess their strengths and weaknesses. Such an assessment will be provided in the first five chapters of this book, followed by a detailed examination of current and possible future electronic payment systems.

2   Cash – Essential or Dispensable?

The average amount of cash in circulation in the UK in the mid-1980s was in the region of £14 billion, of which about 10 per cent was held in bank tills and vaults. These funds are mainly in the form of bank notes, although the total value of coins in circulation is now rapidly approaching £2 billion following the introduction of the £1 coin in April 1983. Most of the money in circulation outside the banking sector is held by private individuals, with an estimated 10 per cent being held by business and government organizations.[1]

There has been a substantial increase in the value of notes and coins in circulation in the last decade, largely as a result of high rates of inflation; for example, the value of cash in circulation increased from approximately £5 billion in the mid-1970s to £14 billion in the mid-1980s. There have been signs, however, that the value of cash in circulation is growing at a much slower rate than total consumer expenditure. For example, official government statistics show that between 1982 and 1985 consumer expenditure increased by about 25 per cent as compared with an increase of less than 20 per cent in cash held by the general public. There does appear to be some evidence, therefore, of a significant change in recent years from cash to other methods of settlement.

CASH AS A PAYMENT METHOD

It has already been suggested that there are in the region of 60 billion cash payments per annum in the UK, although more than half of these payments are believed to be for amounts under £1. The figures in table 1.2

1 Recent Changes in the Use of Cash, *Bank of England Quarterly Review*, December 1982, p. 519.

show that when cash transactions are compared with other forms of settlement over 91 per cent of all payments are in cash. The Inter-Bank Research Organisation (IBRO) has also carried out a survey on this subject and came to the conclusion that if payments under £1 are excluded 86 per cent of all payments are in cash.[2] This compares with figures of 88 per cent in 1981 and 93 per cent in 1976.

More precise information is available of cash transactions in value terms based on detailed surveys. The result of one of these surveys, carried out in the latter part of 1985, is shown in Table 2.1. This survey indicated that 43 per cent of the total value of payments over £3 was at that time in cash. A similar survey, carried out by IBRO in 1976 in respect of transactions over £1.50, showed that 68 per cent of the total value of payments was in cash. Taking inflation into account, this would seem to indicate that there has been a significant fall in the last decade in the comparative importance of cash payments.

Table 2.1   Methods of payment by UK adults

Type of payment	Percentage of total value
Cash	43
Cheques	33
Credit transfers and direct debits	14
Credit cards	5
Other	5
Total	100

Source: AGB Index, London, 1985. The survey covered amounts of £3 and over.

The importance of cash as a payment method will naturally vary according to the range and value of goods sold. One of the few UK retailers that has revealed information on this subject is Debenhams, which has indicated that about 60 per cent of its transactions are settled in cash, although this figure falls to 30 per cent if estimates are made in value terms.[3] These figures are probably much lower than for the retail sector as a whole, mainly because of the comparatively high average value of individual transactions in departmental stores.

Cash is therefore still a very important method of payment, especially in respect of small transactions, although it has become less important in

2 Inter-Bank Research Organisation, *Research Brief*, October 1985, p. 4.
3 Let the Banker Beware, *Banker*, December 1983, p. 65.

recent years. The precise reasons for this change are difficult to establish, although there have probably been several major influences at work; for example, the growing number of bank accounts, the issue of cheque and credit cards and the increase in non-cash methods of remuneration. These influences will all be examined in later chapters.

USER VIEWPOINTS

There are many different users of cash in the UK payments system. The viewpoints of five of these user groups will now be briefly considered:

1 *Private individuals.* There has traditionally been a strong preference amongst a substantial number of private individuals in the UK for settlement in cash regardless of the type of payment, notably wages and government benefits. The major reason for this preference would appear to be that cash provides immediate purchasing power for consumer goods and services. Most of the other payment methods that are currently available require contact with banks and card companies, which are often viewed with suspicion by elderly people and those on low incomes. Attitudes are changing, however, and the number of adults with bank and credit card accounts is growing very significantly.

Cash is also easy to store at home and carry around for shopping purposes and it is extremely convenient for small, uncomplicated transactions. It is impersonal and difficult to trace and it is therefore popular with people who do not wish their transactions to be readily identifiable; for example, tax evaders naturally carry out most of their transactions in cash!

There are, however, some important disadvantages in the holding of cash by private individuals. In recent years the average weekly wage or government benefit has increased substantially, largely as a result of high rates of inflation, and there are justifiable fears of theft, both inside and outside the home. Increasing unemployment may have increased these risks, which are frequently not covered by insurance policies.

It has also been suggested that private individuals are more likely to spend money if it is held in cash rather than a bank account. The truth behind this suggestion is difficult to establish, but it would appear that in some working-class districts there has been a tendency to spend surplus cash after provision has been made for housekeeping and other essential items. It should not be forgotten, however, that there are many greater temptations for an individual to overspend, especially when a credit card account is opened, and the person who relies on cash income will often be limited to the source of funds currently available, e.g. the weekly wage packet.

In the future there will probably be increasing pressure on the private individual to accept remuneration and government benefits by non-cash methods. These attempts to change established practices may be accompanied by incentives of one form or another and promises of improved status, but there will nevertheless be resistance from many private individuals who do not wish to use non-cash methods. In the long term, ideas will probably change as an increasing number of people begin to appreciate the advantages of a bank account. In the meantime, government ministers will undoubtedly be under pressure to introduce legislative changes to enable payers to make payments by cheque or directly into a bank account regardless of the recipient's viewpoint. Whether these pressures should be resisted is a matter that will be extensively debated over the next few years.

2 *Retailers*. In most non-retail organizations, receipts are mainly in the form of cheques or other methods of bank settlement. In the retail sector, cash settlement has always been a major element of trading activity. As a result, spending power is immediately available, provided that cash can be used as a means of payment, and there should be no risk of bad debts. Cash received may, of course, be counterfeit. This has not been regarded as a major problem in past years, although there were suggestions in the latter part of 1985 that forged notes to the value of £20 million were circulating in the UK.[4]

There are, however, numerous costs and problems attached to retail cash-holding activities. These include collection and handling costs, counting, storage, security, insurance and transport, and the possibility of theft, injury and assault. Bank charges may also be very significant, as most banks now estimate that cash handling costs them in the region of 50p per £100, assuming an average collection of notes and coins. These costs may not be passed on in full by the bank to the retailer because of competitive pressures (deficits have in the past been made up by the use of non-interest-bearing current account funds), although many retailers are now being charged between 30p and 60p per £100 for cash handling, depending on the make-up of cash receipts and withdrawals and the size of transactions.

4 Look Out There's a Fake About, *Observer*, 15 December 1985, p. 31.

Speed through the check-out point should also be carefully considered by the retailer, as the various forms of payment may take very different amounts of time. Surveys on this subject seem to indicate that the average cash payment time, including the provision of a receipt and change, is in the region of 30 seconds.[5] This is considerably faster than credit cards (about 75 seconds) and cheques (about 90 seconds). It is possible that the electronic point-of-sale debit card may eventually be quicker than a cash transaction, although there is considerable scepticism regarding this suggestion.

Many of these retailing costs are extremely difficult to quantify, and as a result there is often a lack of appreciation regarding the overall costs involved in handling cash receipts and payments. Ideally attempts should be made by the retailer to estimate these costs and split them into fixed and variable elements so that realistic comparisons can be made between cash and non-cash methods. Many of these estimates will in practice be rather arbitrary, but they should provide some data for comparison purposes. These processes will be considered again in later chapters, when the comparative costs of different methods of payment will be considered in more detail.

3 *Business payers.* In the retail sector cash may be readily available to pay wages and salaries, although this can be a time-consuming practice which may create disputes if recipients do not agree that the correct amount has been paid. If cash receipts are insufficient for payment purposes, cash will have to be drawn out of the bank, involving staff time, transport, security, insurance, bank charges, etc. Cash may also have to be withdrawn from the bank a day or two before it is actually paid over to employees because of the time involved in making up wage packets.

Cash methods of payment carry with them great risks of theft and personal assault, and it is not suprising that many efforts have been made in recent years to introduce non-cash methods of payment. These methods may, however, be unpopular with employees, and past legislation – considered in more depth in chapter 10 – has made it virtually impossible to insist that manual employees should accept non-cash methods. Nevertheless ways forward have been found, especially when savings have been shared between employer and employees.

5 See, for example, *Retail and Distribution Management*, November/December 1982, p. 48, and *Retail Banker*, 18 April 1983, p. 10. There are disagreements, however, about these figures, as is shown by the significantly lower figures quoted in *Which?*, December 1985, p. 570.

Business payments other than those for remuneration are normally made by non-cash methods except in the case of small sums of money and payments to private individuals. Accountants generally prefer to restrict petty cash to small amounts, although it may be difficult to obtain some services if cash is not available; for example, the use of taxis for business purposes. It may therefore be impossible to avoid the holding of small amounts of funds for petty cash expenditure purposes, although the amounts involved should be kept as low as possible.

4 *Banks*. There are substantial costs involved in the collection and issue of notes and coins. Bank notes in the region of £2 billion per annum are issued by the head office and the seven regional offices of the Bank of England (different arrangements apply in Scotland and Northern Ireland), whereas coins are issued by the Royal Mint. In addition, the major banks have over 100 cash centres in different parts of the country to satisfy the needs of branches and customers, and extensive use is made of security carrier services.

These activities naturally produce a large number of direct and indirect costs for the major commercial banks. The most obvious direct costs are the amounts involved in storage, security and distribution. In addition, there are the indirect costs of interest lost through the holding of cash resources. These costs have increased very significantly in recent years and the latest bank estimates suggest that the overall cost of these services to the London and Scottish clearing banks is probably in the region of £500 million to £700 million per annum.[6]

The banks would therefore not be sorry to see a significant reduction in cash-holding activities, although they naturally hope that cash transactions would be replaced by additional bank account activity. Within the banks, employees and their trade unions might not be so pleased to see this type of development, as a reduction in cash-holding could lead to a loss of jobs. This subject will be considered in later chapters, as there are many employment implications in the partial or complete abandonment of cash payment methods.

5 *Central and local government*. In current circumstances UK government ministers would almost certainly prefer to keep out of the controversy concerning the desirability of cashless methods of payment. There are, however, several areas of this subject where there will be pressures on government to introduce or change

6 *Payment Clearing Systems* (Banking Information Service, 1984) appendix 3, p. 94.

legislation; for example, the adequacy of existing legislatoin for electronic payment systems and the removal of restrictions on some non-cash forms of payment.

There are also numerous implications for government expenditure policies. In particular, spending on police, courts and prisons might be significantly reduced if there were fewer opportunities for the theft of cash. It is possible, however, that the long-term result of the introduction of electronic methods could be substantially increased computer fraud!

Central and local government are major employers with many weekly paid workers. Over 70 per cent of the total number of payments made by government in respect of weekly wages is in the form of cash, despite recent efforts to change long-established practices. Industrial organizations are in a similar situation and will be looking towards government for action on this subject.

Large amounts of cash are also involved in the payment of government benefits. The right to receive some of these payments by bank transfer methods has recently been introduced, although very little pressure has been put on recipients to accept these methods. Non-cash methods of payment may be popular with a small number of people – for example, some pensioners may prefer payment directly into a bank account – but any suggestion of compulsion would be extremely unpopular. In addition there could be numerous side-effects if a considerably smaller number of payments were made through the post office system. For example, many rural post offices might have to be closed down.

Government ministers are therefore likely to tread very carefully in this area, as the large-scale abandonment of cash payments, especially for state benefits, could have many unpleasant implications. If electronic transfers are, however, very much cheaper than cash payment systems, it will not be possible in the long term to ignore these issues, although government will probably prefer a gradual changeover policy rather than sudden and dramatic change.

CASH DISPENSING MACHINES

The first cash dispensing machine in the UK (and possibly in the world) was installed by Barclays in 1969. Most of the early machines dispensed only a small amount of cash – usually £10 – which could not generally be varied. Numerous problems were experienced with the machines installed in the late 1960s and early 1970s; for example, there were many breakdowns and the authorization cards were often damaged or retained in the machine after use. As a result, most bank customers preferred to use conventional cashier services, especially in those situations where dispensers were installed inside bank premises.

In the late 1970s and early 1980s the number, placing and reliability of dispensing machines improved and there was a substantial increase in the number of users. The range of services provided by these machines also increased, and the term 'automated teller machine' began to be accepted in the banking community for dispensers that provided several different services, e.g. cash dispensing, account balance data, cheque book and statement ordering, etc. Automated teller machines (ATMs) are examined in more detail in chapter 12; most of these machines are now able to provide instantaneous or end-of-day electronic transfers from the account of the customer to that of the bank.

By the end of 1985 there were about 160,000 ATMs and cash dispensing machines installed in different parts of the world, of which nearly 9,000 were sited in the UK. In well under twenty years, therefore, the automated dispensing of cash has become an accepted part of the banking scene, and bank customers in the vast majority of developed countries are now able to withdraw cash from a bank machine at most (or all) hours of the day or night.

It is rather early, however, to assess the effects of the installation of large numbers of cash dispensing machines. Rather ironically, these machines may in the short term have perpetuated the widespread use of cash for retail and other similar transactions, although the debit card that is used for cash withdrawals may eventually be extensively used for electronic point-of-sale transfers in retail and service organizations. Any conclusions on the effect of debit cards on banking services must therefore be postponed until one can see the overall effect of this card on retail transactions (see chapter 13 for a more detailed consideration of this subject).

SUMMARY AND CONCLUSIONS

Cash is still extensively used in the UK, especially by private individuals in their substantial number of small retail transactions. There is some evidence of reduced use over the last decade, but this still leaves us in a situation in which over 90 per cent of all payments are made in cash. Cash as a means of payment is normally quick and readily acceptable, and it will undoubtedly remain as an important part of the payment scene for many years to come. There are, however, numerous costs and problems associated with the handling of cash, and these costs will probably continue to soar upwards as long as we have labour-intensive methods of handling cash and increasing rates of crime.

Private individuals are therefore much more likely to be in favour of cash transactions than the banks and major retailers. There are increasing signs, however, of a much greater acceptance of non-cash methods of payment, especially amongst the younger generation for whom bank accounts and credit cards are not as frightening as they are for the elderly. The 'black economy' (work done for cash which is not generally reported for taxation purposes) may have held back this movement – one recent estimate has suggested that the annual value of this work may be about £45 billion[7] – although there are many other influences at work which are gradually moving us towards the new electronic methods of settlement.

Dissatisfaction with cash as a means of settlement would not, however, lead to change in the absence of satisfactory alternative methods of payment. Cash has in the past been relatively cheap as a means of settlement, and the alternatives that are available must prove that they are comparable, or preferably cheaper, in cost. As a result, the present and possible future methods of settlement must be examined with particular emphasis on their cost and convenience, as it cannot automatically be assumed that the new electronic methods will produce a means of payment that is preferable to the exchange of cash. A detailed examination of the benefits and problems attached to the new electronic methods of payment must therefore be carried out before it can be decided whether cash payments are essential or dispensable.

7 Black Economy at £45 Billion, *Times*, 3 June 1985, p. 1. This figure of undeclared earnings is well in excess of Inland Revenue estimates, which are believed to be in the region of £20 billion per annum.

3 The Cheque Business

Cheques have been used in the UK for over 250 years, although there are still many private individuals and even a few business organizations that do not make use of the cheque system. There has, however, been a rapid increase in the number of bank accounts in recent years and the latest bank estimates suggest that about 65 per cent of adults have a bank current account as compared with 45 per cent in 1976.[1] A much higher figure, in the region of 87 per cent, would be arrived at if accounts relating to bank deposits, building societies and national savings were taken into account. Building societies and post offices will usually provide a cheque or payment voucher for an account-holder following receipt of instructions, although this is not normally as convenient as making out a cheque in one's home or place of business. Changes in the clearing system in the late 1980s could provide the building societies and other similar financial institutions with the ability to issue their own cheques but this will almost certainly be a long-term process.

In 1985 over 2.4 billion cheques were handled by the London clearing banks, as can be seen from table 3.1. About 76 per cent of these cheques were concerned with transactions in which payer and payee had different banks (described in the table as inter-bank), whilst the remaining 24 per cent took place between different branches of the same bank (inter-branch). In addition, there are many cheques issued for cash withdrawals or for payees at the same branch in respect of which no figures are published. Unofficial estimates suggest that there could be over 400 million cheques in this category. Cheques are also cleared by the banks in Scotland and Northern Ireland; these amount to a total of about 200 million per annum.

The handling of this vast number of cheques naturally creates an

1 Inter-Bank Research Organisation, *Research Brief*, October 1985, p. 2.

enormous amount of work, and in recent years leading bankers have been heavily involved in plans to reduce labour costs and paperwork, especially through the use of electronic funds transfer systems. Nevertheless, the volume of cheques handled by the banks increased by about 5 per cent per annum in the early 1980s; this is, however, a reduction of growth in percentage terms as compared with the late 1970s.

Table 3.1 Cheques handled by London clearing banks
(millions of transactions)

Year	Inter-bank	Inter-branch	Total
1980	1459	495	1954
1981	1506	525	2031
1982	1565	547	2112
1983	1677	553	2230
1984	1777	555	2332
1985	1866	588	2454

Source: *Abstract of Banking Statistics*, 1986. National Giro-bank figures were included from 8 February 1983.

BANK CLEARING SYSTEMS

The clearing system that operates in London has in the past been organized and controlled by the major clearing banks, which have worked through the medium of the Committee of London Clearing Banks (CLCB). These banks have owned the Bankers Clearing House, the function of which has been to supervise cheque and credit clearings in England and Wales. Proposals to change the structure and organization of the clearing system were put forward in the latter part of 1984, and as a result a new Association for Payment Clearing Services (APACS) was set up in December 1985. The effects of the formation of this new organization will be considered later in this chapter.

Table 3.2 shows the different types of clearing systems and their relative importance in volume terms. In 1985 the number of cheques handled made up about 65 per cent of the overall number of money transfers arranged by the London Clearing Banks, although the number of automated clearings is growing very rapidly. Figures in respect of transfers from one account to another at the same branch are not included in these statistics.

The town clearing system deals with a relatively small number of items – about 5 million cheques per annum – although most of these transfers are

Table 3.2 Payments handled by London clearing banks
(millions of transactions)

Year	General debit clearing	Town clearing	Credit clearing	Automated clearing	Total
1980	1948	6	422	485	2861
1981	2025	6	414	537	2982
1982	2106	6	414	597	3123
1983	2224	6	428	682	3340
1984	2326	6	420	798	3550
1985	2449	5	416	912	3782

Source: Abstract of Banking Statistics, 1986.

for very large amounts of money, frequently above £1 million. This system
works on a same-day transfer of funds basis and it is therefore extremely
valuable from the viewpoint of the large financial institutions. More
information about the town clearing service is provided later in this
chapter.

The credit clearing system covers those transactions where money is
transferred from payer to payee by means of paper-based bank transfers.
Funds normally reach the payee's account two working days after the
payer's account is debited. About 416 million transfers were handled in
1985. Credit clearing was fairly static in the early 1980s, mainly because of
the increasing number of transfers now being arranged by automated
methods. Credit transfers will be considered in more detail in chapter 4.

The clearing banks also control the Bankers' Automated Clearing
Services (BACS) organization, which deals with a large number of
electronic bank transfers – credit transfers, direct debits, etc. This
organization has been operating since 1971 and the business is now
growing rapidly. In 1985, 835 million transactions were processed (the
figure shown in table 3.2 of 912 million includes items processed by
individual banks as well as BACS) and it is expected that there will be well
in excess of 1 billion transfers arranged each year by the end of the current
decade. The BACS system will be examined in more depth in chapter 7.

GENERAL CLEARING

The major objective of cheque clearing systems is to transfer funds as
quickly as possible between payer and payee and their clearing banks. This
process normally begins when a customer pays a cheque into a bank
branch account. If this branch is the 'home' bank of the person or business

concerned, it is entered on the bank statement on the same day, although cleared funds will in most cases not become available for two or three working days.

At the close of business for the day cheques are sorted, following which they are encoded with the amount entered on the cheque. Other details regarding the payer and the appropriate account will normally have been encoded before issue of cheques. This type of automation, which is known as magnetic ink character recognition (MICR), has had a considerable effect on the speed of the clearing process. At the end of the day of receipt, detailed lists, together with cheques and control vouchers, are sent to the clearing department of the bank in London, usually in transport arranged by one of the security organizations. Cheques drawn on the same bank and branch are, however, retained by the branch and cleared internally.

Cheques should therefore arrive at the clearing department of the bank in London on the morning of the working day after receipt by the branch. Cheques received from the various branches are then examined and amalgamated, and those which do not involve other banks are processed internally, and sent back to the drawer's branch the same evening. These cheques number more than 2 million each day. The remainder – normally over 7 million – are dealt with through the centralized clearing house system.

The London premises of the Bankers Clearing House are generally open for deliveries of cheques and credit transfers from Monday to Friday (excluding bank holidays) between 9.00 a.m. and 11.15 a.m. Representatives of the member banks will be present at the agreed times, and exchanges will be arranged shortly after the arrival of cheques. The banks on which cheques are drawn will then arrange processing in their own clearing departments. By the end of the day, cheques should have been despatched back to the branch on which they were drawn, and the amounts involved should have been agreed between the appropriate banks. Settlement normally takes place between the banks on the afternoon of the day following the exchange. This is arranged by cheques drawn on the Bank of England.

Cheques should therefore arrive back at the branch on which they are drawn two working days after being paid in at the receiving branch. This is the time at which funds should be available in the drawer's account; if funds are not available and there are no overdraft arrangements, the unpaid cheque will be returned by post to the branch at which the cheque was received and a special claim will be made for an adjustment in the amount agreed at general clearing. In most situations funds will be available, and an appropriate entry will then be made in the drawer's account to reflect the withdrawal of funds. The clearing process of the London Clearing Banks is illustrated in figure 3.1.

Funds for payment of a cheque will therefore normally be required two working days after a cheque has been paid into the payee's bank. This timetable should apply in respect of both inter-bank and inter-branch transactions. Drawers of cheques should note, however, that same-day settlement will be arranged when both parties bank at the same branch of the same bank.

Figure 3.1 The clearing process of the London clearing banks

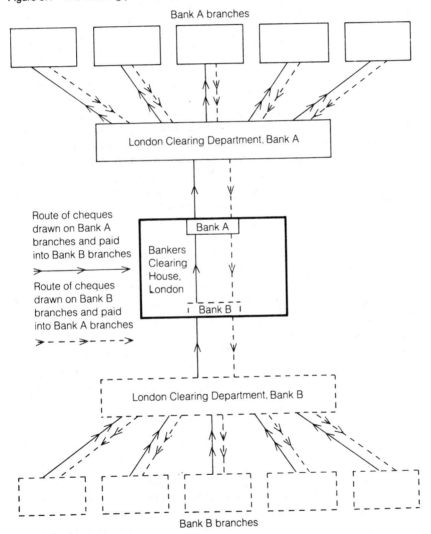

Source: *The Clearing System*, Banking Information Service, London.

With the advent of computer systems, banks now have to make assumptions for programming purposes regarding the speed of clearing on cheques that are received and paid into an account. In most UK banks this delay period is assumed to be three working days, so that a cheque banked on a Monday will not be regarded as cleared until Thursday. Bankers justify this extension from the normal two-day clearing period by pointing to the possible delays within the present system, although they may in competitive situations reduce the three working days to two. Business customers, especially those with an overdraft, should check what assumptions are being used in their particular case.

Payees will find that it is extremely difficult to avoid the clearing delay on cheques paid into a bank account. One method that has been suggested for reducing the clearing period is the 'special clearing' system which can be arranged on payment of a small fee (the minimum amount that has to be paid for this service is likely to be in the region of £3). Under this system, cheques are sent directly to the drawer's bank by the payee's bank using first class postage. Many directors and accountants assume that this saves one day in the clearing timetable; this misunderstanding is often perpetuated at local branch level, where many bankers are not entirely sure how the system works. Discussions with senior bankers suggest, however, that the overall effect of this type of clearing is that the payee gets a speeded-up guarantee of funds, but there will not generally be any improvement in the time at which cleared funds are assumed to be available for interest calculation purposes, primarily because the collecting bank has to obtain payment through the clearing house system.

The special clearing process is therefore mainly concerned with discovering whether funds are available for settlement processes and, if so, ensuring that these funds can be made available for this particular cheque. It should not be assumed that an improvement in the normal clearing period will automatically follow. The payee must therefore consider other bank transfer methods if it is desired to speed up the availability of funds; for example, the town clearing system as provided in the City of London.

TOWN CLEARING

Any business organization that wishes to use the town clearing system must have an account with one of the 'town' branches of the major banks. There are about 100 of these branches belonging to the major clearing banks, all of them being situated within the boundaries of the City of London in close proximity to the Bank of England and the Bankers Clearing House. The cheques that are used for this process are very similar to ordinary cheques, the only important difference being the small 'T' that is printed next to the bank branch code in the top right hand corner of the cheque. All cheques must be for £10,000 or above, drawn on and paid in at a town branch. Organizations outside the City of London can open an account at one of these branches, although there may be transport problems in lodging cheques received at one of these branches.

The major advantage of the town cheque to a payee is that cleared funds normally become available on the same date that a cheque is paid in at one of the town branches. To achieve this result, cheques must be paid in at a town branch before 3.00 p.m. These cheques are then sorted, listed and totalled, and taken to the clearing house for delivery to a representative of the paying bank. Details are then agreed between the two banks after which cheques are delivered to the branch that is responsible for payment. A decision then has to be made as to whether funds are available, as it has been agreed that the receiving bank must know whether the cheque will be paid by 4.45 p.m. If funds are available, a deduction will normally be made from the drawer's account and cleared funds will be made available to the payee. Finally, settlement between the banks that have been affected by these transactions will take place before business ends for the day.

The town clearing system has in recent times handled about 5 million cheques per annum, which is about 0.2 per cent of the total number of cheques handled in the clearing house system. In value terms, however, the town clearing system has in the past handled well over 90 per cent of the total value transferred in debit clearings. The town clearing system has therefore played an important role in the transfer of large amounts of funds in the City of London, although it has become increasingly expensive to operate in recent years, largely because of the labour-intensive nature of the processes adopted for clearing purposes.

The future of the town clearing system is now in some doubt because of the introduction of the fully automated Clearing House Automated Payments System (CHAPS) in February 1984. This system, which is now available on a nationwide basis, is described in more detail in chapter 7. Initial pronouncements from the major banks suggest that, at least for the next few years, the two systems will operate side-by-side, although it does seem inevitable that much of the present business will eventually be transferred to the CHAPS system. There will probably continue to be a need for town clearing for some years, although one cannot really see a long-term future for this system, especially if CHAPS transactions are eventually charged out at a significantly lower rate than town clearing cheques. Attempts will be made by interested parties, e.g. the bank messengers who carry cheques around the City of London, to continue the town clearing system, but it now seems extremely doubtful whether we shall have such a system by the end of the century.

USER VIEWPOINTS

Private individuals and businesses generally find that there are many advantages attached to the use of cheques. Advantages vary from one individual or organization to another, but in most cases the major advantages of using cheques will be found in the following list:

1 convenient to carry or send through the postal system;

2 easy to make out and use for settlement purposes;

3 relatively safe for payment purposes, especially if compared with cash;

4 widely accepted for personal transactions especially since the introduction of cheque guarantee cards;

5 usage need not be restricted because of an unexpectedly large amount, although funds will have to be available at the end of the clearing period;

6 can be 'stopped', i.e. the order to pay can be countermanded before settlement if the cheque was not used with a guarantee card; this is obviously an advantage to the payer but a disadvantage to the payee, and may lead to legal action if there are inadequate grounds for stoppage;

7 a delay period will normally be available to the drawer for settlement purposes because of the operation of the postal system (if used) and clearing procedures; this will be considered again under 'disadvantages', as the payee will in turn have to wait for cleared bank funds.

Most of these advantages are self-explanatory, although a small number may need additional comment or explanation. First of all, some comment is desirable about the safety of cheques, as these documents can obviously be stolen. Ideally, all cheques should be crossed (as is normal with most UK cheques); in this case the cheque has to be paid into a bank account, although it need not necessarily be that of the payee. Funds may, of course, be drawn out of a bank account in respect of such a cheque, but there should in these circumstances be some information or evidence as to who has drawn the funds.

The drawer of a cheque will sometimes attempt to ensure that a cheque is paid into a particular bank account. This procedure should work satisfactorily if a bank branch and account number is specified, although crossings such as 'account payee only' on a cheque made out to, say, J. Smith will not necessarily ensure that the cheque is paid into the account of the right J. Smith. Thieves have been known to open accounts in the name of a person to whom a stolen cheque is made out and to withdraw funds a few days later. Bankers have in the past tried to stop this type of abuse by taking up references or inspecting electoral records, although this can be a time-consuming process. Theft in the post or by other means is fortunately rather unusual, and most users feel that cheques are very much safer than cash.

The use of cheque cards is a relatively new development which ensures that the cardholder's bank will accept as valid a cheque issued by the cardholder up to the limit of the guarantee card, currently £50. The issue of this type of card has had a great influence on payments by private individuals to business organizations, as there was previously a great fear that the cheque might not be honoured at the end of the clearing process. More information regarding these cards is provided later in this chapter.

The cheque has therefore some important advantages when it is compared with cash and other methods of payment. It is important, however, that the disadvantages of cheques should be considered before a decision is reached as to the continued use of this method of payment. The most important of these disadvantages can be summarized as follows:

1 monitoring work will be required to ensure that the bank account is not overdrawn;
2 bank charges will usually be involved in the issue of cheques, although private individuals may be able to avoid these charges by keeping an agreed minimum balance;
3 the preparation, verification and signing of cheques can be a time-consuming and expensive process;
4 cheques will not provide funds for the payee until completion of the clearing process, although banks may allow access to these funds on payment of an overdraft charge; the cheque may, of course, be dishonoured but this is not a common occurrence, especially since the introduction of cheque guarantee cards.

The most important of these disadvantages from the business recipients's viewpoint will probably be the fourth point, as most electronic systems provide instantaneous transfer facilities. It should not be assumed, however, that payers – especially those in the business sector – will be prepared to arrange electronic transfers on the same date that cheques have previously been despatched. Most cheques are sent by second class mail and this frequently means that, by the time they are received, paid in and cleared, about a week has elapsed from the date of postal despatch. Many payers will therefore be reluctant to abandon cheques if they are not offered attractive incentives to change over to an instantaneous electronic transfer system.

In the retail sector the time taken to prepare and approve cheques can be a major problem, although printers located at the point-of-sale may help to solve some of these problems in the future. The cheque guarantee card has also speeded up this process but it still takes about 90 seconds for a typical cheque transaction. The settlement process is, however, only one of several processes at the check-out point that should be considered in arriving at more efficient point-of-sale systems; for example, it is essential that retailers should consider packaging and pricing as well as money transfer systems.

The bank charges structure will also be an important consideration when business decisions are made regarding the desirability of cheque receipts and payments. The major banks are very keen to reduce the amount of paperwork going through the banking system, and this is likely to be an increasing influence on charges for cheques and other paper-based items. The current bank charges structure in the UK will now be briefly examined.

BANK CHARGES

In the UK it has always been difficult to obtain precise data regarding the way in which bank charges are calculated, although the position is now much better than it was a decade ago. Personal customers will on request be provided with a leaflet on charges, and information regarding tariff changes is now beginning to be sent out to customers. Banks have also begun to show on the customer's statement the way in which charges have been calculated. The National Westminster adopted this practice in the latter part of 1984, and it now seems probable that most of the other major banks will be providing this information by the end of 1987. Charges in respect of business customers are likely to be a matter for negotiation, based on guidelines provided for bank personnel, although small businesses may be subject to a standard scale of charges.

In the early 1980s all the major UK clearing banks used a similar charging system for personal customers. This was based on the principle that customers who maintained a balance of £100 or over throughout a charging period (normally a quarter) should *not* be subject to bank charges. In theory, no exceptions were allowed to this rule, although bank managers have nearly always had the power to adjust charges in borderline cases. A person whose balance fell below £100 on one day in a quarter could therefore be charged for the whole of the quarter, unless the account-holder could persuade the local bank manager to cancel these charges.

In recent years there have been some changes of policy on personal bank charges; in December 1984 the Midland joined a small group of other banks, including the Co-operative, National Girobank, Trustee Savings and Yorkshire, in offering free banking to all customers who kept their account in credit. This helped to produce an increase of 450,000 customers in one year for the Midland, and in December 1985 the three other major clearing banks, Barclays, Lloyds and National Westminster, all announced a changeover to free banking for those customers maintaining an account in credit for the charging period.

As a result of these new balance rules, over 60 per cent of private bank customers will pay no bank charges. The remainder will in most cases pay a quarterly charge and a set amount for each payment. For example, in 1986, Barclays made a quarterly charge of £3 to all customers who did not keep their account in credit or have an average credit balance of more than £500. If these balances were not maintained, customers were charged 29p per item for each debit entry. No charges were made for amounts paid into an account. Some banks, e.g. National Westminster, also have a charges abatement linked to the average balance held in the account.

Business customers may be charged on a 'per item' basis or there may be a quarterly or annual fee, often linked to the maintenance of a minimum current account balance. In recent years, however, an increasing number of businesses have been charged on a 'turnover' basis, which is normally associated with the value of transactions on the account. This could include both incoming and outgoing transactions, although the charge is more likely to be based on outgoing items, i.e. debit turnover. Ideally, charges should be clarified in a letter from the banker to the business, but there do appear to be many instances where this does not happen.

On the accounts of most large and medium-sized companies periodic examinations of bank account activity are carried out within the appropriate branch to ascertain the net costs relating to the account. This will serve as a basis for future turnover charges, and any major changes expected over the next year may also be taken into account. For example, if the expected net cost of maintaining a business account over the next year, after taking the appropriate profit percentage into account, is £5,000 and the estimated value of debit items is £500,000, a debit turnover charge of 1 per cent might be levied. This should produce charge revenue in the region of £5,000 if estimated turnover figures turn out to be reasonably accurate. The turnover charge may be 'imposed' in the case of a non-competitive situation or 'discussed' when there are likely to be competitive pressures. The advantage of the turnover system to the banks is that it provides an in-built allowance for the effects of inflation, although this is unlikely to be an advantage to the rapidly expanding business.

Cost guidelines for money transmission services are provided by bank head offices for branch managers. In most cases these lists provide estimated costs for different activities; for example, costs will be specified for the collection and payment of cheques, cash handling, standing orders, direct debits, issue of statements, night safe facilities, stopped cheques, etc. These figures do not generally include a profit element, although managers are expected to consider such matters in producing figures for the customer. It is accepted that in some competitive situations it will not be possible to obtain a full recovery of costs.

If the above charges are incorporated into a turnover charge, careful consideration will have to be given to the range of services that is expected from the bank. A survey carried out in a small number of major companies in 1982 suggested that debit turnover charges at that time ranged from 0.75p to 2.75p per £100 of debit items handled.[2] Charges have, however, increased significantly since 1982, and small businesses often expect advice on many matters which the large business is capable of handling itself. The 'mix' of business is also important, as some businesses have large numbers of small cheques whilst other businesses have small numbers of large cheques. Discussions with senior bank personnel suggest that turnover charges for 1986 will probably range from 3p to £1 per £100 of debit turnover, depending on the level of competition, relationships with the customer, and the make-up of bank transactions. Only the Co-operative Bank is prepared to provide a standard turnover quotation (42p per £100 of debit turnover in 1986), and this is subject to change when there are significant variations from the normal make-up of an account.

Business directors and accountants of companies charged on a turnover basis should therefore enquire as to the way in which this charge has been calculated. There will occasionally be some resistance to disclosing this information; most large and medium-sized companies that are charged on this basis have, however, been able to obtain this information on request. The provision of this data should provide an indication as to how overall charges can be reduced. For example, in the survey that has already been mentioned,[2] it was suggested that charges at that time (1982) for debit transactions (mainly cheques) ranged from 12p to 21p per item as compared with 3p per item for electronic transfers. A company director in possession of this information might therefore be able to negotiate a reduction in the turnover charge for the next year if debtors could be persuaded to settle accounts by electronic transfer methods. Benefits from this type of policy might arise more quickly if a 'per item' charge was made, and there does now appear to be some pressure from the business sector for charges to be made on this basis.

2 D. Hodson, Bank Charges Revisited, *Treasurer*, February 1983, p. 21.

From the figures that have been provided it should be obvious that there are significant costs attached to the use of cheques. Private individuals who are subject to bank charges generally pay between 25p and 35p for each cheque paid out, although in most cases there is no charge for cheques paid into an account. In the business sector the overall level of charges is similar, but costs will usually be split between the payer and the payee. In most cases this will produce a charge in the region of 10p to 20p for cheques received and 15p to 30p for cheques paid out. These charges may be made on a 'per item' basis or incorporated into a turnover charge.

It is very difficult to predict what will happen to bank charges for processing cheques in the future. The banks claim that it costs in the range of 30p to 50p to cover all the costs associated with the clearing of a cheque; Barclays' costs are estimated to be in the region of 30p per cheque, made up of 12p for variable costs, i.e. printing, postage, branch and clearing costs, with the remaining 18p being made up of allocated central and branch overheads.[3] The banks may therefore move towards a higher 'per item' charge with an abatement for the average balance held on the account e.g. Lloyds has recently announced a small business tariff of 50p per item (excluding direct debits and cash dispenser withdrawals) which will be reduced by interest calculated on the average cleared balance (3% per annum in August 1986).

It also seems probable that there will be greater competition for funds in the future. This has already begun to happen, and as a result some of the major banks are now offering interest-paying current accounts and special deposit accounts. The banks are therefore likely to make determined efforts to reduce processing costs through the increased use of electronic methods. The overall effect of these different influences on bank charges is very difficult to estimate. It seems likely, however, that bank charges for paper-based items will increase at a faster rate than charges for electronic transfers, although there may be strong protests from private and business customers if this type of policy is adopted.

CHEQUE GUARANTEE CARDS

Until the mid-1960s it was extremely difficult for private individuals to guarantee that cheques drawn on their UK bank account would be honoured. In 1964, however, the first cheque guarantee card was issued, and by the beginning of 1986 there were over 24 million of these cards in

3 These figures were reported in an article by R. Waters, Banks Battle for Custom, *Account*, 21 November 1985, p. 12

circulation in the UK. Most of these cards are for cheque purposes only, although some guarantee cards are used for cash withdrawal and/or credit transactions.

The cheque card, which should obviously not have been altered or defaced, normally guarantees the payment of one cheque not exceeding an agreed amount (currently £50) as long as the cheque:

1 is signed by the cardholder in the presence of the payee, the signature corresponding with that on the card;
2 is drawn on a document that bears the same name and code number as the card and is dated before the expiry date of the card;
3 has the card number written on the back by the payee.

The cheque card may also be used as a cheque encashment card to obtain cash from most UK banks. A charge may be levied if a cheque is cashed at a bank other than the one on which it is drawn.

The £50 limit for guaranteed cheques was introduced in 1977 (it was previously £30), and it would now be in the region of £100 if adjustments had been made for changes in purchasing power. There have been numerous demands from customers and consumer groups that this limit should be increased,[4] but the banks have not been prepared to respond to these pressures, largely because of the increasing amount of fraud committed with the aid of cheque cards. The limit is currently applied by all the major banks under a registered trade agreement which the Office of Fair Trading has decided not to challenge.

The scale of the cheque card fraud problem has increased significantly in recent years from less than £2 million per annum in the late 1970s to over £25 million per annum in the mid-1980s. The major cause of these fraudulent transactions has been the use of stolen cheques for retail purchases backed up by a cheque card stolen at the same time. No charge is made by the banks for the issue of a cheque card, and it is not surprising therefore that the banks are trying to limit their losses by retaining the 1977 limit of £50. There is a great danger, however, that customers will try to bypass the limit by the use of more than one cheque for the same purchase, although this is not strictly speaking acceptable under the terms of the cheque card agreement.

For many years UK cheque guarantee cards could be used outside the UK, although this policy tended to increase fraud problems. In May 1983, however, use of these cards was restricted to the UK, although travellers going to most West European countries are able to apply to use the

4 See, for example, the results of a market research study carried out by the National Consumer Council, *Banking Services and the Consumer* (Methuen, 1983), p. 135.

Eurocheque system. In most banks this involves the issue of books of Eurocheques backed up by a special cheque card. This card enables the holder to use Eurocheques up to the equivalent of £100 per cheque in 24 European countries (including the UK). The Eurocheque card is now extensively used in Western Europe, mainly for cheque guarantee purposes, and in some countries the card also serves as a debit card for cash withdrawal and point-of-sale transactions.

New cheque guarantee cards were issued by all the major UK banks in 1984/5. The banks claim that the new cards cannot be copied or changed without showing obvious signs of alteration. The means by which the banks hope to achieve these objectives are considered in more detail in chapter 5 on the Credit Card Business. Credit cards share many of the problems of cheque cards when attempts are made to reduce the level of fraud.

Cheque guarantee cards have therefore played an important part in the widespread acceptance of private cheques by retail and service organizations. The continued use of the £50 limit is, however, restricting the use of cheques for large retail transactions. Credit cards, on the other hand, are usually accepted for transactions in excess of £50, and besides many holders of cheque and credit cards prefer the credit card system (if accepted by the retailer) because of deferred payment terms. Nevertheless the cheque guarantee card is likely to continue as an important part of the UK payment system, especially for the encashment of cheques and use in shops not accepting credit cards.

FUTURE DEVELOPMENTS

Recent statistics suggest that there will be very little, if any, reduction in the number of cheques used in the UK before the end of the 1980s. Bankers are therefore actively considering changes in the traditional cheque clearing system as well as preparing for a more widespread use of electronic funds transfer systems.

Probably the major development in the late 1980s will be the reorganization of the membership and control of the clearing system, based on the report of a special committee, chaired by Mr D. M. Child of the National Westminster Bank. This committee recommended in December 1984 that there should be a restructuring of the clearing system and the opening up of membership to a much wider range of banks and financial institutions.[5]

5 *Payment Clearing Systems* (Banking Information Service, 1984), part 1, p. 3.

As a result of these recommendations, a new body, the Association for Payment Clearing Services (APACS), has been set up, as part of which there will be four operating companies. These companies will cover ordinary paper-based bulk clearings (Cheque and Credit Clearing Company Ltd), high-value clearings (CHAPS and Town Clearing Ltd), high volume electronic clearings (BACS Ltd) and eventually point-of-sale transactions (EFTPOS). Several overseas banking institutions have become or are interested in becoming members of the high-value group, e.g. Citibank from the USA. It is also expected that there will be applications from some of the larger building societies, or groups of societies, to become members of one or more of the clearing companies. To become eligible for membership, applicants should have (or expect to have) at least 0.5 per cent of the combined clearing volume of the operational clearings covered by the appropriate clearing group. The UK clearing process may therefore be very much changed by the early 1990s, although there will still be strict entry standards and substantial entry fees attached to membership.

There may also be changes within the clearing system to reduce the amount of paperwork that is handled by the banks. One of the ways in which paperwork might be reduced is by the use of truncation processes.[6] In its broadest sense, truncation involves a stoppage of the physical flow of paperwork before the processing of transactions has been finalized. In the case of cheques, this would almost inevitably mean that the data contained on the cheque would be copied in non-paper form, probably as part of an electronic recording process, and the cheque would then be retained, at least temporarily, at the bank where it was paid in.

There are many legal and technical problems attached to a truncation system but these are not insurmountable, and it has already been shown in Belgium, Denmark and Sweden that cheque truncation processes can be successfully implemented. In its broadest sense truncation has already been partly introduced in the UK through the non-return of cleared cheques to certain customers. This is only a partial system, however, although it was an important first step in what may be a long-term development process.

Changes in a cheque system that has been used for many years will therefore not be easy. In the long term, government involvement may be desirable, especially in respect of legislative changes and control systems.

---

6 Helpful studies of the ways in which truncation might be introduced in the UK are contained in T. Bell, Cheque Trucation – Flight of Fancy or Force Majeure?, *Bankers' Magazine*, March 1980, pp. 10–12 and J. Edwards, Overcoming Obstacles to Cheque Truncation, *Bankers' Magazine*, January 1983, pp. 11–12.

It is possible, of course, that growth in the use of electronic funds transfer systems could be so fast that changes in cheque handling will not be necessary. This seems unlikely, however, as long as the banks continue to encourage private individuals and business organizations to open bank accounts.

SUMMARY AND CONCLUSIONS

Cheques are extensively used in the UK, especially in respect of the supply of goods or services by business and government organizations. In most sizeable transactions cheques have substantial advantages over cash for settlement purposes, although we may soon be entering a situation in which an extensive range of electronic transfer systems will be made available at much cheaper transaction rates than cheques.

In the business sector the settlement of indebtedness has in the past often been part of a power struggle between payer and payee. One of the major reasons why business payers will be reluctant to abandon the cheque system is because it provides a built-in delay factor in respect of postal, paying-in and clearing processes. Powerful suppliers of goods and services may be able to insist on settlement using electronic transfers, but the less powerful will have great difficulty in persuading payers to move away from the cheque system.

The banks will probably not be prepared to act as observers in this power struggle. The enormous amount of paper produced by the use of cheques and credit transfers is very expensive to process, and bank employees will naturally be encouraged to increase productivity and efficiency. The banks are therefore likely to make increasing efforts to persuade customers to use electronic transfers, although opposition from employees may slow down the rate at which change can be effected.

It seems likely, therefore, that the substantial recent growth in the use of cheques in the UK will slow down in the late 1980s and possibly come to an end sometime in the early 1990s. Even so, the banks will probably have well over ten million cheques to process each day, unless there is a very dramatic changeover to electronic funds transfers. The cheque system has, however, provided a good service to its users for many years, and it seems virtually certain that cheques will still be an important method of payment by the year 2000, although by that time we shall almost inevitably have accepted the idea that electronic transfers should be used for a wide variety of business transactions.

4 Credit Transfers and Bank Giro Services

It has been possible for many years for a person or organization to pay for goods or services by the transfer of funds to another bank account. This method of payment, which is usually described as the credit transfer system, involves the provision of funds at any branch of any clearing bank for the account of a person or organization with an account at any other branch of any clearing bank.

The initiator of the credit transfer may incur setting-up costs in those situations where the payee's consent to this method of payment has to be obtained together with details of the appropriate bank account – name, number, address, etc. An increasing number of invoices do, however, provide this information in the expectation that some accounts will be settled by credit transfer. In the absence of this information on the invoice, this can still be a worthwhile settlement method, especially if frequent payments are likely to be made to the same payee, although the costs and time involved in setting up the system must be carefully considered.

HISTORICAL DEVELOPMENTS

The credit transfer system was first used in the 1930s. Initially all credit transfers were arranged by means of credit advices, with information provided by the payer concerning the accounts to which funds should be transferred. Payment was then made to the bank by the initiator of the credit, although one cheque was generally considered adequate to cover any reasonable number of credit advices. Before 1960 the payer's bank would arrange for payment to be made to each payee's bank. Since 1960, however, transactions have been settled through the centralized credit clearing system, except in those situations where both payer and payee have accounts at the same bank and branch.

In its early years the credit transfer system was mainly used for the payment of salaries, although settlements were also make in respect of wages, pensions, trade debts, interest and dividends. The payment of set amounts at regular intervals (the standing order system) was another frequent application, and this system is now widely used for the settlement of regular commitments, such as building society payments.

In the 1960s the direct debit system was introduced by the clearing banks with approved business payees being allowed to initiate bank transfers provided that the payer had agreed in advance. Initially these transactions were for fixed amounts, although the system has now been extended to include variable amounts.

By the end of the 1960s the National Giro system had been introduced into the UK, and after some initial problems this organization (now called the National Girobank) became a major provider of credit transfer services. The setting up of this new bank produced considerable interest in the clearing bank sector as a result of which all the major banks decided to describe their range of credit transfer activities as 'bank giro services'. This description is widely used today, although there are some differences of opinion as to whether direct debits should be included under this heading.[1]

In the early 1970s the Bankers' Automated Clearing Services (BACS) organization was set up by the clearing banks, and this provided for the first time a fully automated system for credit transfers and other similar forms of payment using computer-input methods. There are still many situations, however, where it is not possible for businesses to use this system, largely because of the computer-input criteria laid down by BACS; for example, in the 1970s data had to be submitted in approved magnetic tape form although other forms of computer input are now acceptable. The BACS system is described in more detail in chapter 7.

More changes took place in 1984, when the centralized credit clearing system was partly automated, based on the use of specially encoded paper documents. The paper advice system had previously been organized in a very labour-intensive form, and the banks were obviously hoping that the 'new' system would achieve considerable cost savings.

From 1970 onwards, therefore, there have been two primary methods of arranging direct transfers from one bank account to another. For the business which can provide data on magnetic tape or other approved computer-input methods, the services provided by BACS will probably be

---

1 F. E. Perry, *A Dictionary of Banking* (MacDonald & Evans, 1979), p. 22, states that direct debits are part of the bank giro system, although some senior bank personnel use this term in a more restricted sense.

most appropriate for inter-bank transactions (inter-branch automated transfers are frequently handled by individual banks). Other interested businesses may, however, utilize the paper-input system, especially if payments are being made by private individuals.

CREDIT CLEARING

The system that is currently used in the UK for credit clearing purposes was set up in 1960, and operates in a similar way to the general clearing system. At the close of business for a day when credit transfers are arranged, paying banks send bundles of paper credits and listed details to their head office clearing department. The security van system usually ensures that this material reaches the bank's clearing department on the working day after the transaction. The credit advices are then separated into inter-bank and inter-branch transactions, with inter-branch items being dealt with through the head office of the appropriate bank. Inter-bank transactions are passed through the central clearing process to the clearing department of the bank receiving the payment. Information concerning the transfer is then sent to the branch where the payee's account is maintained. This information should arrive two working days after the transaction has been initiated. Settlement between the banks involved in the transfer is arranged in the same way as the general clearing system.

The efficiency of the paper-based credit clearing process has been considerably improved as a result of the steps that the banks have taken in recent years to automate clearing procedures. This has involved strict specifications regarding paper quality, design and coding in order to ensure that information is 'machine-readable'. From the user's viewpoint these changes have not been popular, as they have frequently involved considerable expense. Some of the banks have, however, made available a service under which payment details can be translated into a suitable form for the BACS system. There is naturally an additional charge for this service. The best-known of these services is the National Westminster Autopay system, which has over 5,000 users generating more than 150,000 transactions each month. Changes introduced in the credit clearing system may therefore persuade some organizations to abandon paper-based credit transfers, and the banks are obviously hoping that there will be a gradual movement towards the more fully automated BACS system.

Table 4.1 shows the level of activity within the paper-based credit clearing system from 1980 onwards. These statistics show that there has been little or no growth in the total number of credit transfers handled in the early 1980s. One contributory cause may be the charges imposed by banks on non-customers from 1981 onwards, although increased use of the automated system is probably the major reason. The current figures – slightly over 400 million transactions per annum – are, however, well above those for the mid-1970s; for example, the total number of transactions did not exceed 300 million until 1976. The value of credit clearings in 1985 was about £404 billion.

Table 4.1 Credit clearing transactions handled by the London clearing banks

Year	Transactions (millions)
1980	422
1981	414
1982	414
1983	428
1984	420
1985	416

Source: Abstract of Banking Statistics,
1986.

The statistics provided in table 4.2 show a very different picture in respect of automated transfers. Most of these transfers are arranged through BACS, which began trading in 1971 and is now handling many more transactions than the much longer-established credit clearing system. The value of transactions handling by BACS in 1985 was about £250 billion. Information about the value of automated transfers handled by individual banks has not been published.

Table 4.2 Automated bank transfers handled by the London clearing
banks

Year	Transactions (millions)
1980	485
1981	537
1982	597
1983	682
1984	798
1985	912

Source: Abstract of Banking Statistics,
1986.

The overall importance of credit transfers should not be overestimated, however, as the number of cheques issued per annum is still well above the number of direct bank transfers (paper and automated transactions); for example, in 1985 the total number of paper-based and automated credit transfers and direct debits was approximately half the number of cleared cheques (excluding cheques cashed or cleared at branches). Cheques therefore still dominate the UK non-cash payments system, although credit transfers and direct debits are becoming increasingly important methods of settlement.

BUSINESS CONSIDERATIONS

There are several matters that should be considered by payers in deciding whether credit transfers (paper or automated) should be used in place of cheques. The most important of these matters from the business organization's viewpoint are:

1 *Obtaining the payee's agreement.* The agreement of major payees should ideally be obtained before a decision is made to embark upon a credit transfer payment system. The knowledgeable payee is likely to welcome this type of initiative as long as the probable date of transfer into the appropriate bank account is earlier than the cleared date of cheques for similar transactions. Proper information and documentation concerning payments should always be provided; this point is important, as much time can be spent by payees tracing the source of credit transfer payments. Discussions with company accountants suggest that there are usually a small number of objections from payees to this method of payment, although it is often very difficult to analyse the precise reasons for this attitude. Unfortunately, there does appear to be considerable ignorance in the UK business sector concerning the way in which the bank clearing system operates, in addition to which the owners of some small businesses seem to have a strange desire to see a cheque or cash in settlement of every transaction rather than an entry on the bank statement! Experience does suggest, however, that if a letter is properly drafted, with all the implications explained, there should eventually be over 90 per cent acceptance from businesses (if failures to reply are properly followed up), and over the course of time this should gradually increase towards the 100 per cent mark. If payments are made to private individuals, there will probably be more objections, as some of them may not have bank accounts.

2 *Effects on administrative costs.* A changeover to the credit transfer system would normally be expected to produce significant savings in administrative costs. Large numbers of cheques will no longer have to be produced, checked, signed and despatched and there should as a result be savings in staff time as well as printing and stationery costs. Postal savings may also be achieved if it is possible to provide sufficient information concerning the payment on the input medium. If this is not possible, as is frequently the case, settlement details will have to be sent through the post. There will, of course, still be administrative costs attached to the preparation of paper-based credit transfer schedules, automated data, etc., but these costs will generally be significantly less than those involved in the cheque system.

3 *Likelihood of errors and security problems.* There is no detailed evidence available regarding the comparative number of errors in cheque and credit transfer preparation, although there will generally be more work involved and therefore more possibility of errors if cheques are used rather than credit transfers. Cheques are also likely to be sent through the post to many different addresses, and there will probably be more likelihood of theft or loss than in the case of credit transfers where distribution takes place through the banking system. It is extremely difficult to attach a value to this type of saving, although much will depend on the efficiency of the system in operation before the introduction of credit transfers.

4 *Cash availability and planning.* Budgeting in respect of cash resources is generally much simpler when payments are made by credit transfer, as the total amount involved for each set of transfers is transferred out of the bank in one lump sum. By contrast, it is much more difficult to estimate when cheques will be presented because of postal, paying-in and clearing delays. There may, however, be advantages in the use of cheques from the cash availability and interest-earning viewpoint. Much depends on the date when credit transfers are initiated as compared with the previous cheque despatch system. If the dates of initiation are the same, there will almost certainly be a loss in interest-earning opportunities if credit transfers are used. There is no reason why attempts should not be made to negotiate a later date – some payers do this automatically without consulting the payee – although any decisions that are made may depend on the strength and accounting systems of the payee and existing knowledge of the bank clearing system.

5 *Bank systems and charges.* The speed of transfer between bank accounts is an important consideration in credit transfer systems. In paper-based systems there is normally a delay of at least two working days between the debit to the payer's account and the credit to the payee's account. In automated systems, such as BACS, the debit and credit entries should be made on the same day, although bank policies on this matter should always be checked, especially with standing orders, where the two-day delay will probably be maintained. Bank charges may also vary significantly between the two systems. Charges for paper-based credit transfers may be slightly higher than those for cheques, although encoding processes are now beginning to reduce processing costs. In the past it was possible for an organization which arranged fifty credit transfers paid for by one cheque to escape with a charge for one cheque, but the more detailed costing records that have been set up by the banks in recent years will now ensure that most businesses will be charged for individual credit transfers. This will generally mean that business charges will be in the range of 20p to 40p for each paper-based credit transfer, although this can be reduced to about 5p per item if automated transfers are arranged through the BACS system or other similar processes.

6 *Compliance costs.* In both paper and automated systems there will be costs involved in meeting the input requirements laid down by the payer's bank. In some cases this will involve the purchase of equipment, although in large companies the appropriate machinery may already be in use. The services of an agency could be used if it is decided not to purchase equipment. The changes that have recently been introduced in the quality, design and encoding of paper-input documents have increased costs in recent years, although the business sector hopes that bank charges will as a result be decreased or at least held constant. The banks expect that an increasing number of businesses will use the BACS system, although there may also be significant costs involved in meeting the computer-input criteria laid down by BACS.

The decision by a business payer to make payments through the credit transfer system should therefore not be made without a detailed study of costs and benefits. In most cases there should be administrative cost savings, although some directors and accountants believe that the interest losses brought about by probable earlier settlement will more than offset these gains. There is no reason, however, why credit transfers should not be restricted to 'small' payments – say those for under £1,000 – in which case interest losses, if any, should not be very significant. The initiation of credit transfers several days later than the date adopted in respect of cheques could also avoid these problems.

CUSTOMER VIEWPOINTS

Extensive use is made by private individuals of credit transfers and standing orders, although there is some evidence of a gradual changeover to direct debit payments in recent years. The vast majority of standing orders and direct debits are now arranged through the BACS transfer system, which will be considered in more detail in chapter 7. Many credit transfers are, however, still initiated on paper-based systems.

There are several advantages available to the private individual in the use of the credit transfer system rather than cash or cheques. The major advantage is that several payments can be made at the same time with the aid of one cheque; thus settlement might be made at the same time in respect of electricity, gas, telephone and credit card accounts. There should also be savings in respect of postage and stationery, and in some cases bank charges. Other less positive advantages arise from avoiding problems associated with cash and cheques – likelihood of theft, assault, loss in the post, etc.

Similar advantages apply in respect of the standing order system, which is normally used in respect of regular payments. Accounts in respect of general household rates, for example, are now frequently split up into ten equal instalments payable monthly from May to February. In this case, however, there is the additional advantage that once an authority is signed, payments will automatically be made on a set date until termination of the order. This can be useful where a person is often away from home or has a bad memory! Bank charges in respect of standing orders have in recent years been strongly influenced by the large number of amendments, usually to increase the amount payable, and as a result costs for private individuals who are subject to charges are frequently the same as for cheques, even if the standing order is paid by automated methods.

Direct debits have similar advantages to the standing order, although there is always a slight risk in the case of variable amount agreements that the payee may arrange for the wrong amount to be transferred out of the payer's account. The payee must, however, agree that immediate refunds will be arranged in the case of error. Banks also stress the fact that these transfers can be initiated only by 'reputable organizations'. The direct debit system is considered in more detail in chapter 8.

The major disadvantage with standing orders and direct debits, as compared with cash or cheques, is lack of flexibility, especially if financial difficulties arise. With cash or cheques, there are a number of delaying tactics that can be adopted by the person owing the money, and it may not become obvious to the payee that there are cash problems until several weeks have passed. With standing orders or direct debits the fact that such a payment has been dishonoured or delayed will soon become obvious, and it may therefore be more difficult to delay payment. As a result, legal action may be started at an earlier date than would otherwise have been the case. These facts are seldom pointed out to the payer, as it would obviously not be in the payee's interests to do so.

SUMMARY AND CONCLUSIONS

This chapter has been primarily concerned with paper-based credit transfers, which have been in use in the UK for about fifty years. In recent years there have been about 400 million of these transactions each year, although this number has been fairly static since 1980, largely because of the growth of the computer-input credit transfer system organized by BACS.

The rapid growth of BACS transfers inevitably means that the long-term continuation of the paper-based bank transfer system must be in some doubt. Virtually all inter-bank standing orders and direct debits are now dealt with by automated methods but there are still large numbers of small businesses and private individuals making extensive use of the paper-based credit transfer system for payment purposes. The recent decision by the banks that credit advices should be encoded in a laid-down form has caused some problems for businesses, although there does not yet appear to be a substantial reduction in the demand for these services.

We may therefore find that both paper-based and computer-input credit transfer systems remain in operation for the next decade. By the end of the century it would seem extremely likely that the vast majority of business organizations – through their own services or those of an agency – will be capable of initiating computer-input transfers through the BACS system. There are, however, many private individuals who use the paper-based system for the payment of accounts relating to electricity, gas, telephone, credit cards etc., largely because of the general convenience of such a system. As a result, this service may have to remain in existence for payments by private individuals, although it is possible that in ten years' time most consumers will be paying their accounts by means of automated direct debits or plastic card systems. The large amount of paperwork involved in credit transfers may therefore be significantly reduced by the mid-1990s and it could have been completely eliminated by the year 2000.

5 The Credit Card Business

The first credit card is believed to have been issued in the USA in 1914 by the General Petroleum Corporation of California – now Mobil Oil.[1] The credit card business did not become properly established, however, until the years following the Second World War, but since then there has been rapid growth and there are now about 1 billion credit cards being used in different parts of the world. The major cardholding country is the USA, where there are over 600 million cards in circulation, although only about 20 per cent of these cards have been issued by banks, as compared with over 50 per cent by retailers.

In the UK, attempts were made by Diners Club and American Express to introduce credit cards in the 1950s, but it was not until the 1970s that the use of these cards began to be widely accepted following the launch of Barclaycard in 1966. The Access card followed in 1972 and by the beginning of 1986 there were about 30 million credit cards in circulation, of which about 65 per cent had been issued by banks and nearly 30 per cent by retailers.

In the last decade, therefore, credit cards have become an important part of the worldwide payments scene, although they have generally been a means of identification for future billing rather than a method of final settlement by the purchaser. These cards have, however, brought with them a considerable amount of paperwork for credit card companies, retailers and private individuals. This paperwork provides proof of transactions for both retailers and consumers, and information for the credit card billing process. More paperwork is then likely to be generated, as settlement frequently takes the form of a cheque or credit transfer; these transactions have, however, almost certainly been reduced in volume terms from what they would otherwise have been, as many consumers in the

---

1 A. C. Drury and C. W. Ferrier, *Credit Cards* (Butterworth, 1984), p. 19.

absence of such a card would probably have used several cheques or transfers to pay for some or all of these items. Major efforts are now being made to automate credit card processes, although interested organizations are obviously trying to ensure that this does not slow down the present boom in the number of transactions.

TYPES OF CARDS

The bank credit card, as it has evolved in the UK, provides the owner of the card with short-term credit up to an agreed limit, which in most cases is between £300 and £1,000. On a set day or week each month, a statement is sent out to the cardholder by the credit card company giving full details of transactions for the previous month and the amount outstanding. This statement can be paid in full by a specified date – usually 25 days after the statement date – in which case there will be no interest charge. Alternatively a small minimum payment – usually £5 or 5 per cent of what is owed, whichever is the greater – can be made, with the amount outstanding then subject to an interest charge. The two major providers of the 20 million or so bank credit cards are Access and Barclaycard, as can be seen from an examination of table 5.1.

An increasing number of retail groups also provide credit card services; these are usually known as 'store cards'. About 8½ million of these cards were in circulation at the beginning of 1986. Some of these schemes are organized and administered by the UK banks, although the general public are frequently not aware of this fact. Finance companies, e.g. Welbeck Finance, and overseas banks, e.g. Citibank, are also involved in the administration of these schemes.

Retailers provide credit facilities in several different ways. Some have monthly or option accounts, which usually have to be paid within two or three weeks of the invoice date. Others have budget accounts with a limit of 20 to 30 times the cardholder's monthly payment. Rules regarding credit limits and interest payments vary tremendously. Most of the major UK retail groups are now involved in the issue of credit cards. Marks & Spencer, for example, which does not accept bank credit cards, introduced its own nationwide credit card scheme in April 1985, and issued over a million cards in the first year of card trading. The most popular UK store card at the beginning of 1986 was that of Debenhams with about 1.2 million cardholders.

The third major type of credit card is the 'travel and entertainment (T & E) card'. It is sometimes suggested that these cards are not credit cards as the cardholder is expected to pay in full on receipt of the monthly statement. As a result the description 'charge card' is sometimes used. The cardholder is not, however, expected to pay for goods or services at the time of delivery, and these cards will therefore be considered under the heading 'credit card' in this chapter. The major providers of these cards are American Express (about 800,000 UK cardholders) and Diners Club (300,000 UK cardholders).

A fourth major type of credit card is now emerging in the UK – the petrol or fuel card. In the USA there are over 100 million of these cards in circulation, and it seems probable that an increasing number of these cards will be issued in the UK over the next decade. This type of card may well prove to be attractive to business users, especially for issue to senior management and sales staff; these cards are usually described as 'company cards'. It has been estimated that there are currently about 800,000 petrol cards in circulation in the UK.

In recent years the credit card companies have also started to issue 'premier' or 'gold' cards to high income earners – usually those earning above £20,000 per annum. These cards often carry the right to 'no limit' credit card facilities and a variety of other privileges such as unsecured overdraft facilities and the ability to withdraw large amounts of cash in an extensive range of home and overseas banks. There is normally an annual charge – £40 to £50 – and amounts outstanding must be paid by the due date. There are currently about 200,000 of these cards in circulation in the UK.

There are many other types of plastic cards in circulation, although most of them are not intended to be used as credit cards. The banks issue special cash cards for withdrawals at cash dispensers or automated teller machines (ATMs). These were considered in chapter 2. Cheque cards are also issued and in some cases, for example Barclaycard, a card may serve the purpose of both credit card and cheque card; cheque cards have already been considered in chapter 3. In the future we shall almost certainly have cards for point-of-sale transactions, and memory cards may also be introduced. Memory cards will be briefly considered in this chapter under 'future developments' and also in chapter 14.

Existing credit card business can therefore be divided into bank credit cards, store cards, travel and entertainment cards, and petrol cards. These cards are mainly held by private individuals, although there is a small but growing market in company cards. Table 5.1 shows the estimated state of the overall UK credit card market at the beginning of 1986. The issue of cards is expanding at a rate of 20–25 per cent per annum, so the state of business at the end of the 1980s will obviously be very different from what it is today.

The credit card market in the UK is dominated by the bank credit card

Table 5.1   Credit cards in circulation in the UK (millions)

Bank credit cards		
Access	8.6	
Barclaycard	8.0	
Trustcard	2.4	
Other cards	0.5	
	⎯	19.5
Store cards		8.5
Travel and entertainment cards		
American Express	0.8	
Diners Club	0.3	
Other cards	0.1	
	⎯	1.2
Petrol cards		0.8
		⎯⎯
		30.0

Sources: Published and estimated data (1986) from credit card companies and other trade sources.

companies, and in particular by Access and Barclaycard, both of which have over 8 million cardholders with turnover in the region of £5 billion each. The Trustcard organization is also growing rapidly, and has about 2½ million cardholders. Many private individuals have accounts with more than one card company, and as a result the total number of individuals with bank credit cards is less than one would expect from the data shown in table 5.1. Most current estimates suggest that there are over 16 million credit cardholders, of whom about 12 million have bank credit cards.

In recent years the UK bank card companies have become part of vast international credit card networks. Barclaycard and Trustcard are linked to the Visa International network together with several of the smaller banks, e.g. the Bank of Scotland and the Co-operative Bank. The National Girobank is also a member of Visa and issued cards for the first time in 1985. There are currently more than 132 million Visa cardholders worldwide with over 4.7 million retail outlets in 160 different countries.

The Access credit card service is administered by the Joint Credit Card Company on behalf of Lloyds, Midland, National Westminster, Royal Bank of Scotland and several smaller banks. Access is now part of the Mastercard international network, which has over 100 million cardholders. As with Visa, there are more than 4 million retail outlets in 160 countries. Access is also affiliated with the Eurocard scheme operative in most Western European countries.

Detailed statistics regarding the Access and Barclaycard operations are provided in tables 5.2 and 5.3. Both of these organizations now have over 200,000 retail outlets in the UK, although there are, of course, many shops which are linked up with both Access and Barclaycard.

Table 5.2 Access credit card statistics

	1980	1981	1982	1983	1984	1985
Credit outstanding (£ millions)	564	760	984	1258	1504	1901
Number of cards issued (000s)	4863	5418	6056	6823	7589	8515
Number of accounts (000s)	4010	4423	4924	5529	6133	6923
Number of UK outlets (000s)	158	175	190	205	218	236
Value of turnover (£ millions)	1390	1833	2384	3152	3955	5032
of which cash advances	131	177	205	274	351	446
Volume of turnover (millions of transactions)	69	81	103	129	156	177
of which cash advances	3	4	4	6	7	8

Source: Abstract of Banking Statistics, 1986.

There are therefore many different types of credit cards in circulation in the UK and the number of promoting organizations will probably go up substantially in the future, with an increasing number of retailers and providers of financial services offering credit card facilities to their customers. Interested parties – card issuers, retailers and consumers – should obviously examine the related costs and benefits in some detail, as there will almost certainly be losers as well as gainers in this type of operation. In the remainder of this chapter an attempt will be made to examine the credit card system from the viewpoint of all major users, with particular emphasis on retail benefits and problems.

POTENTIAL RETAIL BENEFITS

There are a number of very important reasons why retailers accept credit

Table 5.3   Barclaycard statistics

	1980	1981	1982	1983	1984	1985
Credit outstanding (£ millions)	553	698	853	1068	1322	1668
Number of cards issued (000s)	5511	6113	6607	6804	7338	7947
Number of accounts (000s)	4577	5119	5476	5639	6049	6540
Number of UK outlets (00s)	153	177	192	202	216	235
Value of turnover (£ millions)	1358	1691	2179	2723	3376	4413
of which cash advances	124	187	254	302	359	455
Volume of turnover (millions of transactions)	74	84	99	116	136	164
of which cash advances	4	5	6	7	8	9

Source: Abstract of Banking Statistics, 1986. A changed basis of reporting produced a reduction in the number of accounts (and cards issued) of about 300,000 in 1983.

cards. These reasons will be examined under three main headings, together with a fourth heading which brings together several other small points which on their own might not be regarded as particularly important:

1 *Expectation of increased turnover and profit.* Those retailers who accept credit cards have in most cases decided to adopt this method of settlement because of the expectation of increased business which they hope will produce profit in excess of the charges of the credit card company. Whether these hopes are fulfilled will always be difficult to assess, especially when the goods that are sold and their prices are frequently changing. Nevertheless, one would expect that at this stage in the development of credit cards retailers should have some evidence as to whether increased sales and profit have been achieved, although it is obviously extremely difficult to assess what would have happened in the absence of cards.

The most detailed canvassing of retailer opinion to date was arranged by the Monopolies and Mergers Commission prior to its report *Credit Card Franchise Services* in September 1980.[2] The report certainly gives the impression that there are strong differences of opinion on this subject. On the one hand, some retailers believed that 'they were likely to receive additional business from the availability of a larger potential market, including overseas tourists', whilst on the other hand some were 'sceptical about the possibility of increased sales' (paras. 8.4 and 8.6).

Trade organizations were also asked for their views on credit cards. The National Chamber of Trade stated that 'some traders had told it that the amount of additional trade they received was appreciable and identifiable, whereas others had said it was negligible, but no one who responded to the Chamber's enquiries placed the total retail sales involving credit cards at more than 3 per cent of turnover and most thought it considerably less. From that figure the Chamber deduced that the overall increase in sales was not likely to be substantial' (para. 8.6).

It seems obvious, therefore, that there is a considerable amount of disagreement in the retail sector as to the additional business, if any, that is generated by the acceptance of credit cards, although views may have changed in the seven years that have passed since the publication of the Monopolies and Mergers Commission report. Credit card activity has expanded considerably since 1980, and new methods of using cards – telephone orders are probably the best example – have been adopted. There does appear to be a developing consensus, however, that by accepting credit cards many retailers avoid the penalty of lost business which would go to competitors if credit cards were not accepted. If this viewpoint is accepted, there are certainly some benefits to be obtained through the acceptance of credit cards, although the result of credit card transactions for some retailers could be a reduced net profit, as the charges of the credit card company will have to be met out of a turnover figure which may in some cases be maintained only in volume terms.

2 *Improved cash flow and guaranteed payment.* In the absence of credit card facilities, the retailer will probably have to accept cheques and grant credit facilities. Cheques may, of course, be dishonoured, especially if the amount involved is above the cheque card limit – currently £50. The granting of credit facilities will almost inevitably produce some overdue accounts and bad debts, especially in times of high unemployment.

The retailer who offers a credit card service may still have to accept

2 The Monopolies and Mergers Commission, *Credit Card Franchise Services*, (HMSO, 1980).

cheques and offer credit facilities, but these will probably be on a reduced scale as compared with the situation before the introduction of credit cards. Bank credit card vouchers, when paid in at an appropriate bank, e.g. Barclaycard vouchers paid into a Barclays Bank account, will be treated in the same way as cash receipts for bank calculation purposes, and there will be no clearance delay as in the case of cheques. There will, however, be a longer payment delay in the non-bank credit card companies such as American Express and Diners Club. In most cases, therefore, there should be improved cash flow and reduced bad debts as a result of the acceptance of bank credit cards, especially as compared with cheques and credit accounts.

The credit card company's charges will once again have to be carefully considered in reaching a decision about the real value of these potential benefits. Delayed payments and bad debts vary considerably from one credit-granting retail organization to another, and the frequency and size of past delays in payment and bad debts will obviously have to be considered in deciding whether this is a worthwhile potential benefit.

3 *Reduced administrative costs and bank charges.* Bookkeeping costs may be significantly reduced if cheque and credit account facilities are partly or wholly replaced by the use of credit cards. Other administrative and clerical costs may also be reduced, although there are still going to be handling costs involved in recording and paying in credit card vouchers. The procedures involved should, however, be readily understandable and simple to operate.

If cash receipts are replaced by credit card transactions, there may be some small internal and external cost savings before the charges of the card company are taken into account. For example, cash handling and security costs should be reduced, and there should certainly be a reduction in bank charges based on the reduced volume of cash transactions. Bank processing charges for small cash transactions will in some cases be greater than those for dealing with credit card vouchers, although there will obviously be no credit charges to meet in the case of cash receipts.

The size of these potential savings could be difficult to determine, as there may be little information available concerning the costs existing before the introduction or consideration of credit cards. Some retailers regard these savings as insignificant, although this may be at least partly due to an absence of information concerning the administrative costs and bank charges incurred in the handling of cash, cheques and credit transactions.

4 *Miscellaneous benefits*. If additional business is generated by the acceptance of credit cards, there should be numerous associated benefits to consider; for example, improved employment prospects. This may be particularly true in those organizations that deal with overseas tourists who might not otherwise spend their money in the UK. The international links of the credit card companies with Mastercard and Visa have been particularly useful in this respect. It should not be forgotten, however, that the widespread international acceptance of credit cards may persuade UK residents to buy goods overseas that they would otherwise have bought in the UK. This is illustrated by the fact that in 1985 Mastercard and Eurocard holders from overseas spent £208 million in the UK whilst Access cardholders spent £173 million abroad.

The advertising and promotional activities of the credit card companies may also help to bring additional business to the retailer: numerous leaflets and brochures are sent out by the credit card companies. The real value of this type of promotion may, however, become less important to the individual retailer as an increasing number of organizations accept credit cards, although it is possible that the number of 'special offers' may be significantly increased in the future.

Current and future developments in the credit card business may increase the list of potential benefits. Retailers are likely to be interested in the development of point-of-sale systems under which instantaneous or end-of-day electronic transfers are made to a shopper's credit card account. This should reduce the amount of paperwork that is necessary at the present time. These developments and other possible future changes, such as the introduction of memory cards, will be considered in chapter 14. Some of these new cards may not be primarily used for credit purposes, although they will probably become part of a comprehensive future range of plastic card services.

RETAIL COSTS AND PROBLEMS

The costs and problems that are likely to arise from the retailer's acceptance of credit cards will now be considered under three main headings:

1 *Credit card company charges*. The charges made by credit card companies are a frequent subject of conversation amongst retailers.

The 1980 Monopolies and Mergers Commission Report suggested that the range of bank credit card charges to retailers at that time varied from 0.5 to 8 per cent of turnover, although charges in excess of 5 per cent were rare (para. 11.83). Average charges are currently in the region of 2–3 per cent; for example, the average Barclaycard service charge in the early 1980s was between 2.3 and 2.5 per cent of total turnover. There is also a small retailer entry charge – normally in the region of £40. Charges are debited to the retailer's bank account on a monthly basis.

From the retailer's viewpoint it is naturally extremely difficult to assess whether the rate quoted in response to an initial enquiry is comparable to that given to other similar retailers or whether there is an element of negotiation involved in these processes. The large national company may be able to negotiate a lower rate than the small firm because of bargaining power and a better knowledge of the current market situation. A small element of competition does exist in this market, although experience suggests that there are unlikely to be any large differences between the three major bank credit card companies – Access, Barclaycard and Trustcard.

The probability is therefore that a bank credit card rate of between 2 and 5 per cent of turnover will be negotiated initially in respect of the retailer who does not have widespread national interests, with the rate probably being higher than normal in the first year or so of usage. This rate is likely to be strongly influenced by the level of turnover, although numerous other factors will be taken into account. For example, charges on petrol transactions, where margins have traditionally been rather low, are now in the region of 2 per cent of turnover. At one time in the extremely competitive conditions of the late 1970s credit card charges were alleged to take 50 per cent of the typical gross profit margin. Since that time, however, the average credit card charge for this type of service has been reduced to take account of low profit margins.

2 Price discrimination clauses. Many retailers have argued that, if a credit card system is being used, they should be able to offer discounts to customers for cash settlement. The bank credit card companies have consistently opposed this approach, and retailers have to sign an undertaking that they will not discriminate against credit card customers. This means that if a retailer charges more for a credit card deal than for a cash transaction the credit card company might withdraw its services. The Monopolies and Mergers Commission recommended that the 'no discrimination clause' should be abandoned (para. 11.107), but the government decided in 1981 that it could not support this recommendation, largely on the grounds that differential pricing might lead to higher charges for credit card customers and a resulting increase in the cost of living.

The retailer who accepts credit cards but also desires to encourage cash transactions has therefore been placed in an extremely difficult situation by this decision. The credit card companies are unlikely to be informed of most transactions involving discounts for cash, but there is nevertheless a risk that a retailer's credit card facilities might be withdrawn if cash discounts are offered and a complaint is made by a credit card customer. This is an illogical situation, but one with which retailers have had to live for several years.

3 *Time involved in checking cards and credit limits.* Credit card company regulations lay down that retailers should check all credit cards for signature, validity, etc., and ensure that there are no suspicious circumstances. Retailers are frequently provided with lists of stolen or missing credit cards which should be checked to ensure that all is in order on any proposed transaction. Credit limits for customers are also laid down and if the 'floor limit' is to be exceeded a telephone call must be made to the credit card company headquarters for approval, following which an authorization number will be provided for entry on the sales voucher. The size of this task is illustrated by the fact that in 1985 Access handled over 13 million authorization calls.

These procedures are likely to be time-consuming, although the credit card companies often refund the cost of telephone calls. In addition, there is obviously a risk that the credit card company will pass on any losses incurred if all the laid-down procedures are not observed. In practice this has not appeared to happen very often, if at all, although the increasing number of fraudulent transactions may produce a stricter attitude on this subject in the future.

In a busy retail store the required procedures may produce delays at check-out points, especially on a Friday or Saturday, when there may be a large number of customers waiting for attention. The time involved in these activities must be considered side-by-side with the administrative savings considered earlier in this chapter.

It is therefore extremely difficult for the retailer to decide whether credit cards should be accepted. There are now, however, over 300,000 UK providers of goods and services accepting credit cards and in those sectors where credit cards are very popular, e.g. the motor trade, hotels, restaurants, etc., it could be extremely difficult to increase trade if credit cards were not accepted. Nevertheless, the costs and problems involved in credit card acceptance should be carefully examined before a decision is made to accept cards of this nature.

The retailer, or his adviser, should consider customer viewpoints on credit cards in some detail, as the acceptance of these cards could help generate additional business. Five possible consumer advantages of credit cards, together with attached problems and disadvantages, will therefore now be considered:

1 *Speed and convenience*. Possession of a credit card generally ensures that the consumer does not have to carry large sums of cash for retail purchases, with the attendant risks involved in cash-holding activities. Cheques have to some extent fulfilled this function in the past, although it is often a time-consuming task to prepare a cheque and get it accepted by a retailer, especially if the transaction is over the cheque guarantee limit of £50. In most cases the consumer will find it quicker to use a credit card at the check-out point rather than arrange cheque or credit account facilities. Cash is, however, currently the quickest method of settlement.

There are, however, many retail organizations that will not accept credit cards – for example, most food retailers. This is largely due to low profit margins on turnover, which may not provide adequate cover for credit card charges. Growth in the number of shops accepting credit cards will obviously be limited by the large number of small retailers who, even if they could obtain approval from the card company, will generally find it uneconomic to use credit cards.

There is also likely to be a limit on the amount of credit card business that a consumer can arrange. The average personal credit limit is currently in the region of £700, although there will obviously be many credit limits above and below this figure. In most retail transactions, however, the credit card provides a speedy means of settlement which could become even faster in the future if electronic communication systems are introduced at the point-of-sale.

2 *Provision of credit facilities*. The holders of bank credit cards operating within their credit limit can automatically obtain flexible credit facilities with variable repayment terms based on a minimum payment per month – usually £5 or 5 per cent of the total amount outstanding, whichever is the greater. This type of extended credit is *not* offered by the travel and entertainment card companies. No

interest is payable to the bank credit card companies if the total amount outstanding is received within 25 days of the monthly statement date. The customer will therefore receive an average of 40 days interest-free credit with a possible maximum of 55 days (assuming a 30-day month) if goods are purchased at the beginning of the monthly account period. This period may become greater if the retailer does not pay credit card slips into the bank on the day of purchase.

There is, of course, a danger, as with all credit facilities, that consumers will purchase more than they can really afford. In the UK the average amount outstanding on an active bank credit card account is about £300, with repayments in the region of £60 per month. If the account is not paid in full, interest charges can become a real burden, especially if the payments made on account are small. The interest rate adopted by most companies in the latter part of 1986 was 2 per cent per month, which amounted to a true rate of about 26.8 per cent per annum using official government calculation methods. The latter rate was significantly in excess of normal bank overdraft charges, although credit card finance will usually be for a much shorter period than an overdraft. The importance of the interest charge in credit card company finances can be judged from the fact that at the beginning of 1986 Access were owed £1,928 million, of which £1,213 million was interest-bearing. The provision of credit facilities without any complicated paperwork (apart from the initial application) is, however, a great advantage to the customer, although it can lead to a situation in which the cardholder finds that it is extremely difficult to pay off the total amount outstanding.

3 *Protection against faulty goods and services.* The Consumer Credit Act gives the consumer the right in stipulated circumstances to claim against a lender where the goods or services received are unsatisfactory. The bank credit card companies have reluctantly accepted this liability, and as a result have been involved in some costly settlements. These provisions are not considered to apply, however, to travel and entertainment cards, where debts should be settled on an agreed date.

From the consumer's viewpoint, these provisions are helpful, as there will be a second party to claim against if goods or services are unsatisfactory. The bank credit card companies are naturally concerned about the legal position, as there does appear to be an open-ended commitment in this type of situation. The Consumer Credit Act was, however, changed from 1 January 1984, and the Act no longer applies to transactions under £100 or over £30,000. The new lower limit should provide some relief for the credit card companies on small transactions, although liability will remain in most travel and holiday bookings – a sector where there have recently been a significant number of business failures.

4 *Expenditure records*. Many private individuals find it difficult to keep records of personal and business expenditure. Credit cards should help in this process, although there will, of course, be some expenses that it will not be possible to charge to a credit card, e.g. small food and drink purchases may not be available on credit card facilities. Companies are also likely to welcome the vouchers provided by credit card companies, especially in the case of sales personnel, who often have a bad reputation for keeping details of costs incurred on business duties.

Credit cardholders now appear to be making much greater use of their cards, presumably because of the rapidly increasing number of retail outlets that accept credit cards. For example, Access has reported that the average cardholder used his/her card 29.4 times in 1984 as opposed to 21.1 times in 1980. Improved records of expenditure should therefore be available, especially in respect of business transactions. The increasing number of company cards should help in this connection, although there are obviously some dangers to the sponsoring company in the widespread use of these cards.

5 *Miscellaneous advantages*. The consumer who has the use of a credit card is not limited to purchases of goods or services in the UK. Items can be purchased with a credit card in many overseas countries, details of which can be obtained in the UK. It is also possible to obtain cash advances – usually up to £100 per day – in the UK and certain overseas countries, although there is a charge for this type of service; for example, in 1985, Barclaycard levied a charge of 1.5 per cent of the amount withdrawn. The credit card can therefore be extremely useful when emergencies arise.

One facility that may be of great value to credit card holders is the ability to order goods by telephone. This service is being increasingly used in respect of debts arising from advertisements, charity contributions, holiday or hotel bookings, mail order business, theatre ticket bookings etc. There does seem to be considerable potential growth in this type of business, although the retailer or provider of services does not have a signature in the case of dispute.

The credit card company may also offer discounts or special prices to cardholders. For example, discounts on health insurance and car rental charges, as well as personal accident insurance are currently being offered to some cardholders. Price reductions of this nature may, however, be of interest to only a small number of cardholders, although it does seem probable that more of these offers will be made in the future.

The average retailer is therefore likely to be dealing with an increasing number of customers who are looking for credit card facilities. This trend is likely to increase as long as the UK bank credit companies retain their present policy of not charging consumers for the use of their card (though the travel and entertainment card companies do make an annual charge). The typical transaction may not be very large – current figures suggest that the average bank credit card purchase is about £25 – but there will nevertheless be a reasonable opportunity for increased business. Cardholding consumers are likely to prefer the shop that offers credit card facilities, especially if there is little or no difference in pricing policy, and retailers will obviously have to take this factor into account in deciding whether to provide credit card services.

CARD ISSUER VIEWPOINTS

In most credit card operations it takes several years for the whole operation to become profitable. Barclaycard, in its evidence to the Monopolies and Mergers Commission in the late 1970s, stated that its credit card activities did not become profitable until 1977 (operations began in 1966). It was difficult, however, for realistic profit figures to be produced for credit card activities as there were some important shared facilities within the Barclays group, e.g. computer services. Despite these difficulties, the Monopolies and Mergers Commission did attempt to measure profitability, and subject to some qualifications came to the conclusion that in 1978 the return on average capital resources was 28.9 per cent (para. 3, sections 107–29), an attractive return in the conditions existing at that time.

Comparative figures for the Access organization were much more difficult for the Monopolies and Mergers Commission to obtain because of the complex structure of the group. Returns on capital were, however, lower than was the case with Barclaycard, although Access began operations six years after Barclaycard. It is also interesting to note that Access was in profit six years after commencement, as compared with eleven years in the case of the Barclaycard operation, although Barclaycard was of course the pioneer in the UK bank credit card sector.

In the years following the Monopolies and Mergers Commission Report there has been no similar detailed study of costs and profits, and the banks have naturally not been keen to disclose similar information to non-government organizations or individuals. In recent years, however, it is believed that bank credit card activities have been very profitable. For example, it has recently been suggested that Barclaycard made a profit of £100 million in 1985,[3] although there have probably been substantial variations from one year to another because of changes in interest rates, fraud and other associated factors.

In their attempts to achieve satisfactory levels of profits, the credit card companies have encounted several important problems. Some of these have now been largely overcome by, for example, computerization of the monthly statement process, but there are still two extremely important matters that have not been resolved; the amount of paperwork required to record transactions and the high level of fraud.

The paperwork burden has increased rapidly in recent years. The major factor in this process has been the increase in the number of transactions, which have more than doubled since the beginning of the 1980s (see tables 5.2 and 5.3). These increases in paperwork have inevitably played their part in pushing up clerical costs and in particular the number of staff employed. The scale of this problem is illustrated by the fact that in 1985 Access processed 222 million sales vouchers with a daily peak of 2.1 million vouchers on 30 December. Payment vouchers for retailers also present a major problem – 51 million were processed by Access in 1985.

There will probably be no short-term solution to the paperwork and staffing problems; indeed they may become much worse in the late 1980s. The long-term solution must lie in the electronic communication of transaction data at the point-of-sale. The way in which these changes are beginning to take place will be considered under 'future developments' in this chapter and also in chapter 14.

The fraud problem is another area of major concern. Total fraudulent transactions in respect of cheque and credit cards are believed to be rapidly approaching £50 million per annum, of which nearly £20 million relates to credit cards. Access fraud losses for 1985 were £6.5 million, although this represented a small reduction as compared with the previous year (£6.9 million). Barclaycard's 1985 losses were £7.9 million as compared with £8.6 million in 1984. These statistics do not look quite so serious when they are related to the total number of cards in circulation or to turnover; annual losses amongst the major bank credit card companies have in recent years been less than £1 per card or 20p per £100 of turnover. These figures

3 N. Collins, The Plastic Jewel in Barclays Crown, *Sunday Times*, 16 February 1986, p. 49.

have tended to fall in the last year or two, probably because of improved security methods, although greatly increased turnover has produced a situation in which it has until recently not been possible to reduce the overall level of fraud.

Most of the fraudulent credit card transactions in the UK come about as a result of loss or theft rather than the illegal reproduction of cards. In the USA there is a substantial amount of illegal reproduction, but this type of activity has not yet spread to the UK on any significant scale. Most fraudulent activity in the UK has in the past taken place when cards have been 'doctored' to remove the signature, and thieves then provide their own style of signature to correspond with the name on the card.

In response to these problems, the credit card and cheque card companies have taken action on three major fronts:

1 *Public awareness of fraud.* The major action that the banks have taken on this front has been to launch campaigns to alert the public in general and cardholders in particular to the risks involved in holding cheque and credit cards. Posters and leaflets have been issued to alert cardholders to the dangers of leaving cards in unattended handbags and other places to which thieves have relatively easy access. It is difficult to judge the effects of such a campaign, although the banks seem to be convinced that the campaign has produced positive results. It is also possible that the credit card companies may decide to make more use of the clause under which most issuers have the right to charge the cardholder with the first £25 of losses incurred when a card is lost. This clause does not appear to have been used very much, if at all, in the past.

2 *Authorization procedures.* The credit card companies normally lay down limits as to the size of transaction that individual retailers can arrange without obtaining approval. Until relatively recently, the only way in which this could be done was by means of a normal telephone call, which could be very time-consuming. It is now possible, however, to install special transaction telephones which can also be used for other purposes. Under this system the credit card (this is likely to be every card, not just those exceeding the store limit) is passed through a card reader unit which is built on to the side of the telephone. As a result of this process, a connection is established to the computer centre of the card company. The card is then automatically checked to see if it is valid and whether the credit limit is being exceeded (the proposed amount is typed in beforehand). If the transaction is acceptable, an authorization code appears on the telephone's display board. On the other hand, the

transaction may be rejected or the retailer could be put into contact with the card company or instructed to re-dial. This type of authorization process takes an average of 25 seconds. and it has already led to the recovery of many stolen cards.

There were about 5,000 transaction telephones in use in the UK in the early part of 1986 by both retailers and banks with rapid expansion envisaged over the next five years. The cost of these units, which are supplied by several manufacturers, is currently in the region of £300, with most units being programmed to accept up to 15 issuers' cards. The major card companies have set up a special marketing organization – On Line Card Services – to provide this equipment, which will in most cases be leased to the retailer at about £10 per month. The capital expenditure incurred in the widespread use of these systems could, of course, be substantial, and it will be interesting to see how far this movement progresses in the retail sector.

3 *Card security systems and retailer checking procedures.* The card companies have always had power to charge retailers with losses involved in fraudulent transactions where these losses arise because of the fault of the retailer, e.g. failure to check signatures. In the UK, however, very little action has been taken against retailers in these situations. As a result, checking procedures have often been extremely lax. Numerous safeguards are now available to the card companies if they wish to take more security precautions; signature verification systems, provision of photographs, finger and hand prints, voice analysis, etc. Unfortunately for the card companies the cost of these techniques is still unacceptably high; for example, the provision of a photograph on a credit or cheque card might double the cost of a card.

Action currently being taken to improve the security of cards includes the use of sophisticated colour-printing techniques, the provision of tamper-proof signature panels and the inclusion of a hologram (a three dimensional photograph which changes with the viewing angle) on the front of the card. Steps are also being taken to stimulate retailer interest in checking procedures. For example, more attention is being devoted to rewards for retail employees who spot frauds. Over £1 million was paid out in rewards by bank credit card companies in 1985, mainly in the form of £50 payments to retail employees.

The banks are therefore actively seeking to improve procedures for the detection of fraud, although experience in the USA would suggest that success will have to be measured in containment terms rather than a dramatic reduction or complete elimination of fraud. It is difficult to see a long-term solution to the fraud problem using cards at present in circulation, although the paperwork problem may eventually be at least partly solved through the use of electronic communication methods.

FUTURE DEVELOPMENTS

Credit cards have become an important part of the consumer credit scene in the UK in a relatively short period. Table 5.4 shows the major forms of consumer credit, together with estimates of their current importance. From this table it will be seen that credit cards provide almost one-quarter of total consumer credit and are exceeded only by bank loans and overdrafts as a source of credit.

Most of the major developments in credit card finance have taken place in the last decade. It is difficult, therefore, to estimate what changes and developments one will see in the next decade. It does seem inevitable, however, that credit card growth will continue and the number of adults holding cards in the UK could well increase to 20 million, with many of these individuals holding several credit cards (the average UK bank cardholder has fewer than three cards as compared with a figure of about eight in the USA).

Table 5.4 Patterns of consumer credit in the UK

Type of credit	Percentage of total value
Bank loans and overdrafts	30
Credit cards	24
Direct finance house loans	19
Indirect finance house loans	14
Mail order	4
Retail store accounts	4
Other	5
Total	100

Source: AGB Index, London, 1985.

The growth in the issue of credit cards over the next decade may, however, come more from non-bank sources as the banks, especially Barclays (about 70 per cent of Barclays customers now have a Barclaycard), have probably recruited most of their interested account-holders.

We may, therefore, see a substantial increase in the number of store and petrol cards, and non-banking financial institutions could eventually become a significant influence in the market. Links between large consumer and professional organizations and some of the credit card companies may also become popular. For example, the Law Society and Access have recently announced a scheme under which it will be possible for solicitors' clients to pay their accounts by credit card. A joint scheme has also been announced by the Automobile Association and the Bank of Scotland under which a Visa card will be issued to all approved applicants.

Bank credit cards are, of course, already used extensively in stores and petrol stations. Leading stores and oil companies will obviously have to take this into account when discussions take place as to whether new cards should be issued. The store card can encourage customer loyalty and it should help in the building up of a customer mailing list. It may also be cheaper from the large retailer's viewpoint than the use of bank credit cards, although much will depend on the number of outlets, the amount of turnover, the availability of finance and the efficiency of marketing and administration. Administration is often managed by a bank or finance company rather than from within the company. A retailer will therefore have many matters to consider before issuing a store card, although recent events, e.g. the entry of Marks and Spencer into the credit card business, seem to indicate that a big expansion in the number of store credit cards may be on the way in the next decade.

There may also be significant changes in the types of businesses that accept credit cards. In the past credit card business has been dominated by retailers in clothing and footwear, travel and entertainment, household goods and furniture, consumer durables and the motor trade. In recent years, however, determined efforts have been made to 'sell' the credit card system to the service sector, with particular emphasis on insurance and utility payments. An increasing number of local authorities and nationalized industries are now accepting credit card payments, although billing may have to be made automatically at the time of invoicing rather than at the consumer's discretion.

Attempts are also likely to be made to persuade major food stores to accept credit cards. This has proved to be a difficult task in a competitive environment in which gross margins can be very low. It is possible that ideas will change if paperwork and delays at the check-out point can be reduced, although credit card company charges will probably continue to be the major obstacle if significant reductions in rates cannot be negotiated. Future developments may be strongly influenced by the decision of Tesco Stores in December 1985 to accept Access and Visa cards for all types of food transactions.

It also seems probable that increasing attempts will be made by the card issuers to persuade companies to apply for cards for use by senior members of staff whilst on business duties. Barclaycard is the only company that has in the past provided detailed statistics on this subject; for example, at the end of 1985 there were over 100,000 Barclaycard company cards in circulation controlled by about 27,000 companies. Cities and towns may also distribute cards in a similar way to companies. Wilmslow was the first town to move in this direction in early 1985, and Tunbridge Wells issued a similar card in 1986.

Future developments may be strongly influenced by the debate on the introduction of electronic funds transfer systems at the point-of-sale (EFTPOS). Originally it was envisaged that the primary objective of these systems would be to arrange the instantaneous transfer of funds from the customer's account to that of the retailer. The credit card habit is, however, so firmly ingrained in the UK that it may be extremely difficult to persuade shoppers to accept the idea of instantaneous bank settlement. It now seems extremely likely, therefore, that provision will have to be made for electronic transfers to credit card accounts, especially in the non-food sector where credit cards have been used for many years. Several experiments of this nature are taking place in the UK, mainly at retail stores and petrol stations. Plastic card developments will be considered in more detail in chapter 14.

There may also be a place in our future payments system for the 'memory card', which is currently being experimented with in France. This card involves the use of one or more built-in microprocessors to record transactions and, if necessary, set them against a bank balance or credit limit. It is possible that at some future date credit card transactions could be recorded in this way, although there are still some doubts regarding the probable cost of this type of card and its ability to stand up to extensive usage.

Technological change is therefore likely to dominate the credit card scene over the next few years, although this will not mean that the more traditional areas of expansion and improvement will be neglected. Those credit card companies which ignore technological developments may well find themselves in difficulties, as there is little doubt that the credit card sector will be much more competitive in the next decade.

SUMMARY AND CONCLUSIONS

The credit card business has achieved remarkable growth and acceptance in the last decade, although current UK statistics indicate that cards of this nature are responsible for less than 1 per cent of transactions in number terms and about 5 per cent in value terms. Credit cards are, however, used for about 10 per cent of non-cash transactions, and use is expanding very fast, with annual growth exceeding 20 per cent per annum in numbers of cards issued and 25 per cent per annum in turnover terms.

The rapid expansion in the number of credit card transactions has brought with it a paper mountain which has more than doubled in the last four years to about 500 million transactions per annum worth considerably above £15 billion. This paper mountain has proved to be difficult and expensive to handle, and it has given added urgency to the challenge of introducing electronic communication systems at the point-of-sale.

Credit cards, like cheques and credit transfers, have therefore been reasonably satisfactory methods of arranging retail settlement in the past, but they have created a vast amount of paperwork which is very costly to handle, and also numerous fraud problems. The new electronic systems, when they become widely available, must of course be acceptable to retailers and consumers, although if the problems can be overcome there should be considerable cost savings. The banks and credit card companies will not find this easy, but it is a task that must be attempted if paperwork and fraudulent activity are to be kept under control.

6 Electronic Payment Systems

In the last twenty years there have been many technological developments in banking which have, amongst other things, produced a situation in which substantial changes are possible in payment practices. Where developments of this nature have already taken place, long-established systems have often been changed, or improved, and some new methods of effecting payments have been introduced. New technology will, however, never be easily accepted, and there are still many doubts amongst bankers and other interested parties as to whether all proposed electronic payment systems will prove to be cost-effective and whether changes will be acceptable to employees and customers.

This chapter provides a brief introduction to electronic payment systems – past, present and future. Some important developments have already taken place in the UK in the last fifteen years through the services provided by Bankers' Automated Clearing Services (BACS) and the Clearing House Automated Payments System (CHAPS). CHAPS was set up in 1984 and it is too early to make any realistic assessment of its achievements. BACS has, however, been remarkably successful since its formation in 1971, and current estimates suggest that by 1987 this organization will be electronically processing over 1 billion payments per annum. Individual banks have also been heavily involved with electronic developments, and nearly 9,000 cash dispensers and automated teller machines have been installed in the last fifteen years.

The electronic era has therefore already arrived in the banking sector, although there are additional changes on the horizon which may produce dramatic changes in payment systems over the next decade; for example, funds transfers at the point-of-sale, home and office banking, memory cards, etc. All these developments will be briefly examined in this chapter, with more detailed coverage provided in later chapters.

ELECTRONIC FUNDS TRANSFERS

There is no agreed international definition of electronic funds transfer (EFT) systems. In some books and articles this term is used in a very comprehensive all-embracing sense whereas other authors use the term much more restrictively. The broadest type of definition usually suggests that EFT systems should cover all money transfers in which processing is carried out partly or completely by electronic methods. Under this type of definition it is often not made clear in what form the transaction should be initiated and completed. It is therefore the electronic nature of the processing which is important rather than the input and output processes.

A good illustration of the definition problem is provided by the cheque as it is currently processed by most UK banks. Magnetic ink characters at the bottom of the cheque – partly filled in before issue of the cheque book and partly after lodgement – have transformed a significant part of cheque clearing into an electronic process. Documentation is, however, in a paper form, and cheques normally have to be returned to the payer's branch at the end of the clearing process. Truncation processes may eventually remove this need, although it seems highly probable that cheques will remain in a paper form for many years to come.

It might be argued, therefore, that cheques can now be classified as EFT transactions, although the vast majority of writers on this subject agree that EFT statistics should include only those payments which are wholly or largely initiated by electronic processes and completed in a similar form. Such an approach would rule out cheques, paper-based credit transfers and cash lodgements processed by electronic methods but which are still primarily paper transactions.

The approach outlined in the previous paragraph is similar to the one that was favoured by the US National Commission on Electronic Fund Transfers,[1] which in 1977 defined the EFT system as 'a payments system in which the processing and communications necessary to effect economic exchanges and the processing and communications necessary for the production and distribution of services incidental or related to economic exchanges are dependent wholly or in large part on the use of electronics'.

This rather complex definition emphasizes the importance of the communications process, and stresses the fact that both processing and communications should be dependent – wholly or in large part – on the use of electronics. Under this definition input and output processes would normally be in electronic form, although a limited use of paper methods would presumably be acceptable.

1 *EFT in the United States*, (US National Commission on Electronic Fund Transfers, 1977).

One of the earliest UK attempts to solve the definition problem was provided in a study published by the University of Wales Press in 1979.[2] This suggested that EFT systems should cover 'the provision by financial institutions of the maximum range of services that it is at present operationally feasible to offer through computer linked terminals located either on or off bank premises and linked to current, deposit or other forms of account'.

This definition would probably have satisfied most people with an interest in EFT at the time of publication, although there have been some important developments in the years that have passed since this book was published. In particular, it now begins to look as if the banks will not dominate the EFT sector as was originally envisaged. For example, retailers have already set up EFT systems in the USA and some European countries, and building societies are taking a very active interest in the UK and some Commonwealth countries. The banks will inevitably be involved with most of these schemes, although they will not necessarily play a leading role in the provision of finance, personnel, etc.

It is also debatable as to whether EFT installations should be on-line, off-line or a combination of the two processes. Under an on-line system, data can be transmitted to an external computer instantaneously or at another convenient time. This would normally involve the use of telecommunication services, which can be very expensive in terms of both capital and revenue expenditure. Costs can be reduced through the use of off-line systems, under which data can be physically transmitted at the end of the day by tape, disc, etc. Security under such systems can be suspect, as on-line authorization is not possible, although it may be possible to use a combination of on-line and off-line techniques.

If telecommunications services are used as part of an EFT installation, it is important that there should be an appreciation of the various systems that are available. In the UK it has been possible for over twenty years to transmit computer data by telecommunications links through the public telephone network or leased lines. In the late 1970s and early 1980s, however, a new packet switching facility became available, and this produced significant improvements in the carrying and distribution of telecommunications messages. The packet switching service provides the ability to break down messages into parts so that data can be sent by the shortest and cheapest route; messages are converted back into their original form at the end of the communication process. British Telecom provides these services in the UK under the name of Packet Switch Stream

---

2 D. Hopton, *Electronic Fund Transfer Systems: The Issues and Implications* (University of Wales Press, 1979).

(PSS), and it is currently developing several other communication systems based on digital technology which should speed up transmission times very significantly. Booklets on this subject can be obtained from British Telecom.

Despite these and other recent changes it is considered desirable that a simple, readily understandable definition of EFT should be provided in this book, as most readers will not be specialists in electronic engineering or other related subjects. EFT will here be assumed to cover all those transactions in which funds are transferred from one account to another by electronic techniques, with input and output methods being largely or completely in electronic form. This definition may not satisfy all interested parties, as some technical aspects of the subject are not taken into account; but as this is not a highly technical book, it is considered to be adequate, bearing in mind the subject matter under discussion.

CURRENT OPERATIONAL SYSTEMS

Some accountants and business men think of EFT systems as a development of the future rather than something that is already with us. A reading of the tables provided in chapter 3 – see for example, table 3.2 – should, however, have indicated that automated systems are already in widespread use in banking, and the BACS organization is now processing well over 20 per cent of the non-cash payments handled by the major clearing banks. Payments processed by BACS have to be in an approved computer-input form, but this is becoming less difficult as the range of acceptable input methods is extended and an increasing number of businesses install or have access to computer systems.

BACS currently dominates the EFT payment scene in the UK as far as the number of domestic UK transactions handled is concerned – 835 million transactions in 1985 for more than £250 billion. In value terms, however, the CHAPS system has already become more important, as this method of payment has been specifically designed for large payments (over £10,000). In 1985 2.2 million payments were arranged for £2,355 billion.

Most BACS and CHAPS transactions involve customers who have accounts with different banks. In addition, there are many transactions which involve customers who bank with different branches of the same bank. This type of transfer has been heavily promoted by the National Girobank as well as some of the other clearing banks. Opinions appear to vary amongst bankers as to whether it is more cost-effective to use BACS or internal electronic transfer systems for inter-branch transfers.

International payments are also an important element of banking transactions. The electronic system provided by the Society for Worldwide Interbank Financial Telecommunication (SWIFT) has produced considerable improvements in international bank communication methods in recent years. The services provided by BACS, CHAPS, National Girobank and SWIFT will be considered in more detail in chapter 7.

Electronic systems can be used for a wide range of payments made by central and local government, nationalized industries, commercial and industrial organizations and private individuals. Four chapters (8–11) will therefore be devoted to separate studies of direct debit agreements, purchase ledger payments, wages and salaries, and government benefits. Chapter 12 will be concerned with automated cash dispensing transactions, many of which are processed by electronic methods.

EFT systems have been in operation in the UK for over a decade, although growth in the number of transactions was not very substantial until the early 1980s. In 1986 the number of domestic electronic funds transfers (including automated cash withdrawals) should be over 1½ billion, and this could be the start of a rapid expansion period which might lead to more than 10 billion EFT transactions by the end of the century.

FUTURE DEVELOPMENTS

EFT developments in the late 1980s and the early 1990s will be a combination of expansion of existing facilities and the introduction of new services. Some of the new applications are already being experimented with in the UK and overseas; other which have not yet been seriously considered could develop in the 1990s. Bankers are, however, very conservative individuals, and it seems unlikely that new systems will be introduced at short notice. EFT systems could, of course, be set up by non-banking institutions, e.g. building societies, finance companies and retailers, although the capital and expertise required will probably restrict the initiation of these schemes to large or very progressive organizations.

The major new development in EFT systems in the late 1980s will probably be the introduction of electronic funds transfers at the point-of-sale (EFTPOS) in retail and service organizations. Experimental projects have already been set up in the UK, USA and a growing number of countries in Europe, Asia and Australasia. In the UK, banks, building societies and major retailers are now in the process of examining systems and applications, and it is hoped that several major projects, set up in 1986, will provide further operating experience. This could lead to a nationwide scheme in 1988, although no firm commencement date has yet been set. The EFTPOS system is considered in more detail in chapter 13.

Electronic developments in the credit card sector are also likely to receive much attention over the next decade. Credit cards produce a considerable amount of paperwork, and extensive efforts are being made to introduce electronic communication systems. Experimental projects are already taking place in which electronic transfers are made to the cardholder's account at the time of sale or at the end of the same day. Memory cards with an in-built microprocessor are also being experimented with, especially in France, although there are doubts about the cost and durability of these cards. These developments are considered in chapter 14.

Home and office banking systems are also being used on an experimental basis in the UK and several overseas countries. These systems will probably provide bank statement or other similar data by means of computerized telecommunications links, and there may be facilities to arrange certain payments or transfers by typing in instructions from the home or workplace. There are some doubts in the banking sector about the viability of these schemes, although there does seem to be a growing consensus amongst bankers that businesses are more likely to be prepared to pay the costs involved than private individuals. Home banking is considered in chapter 15 followed by an examination of corporate cash management systems in chapter 16.

There are, therefore, many possible new developments that could take place in EFT systems over the next decade. The technology for most of these systems is already available, although it is by no means certain that all the systems which have been mentioned will eventually be introduced on a national or international scale. Extensive experimentation is, however, taking place, and this should enable us to see more clearly over the next few years the effects and implications of the introduction of these systems. This very important aspect of the EFT debate will be examined in chapter 17.

SUMMARY AND CONCLUSIONS

In the 1970s and early 1980s there was significant progress in the UK in the introduction of EFT systems. As a result, there are expected to be about 1½ billion EFT transactions in 1986, although this will make up less than 2 per cent of all payments. If cash payments are ignored, however, EFT transactions should make up well over 20 per cent of non-cash payments, which perhaps provides a fairer indication of the growing importance of the EFT movement.

In the late 1980s and early 1990s existing EFT systems will probably expand rapidly, and there is likely to be a development of new systems, especially in the retail sector. This should have a significant effect on cash and cheque transactions, although we may have to wait until the 1990s for an extensive use of EFT systems.

Electronic communication systems in the home and the business organization should also lead to a greater use of EFT systems, despite some doubts about the cost-effectiveness of these systems. The credit card companies are also likely to make extensive use of electronic systems, although the objective of these processes will be an entry in the credit cardholder's account rather than an immediate transfer of funds.

Payment systems may therefore be revolutionized over the next two decades by the widespread use of electronic systems. The remaining chapters of this book will examine existing and possible new systems, with a detailed study of present and future applications. It is hoped that the end-result will be a much better appreciation of the electronic payment systems that will probably be in widespread use by the end of the current century.

7 Funds Transfer Agencies

The movement towards EFT systems in major developed countries has in most cases been greatly assisted by the creation of specialized bank agencies which have been given the responsibility of providing electronic transfer services at a central or regional level. These agencies are usually called automated clearing houses (ACHs), although other descriptions are sometimes adopted. In Western Europe ACHs tend to operate on behalf of most, if not all, of the major banks in a particular country, although in the USA there are over 30 ACHs, most of them operating on a regional level. Individual banks may, of course, have their own EFT communications network for inter-branch and other related transfers, although these facilities are unlikely to be satisfactory when transfers are required at short notice to accounts with other banks.

In the UK the first major development in this direction was the setting up of Bankers' Automated Clearing Services (BACS) in 1971. This has been an extremely successful operation, which now handles well over 20 per cent of all bank clearance items. In more recent years another important development has taken place in the setting up of the low-volume, high-value Clearing House Automated Payments System (CHAPS), which was officially launched in February 1984. It is rather early to assess the success of this new venture, although it is already being predicted that this organization will have taken over most, if not all, of the high-value clearing business by the early 1990s.

The National Girobank is another major provider of electronic banking services. This organization was set up in 1978, although there had been a post office giro system in operation since 1968. The primary objective of the National Girobank was initially to provide funds transfer services, although in recent years it has begun to provide a much wider range of bank services. The National Girobank is therefore beginning to bear some similarities to other clearing banks, although a separate section in this chapter was considered to be justified in view of its highly specialized funds transfer activities.

The BACS, CHAPS and National Girobank organizations are all involved in domestic electronic banking operations. In many cases, however, funds have to be transferred overseas at short notice, and coverage will therefore be provided of the services provided by the Society for Worldwide Interbank Financial Telecommunication (SWIFT). This organization is an international banking telecommunications agency, through which many instructions for international transfers of funds are arranged. It is *not* strictly speaking a funds transfer agency, although many SWIFT messages lead to funds transfers.

BANKERS' AUTOMATED CLEARING SERVICES

The Committee of London Clearing Bankers has been heavily involved in computer developments over the last 30 years. In the late 1950s an Electronics Sub-Committee was set up, one of its major assignments being the production of plans regarding automation of bank payment processes. In the 1960s further projects were considered and a working party was set up in 1965 to examine ways in which electronic payment data might be exchanged between banks. In 1969 an important part of this project was completed when it became possible for the first time for interested organizations to provide instructions on magnetic tape for funds to be transferred from their bank accounts to those of other account-holders.

Initially, the bank transfer automation process came under the Inter-Bank Computer Bureau, but in 1970 it was decided to set up a separate company – Bankers' Automated Clearing Services (BACS) Limited – to handle automated clearing processes. BACS began trading in December 1971, initially from temporary accommodation, although a new building was taken over in June 1972. BACS is still located at these premises in Edgware, about 11 miles from the City of London; there is a small London office (in Bread Street) and additional premises have now been built at Dunstable to provide a contingency operational centre. These facilities should be adequate for the remainder of the 1980s, although the overall number of transactions handled could increase dramatically in the 1990s, especially if the leading building societies are allowed to initiate BACS transactions.

Table 7.1 shows the way in which BACS activity has expanded since the early 1970s. The number of transactions processed passed the 200 million mark in 1974, 400 million in 1980, 600 million in 1983 and 800 million in 1985. This is greater than the ACH figure for the whole of the USA – about

600 million transactions. Current estimates suggest that BACS will be processing over one billion transactions by 1987 and there are hopes that in the early 1990s the two billion transaction mark will be reached. These projections suggest that by the mid-1990s BACS transfers could make up over 40 per cent of all items processed in bank clearance procedures as compared with about 15 per cent in the early 1980s.

Table 7.1   Items processed by Bankers' Automated Clearing Services (BACS)

Year	Transactions (millions)	Percentage growth rate
1972	165	–
1973	198	20
1974	216	9
1975	238	10
1976	261	10
1977	296	13
1978	335	13
1979	384	15
1980	432	12
1981	485	12
1982	544	12
1983	609	12
1984	723	19
1985	835	16

Source: Adapted from the BACS publication *A Better Way to Pay*. The large initial 1972 figure is due to the fact that the Inter-Bank Computer Bureau carried out similar activities between 1969 and 1971.

In value terms BACS transfers are not as great as one might expect, since most large transactions are settled by cheque or through CHAPS (see next section of this chapter). Nevertheless, BACS is now handling transfers worth over £250 billion per annum, and this figure is increasing very fast. BACS has therefore been a great success story to date with about 25,000 business users, many of whom are making payments through BACS for several different purposes, e.g. salaries, trade payments, interest, dividends, etc.

Data processing

Business organizations have to be 'sponsored' by their own bank before they can use BACS services. If past trading activity, workload and potential cost savings appear to justify the use of the BACS system, arrangements can be made for a discussion with a BACS representative. In recent years the BACS system has been heavily promoted by the banks at branch level and in newspaper advertisements; Lloyds, for example, has recently arranged several large advertisements.

Methods of computer input to the BACS system must be carefully considered. Half-inch magnetic tape has traditionally been the most popular form of input, although it is now possible to use cassette and diskette facilities (5¼ and 8 inch). The appropriate criteria for BACS submissions are laid down in an official publication, and the prospective business customer will have to assess whether these can be complied with using present or possible future equipment. A computer bureau might be used if the costs involved in such an exercise could be justified.

The most important recent development in BACS input systems has been the introduction of telecommunications links. As a result, business customers can use connections arranged through the public telephone network, leased lines or a private circuit. Data can be transmitted to BACS under either an on-demand or a scheduled service; in the latter case a time slot is allocated prior to each connection.

The BACS telecommunications service (usually described as BAC-STEL) operates from Monday to Friday (excluding bank holidays) from 8.30 in the morning to 9.0 in the evening with an immediate reporting back process through an acceptance (or rejection) advice. Files can be transmitted up to 31 working days before the specified processing date. The system can operate at a very high speed (2,000 items can be transmitted in about 5 minutes using private circuits such as Kilostream), and it avoids the need for data to be transported to Edgware or the BACS city office. Telecommunications links have been available for BACS transactions only since 1983 (apart from some experimental projects) but there is already considerable evidence that this is going to be a popular addition to BACS services, especially for payments which cannot be calculated well in advance, such as weekly wages. Figure 7.1 provides an illustration of the way in which the BACSTEL system operates.

Magnetic tape, cassettes and diskettes will for the time being continue to be extensively used for BACS purposes, with magnetic tape submissions currently making up over 80 per cent of the total number of items processed. For all these forms of input, arrangements will have to be made for transportation to BACS premises. Some of the major clearing banks will assist in this process, although security vans and post office services (Datapost) are frequently used. Processing of data takes place on a 3-day schedule covering 36½ hours. This timetable lays down that if payment tapes are received at Edgware before 9 p.m. on day 1, cleared funds will be made available for the payee by 9.30 a.m. on day 3 (or up to 31 working days later if required). The debit and credit entries are usually recorded on day 3; the previous day and two nights are required for processing

Figure 7.1   Relationship between the BACS system and telecommunications network

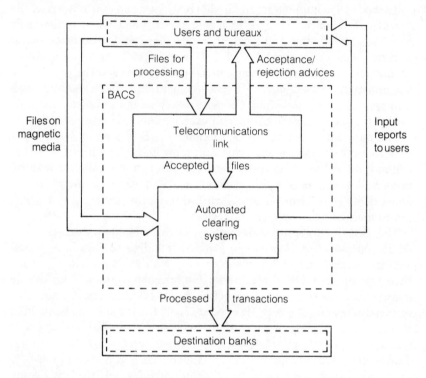

Source: BACS leaflet: *Telecommunications*, 1985.

purposes by BACS and the banks concerned with the transaction. The same timetable is used for BACSTEL, although the time required for delivery to BACS premises should no longer be a major concern.

The larger business with sophisticated computer and telecommunications links will usually be able to use the BACS system without any substantial additional capital expenditure. Small and medium-sized businesses may come up against more difficulties, and it may be appropriate to use a computer bureau if the volume of work justifies such a system. Some of the major banks are also prepared to produce input data from paper material, although there will, of course, be an additional charge for this service. Operational costs should always be carefully considered, especially those relating to telecommunications services, which can add up to a very significant amount over the course of a financial year.

Applications

Initially the BACS system was most heavily used for standing orders arranged by both private individuals and business organizations. Before the introduction of BACS there were many standing orders in existence, and it was not a difficult task to automate these payments. In many cases private individuals were not aware that these payments had been automated, as the effect was virtually identical to that achieved under the previous paper-based system. From the payee's angle, there were hopes that funds would arrive two days earlier than was previously the case, although the UK banks are still maintaining this delay period, mainly because of the possibility of cancellation on the day of debiting and the fact that there are still a significant number of paper-based standing orders. In the future there will probably be pressure for this delay period to be reduced or eliminated on automated transactions, as same-day transfers are normally arranged for other BACS items.

Direct debits had also been in use before the BACS system was introduced, but they were not as popular as standing orders for regular commitments – BACS figures for 1972 were 98 million standing orders and 55 million direct debits. By 1985, however, the number of direct debits processed by BACS was considerably higher than the number of standing orders – 346 million direct debits as compared to 235 million inter-bank standing orders – although there were also 75 million inter-branch standing orders processed by individual banks. Direct debits are now extensively used in respect of payments for insurance premiums, hire purchase, general and water rates, utility bills (electricity, gas, etc.), subscriptions, loans and TV rentals. Payment instructions are, of course, initiated by the payee (*not* the payer) when the direct debit system is in operation.

Credit transfers in respect of remuneration were also in use to a small extent before the introduction of the BACS system, although almost entirely restricted to monthly salaries. The popularity of this method of payment has, however, increased very significantly in recent years, and over 70 per cent of salaries and 40 per cent of occupational pensions are now paid through BACS. Weekly wage payments through BACS are more restricted – less than 10 per cent of total payments – although there are still well over 1 million wage payments made each week through BACS.

BACS transfers may also be initiated by businesses in respect of indebtedness for goods, services, interest, dividends, etc., and by government organizations in respect of state pensions, child benefits and other similar payments. As yet few government payments are made by BACS, and there is room for far more use of the system in the future.

There are therefore many potentially valuable applications for the BACS system. The various applications will be considered in more detail in later chapters, as the case for automation cannot be considered entirely separately from the special issues that affect individual applications.

Costs

The charges made in respect of a BACS transaction are normally agreed with the bank which arranges the transfer. In the case of payments by private individuals, e.g. standing orders, there is generally a scale of laid-down charges for those customers subject to bank charges. In the business sector, accountants and treasurers should have some appreciation of the charge made by BACS to individual banks – 3.3p per transaction in 1986. In addition to this charge, there are generally some branch costs to add on to cover the expenses involved in initiating BACS business. In a competitive situation total charges are unlikely to exceed 5p per transaction. This should be considerably less than the charge for a cheque or paper-based credit transfer.

Bank charges are, of course, not the only costs involved in BACS transactions. For example, there are data preparation and software costs, to which must be added delivery charges and BACSTEL communication costs. Additional capital expenditure may also be incurred, such as purchase of a modem for communication purposes. Nevertheless, the average cost incurred per transaction should be significantly less than would be the case with other money transfer systems, especially if sophisticated computer and communications systems are already in operation.

Benefits

The assessment of benefits received through use of the BACS system may be difficult to determine with any great precision, although the following benefits will usually be obtained if cheque receipts and payments are replaced by BACS transfers:

1 *Improved control systems.* The debit and credit element of a BACS transaction (apart from standing orders) are usually made on the same day. It should therefore be possible to make more reliable estimates regarding the timing of receipts and payments, and control systems should consequently be improved. Many payers, however, prefer the uncertainty of cheque processing – due to postal, paying-in and clearance delays – rather than the certainty of the

BACS system, under which it is possible that funds will have to be made available on an earlier date than was previously the case.

2 *Reduced costs.* The costs involved in the preparation of BACS input material will generally be significantly less than lengthy cheque preparation, signing and despatch costs. Bank charges should also be very much reduced if the BACS system is used. The average expenditure incurred in using a cheque for payment purposes (including internal administrative costs and bank charges) is now believed to be in the region of £2 per cheque as compared with less than 20p using the BACS system. From the business payee's angle there should also be reduced costs, in addition to which there should be greater certainty regarding the time of receipt. It is important, however, that adequate reference material should be provided as the tracing of payments can be a time-consuming process.

The above benefits will generally vary from one application to another, and a rather more detailed study of costs and benefits will therefore be provided in chapters 8–11, dealing with the different types of applications.

Overall assessment

The UK now has one of the most efficient automated clearing houses in the world in BACS, although the two-day notice period causes problems for some business users. Most BACS payments are made by or to private individuals, but the initiative for these payments must come from the organization which is involved with the transaction. There is still some resistance to payments by this method, but this seems to be decreasing as more people become famililar with automated banking systems.

BACS transactions between business organizations are still very limited, however, largely because payers are reluctant to settle debts by payment through this system. The main reason for this attitude is the speed of the BACS funds transfer process – very different from cheques, where there are usually postal and clearing delays. If incentives were offered for payments through BACS, there might well be much greater use of these processes, as there will generally be significant cost savings in the use of the BACS system. This is a challenge that accountants must seriously consider in the next decade.

CLEARING HOUSE AUTOMATED PAYMENTS SYSTEM

In the late 1980s and early 1990s the Clearing House Automated Payments System (CHAPS) will almost certainly take over a substantial part of the role fulfilled in the past by telephonic transfers and the town clearing process. The latter system, which has already been considered in chapter 3, provides a same-day settlement service for amounts over £10,000 in respect of cheques drawn on and paid in at bank branches in the City of London. Clearance is largely achieved by manual methods, with messengers carrying cheques and bankers payments from one part of the City to another. The telephonic transfer system has also been very labour-intensive, although it has been possible to arrange transfers of this nature in most parts of the UK as long as the amount involved was above £10,000. It is not surprising, therefore, that the banks have been seeking to automate these processes for more than ten years.

Discussions started in the early 1970s as to the way in which same-day settlement services might be automated. At one time it was envisaged that there would be one large central computer with all the major banks connected to it. New developments in technology, fears concerning security, and increasing numbers of users changed these ideas, and by 1980 it was accepted that a much more decentralized system was desirable, with the banks sharing little more than a common program for the specialized computers (made by Tandem) which all the major banks had agreed to purchase.

By February 1984 the problems involved in the introduction of an automated system had been largely overcome, and CHAPS was launched with the support of all the London and Scottish clearing banks. Under this system all the major settlement banks provide their own 'gateway' through which payment messages are exchanged via the packet switching service of British Telecom. Other banks can arrange to share a gateway, although the overseas banks have been extremely annoyed by the early cut-off time (3 p.m.) and the lack of standardized software, which makes it extremely difficult to use the services of more than one settlement bank (as has been the custom in the past). As a result, there has been a boycott by some of the overseas bank associations, e.g. the Foreign Bankers Association. It is hoped, however, that a common interface system will be developed in 1986/7. Settlement is effected by each debtor bank sending a payment message to the Bank of England, which acts as banker to all the participating banks.

There are three major objectives behind the CHAPS system:

1 to enable same-day sterling payments to be made by automated methods;
2 to allow settlement to be effected by participant banks;
3 to provide information about payments to the banks and customers involved in transactions.

The new system should therefore provide information regarding transfers more quickly than was previously the case, and funds will now be guaranteed. It is possible, although very unusual, for cheques to be dishonoured under the town clearing system. It is also expected that customer charges will be significantly reduced as compared with telephonic transfers. Most of the major banks appear to be charging between £4 and £8 for a CHAPS transfer, as compared with £10 to £20 for a telephonic transfer. Some banks are, however, still charging a lower amount for a town cheque than a CHAPS transfer; this method of charging will obviously have to change if there is to be a large-scale changeover from town clearing. The CHAPS system will eventually operate on a nationwide basis with no lower limit (transactions below £10,000 are not currently accepted), although the comparative efficiency of bank networks in different parts of the country can vary very significantly.

The CHAPS system is believed to have cost the settlement banks more than £30 million in central and individual bank expenditure, but it is considered that this will be a good long-term investment. The estimated volume of use was initially very difficult to predict. In 1985 it was well in excess of 2.2 million transactions for over £2,355 billion. This level of use is expected to increase substantially in the late 1980s and 1990s, especially when all the settlement banks have installed fully integrated national networks providing access to SWIFT and other similar international services.

With many billions of pounds changing hands each day, security must naturally be an extremely important part of the CHAPS system. There are fears amongst bankers and computer specialists that some substantial fraudulent transactions will eventually take place through this system, although spokesmen for the CHAPS team have given assurances that the project would not have come into operation if the member banks had not been satisfied about security arrangements. Nevertheless there are bound to be temptations if large sums of money are changing hands each day, although the security systems that are being used have been extensively tested in both the UK and the USA.

Communications between individual business organizations and the bank will also have to be considered in this overall process of speeding up communications and money transfers. Under CHAPS the clearing process is initiated by the payer (unlike the town clearing system). Instructions may be given to the payer's bank by personal visit, telephone, telex, mail or electronic communication links. In the larger organization it seems likely that most attention will be devoted to computer and telecommunications links. In this case the CHAPS system will probably become a logical extension of the banks' electronic cash management services, which are considered in more detail in chapter 16. In small and medium-sized companies CHAPS transactions may be largely initiated through personal visits or telephone conversations, although there should be much greater use of computers and telecommunications links in the 1990s.

The attitude of the business debtor to this type of development will be very interesting to observe. Business debtors have traditionally preferred to take advantage of postal and clearance delays in making payments, especially those for large amounts. There are situations, however, in which a same-day payment is highly desirable, e.g. purchases of high-value investments. Most of these payments have in the past been made through the town clearing system, but many of them will undoubtedly be transferred to CHAPS processes by the end of the 1980s.

It is much more debatable whether there will be a large amount of 'new' business deriving from items that did not previously go through the town clearing system or telephonic transfer processes. Some companies may offer incentives to payers to use the CHAPS system if immediate payment is not a condition of the contract. It should, however, be remembered that BACS provides a same-day money transfer service, although two days' notice must be given to transfer requirements. CHAPS will therefore be primarily concerned with large amounts which must be paid at very short notice, although ideas may change if transaction costs fall.

In personal transactions, house purchase payments may become an ideal CHAPS application, especially in large conveyancing practices, as there have been many problems in the past in arranging same-day transfers of funds. It will be essential, however, that bank networks are capable of dealing with these transfers, especially if instructions are received only shortly before the cut-off time of 3 p.m.

The services provided by CHAPS should therefore provide a welcome addition to the range of payment services that is currently available to business organizations and private individuals. The number of payments made through the CHAPS system will probably never be large, although in value terms there will be substantial amounts involved. It will never be easy, however, to persuade business payers to accept the idea of instantaneous bank transfers, although it will probably become increasingly difficult in the future to take advantage of postal and clearance delays when large amounts of money are owed.

NATIONAL GIROBANK

The UK national giro system was set up by the Post Office in the late 1960s, and business began in October 1968 from an operational centre in the Merseyside area. The objective of the organization at that time was seen as the provision of a simple, cheap and efficient funds transfer service for personal and business customers.

Developments were slow initially, although there was an excellent computer back-up system, which is still claimed to be one of the most advanced in Europe. Political objections also had to be overcome; for example, there were fears for a time that the Conservative government would abolish the bank, but it was eventually announced in November 1971 that the bank would continue in existence with a strengthened management structure.

After a period of uncertainty, therefore, the giro system began to expand and in July 1978 the bank's title was changed to the National Girobank. In the years that followed the range of services was increased; for example lending facilities were introduced for private individuals and business organizations. The bank also became a member of the Bankers Clearing House and funds transfer facilities were improved through use of BACS, CHAPS and SWIFT.

In 1986 the number of National Girobank customers reached 1.9 million. The bank is not prepared to reveal the number of corporate customers, although it has disclosed that corporate deposits are over £32 billion. Growth in the number of customers was above 6 per cent in 1985/6, and there is now considerable confidence that growth will be even faster in the future.

From the business viewpoint, most large retailers and many small businesses are now using the National Girobank system because of the large numbers of branches (there are over 20,000 post offices), the attractive opening hours (significantly longer than the other major commercial banks), the excellent money transfer facilities, and the preparedness of the bank to handle cash on a much lower charge basis than most of the other banks. It has already been mentioned (chapter 2) that most banks are now charging in the region of 30p to 60p per £100 for handling cash, depending on the number of notes, coins, etc. The Girobank welcomes cash because of the large demands in post offices for cash for paying government benefits. As a result, cash lodgement charges can be significantly lower than those quoted by other banks; a rate in the region of 10p per £100 is by no means unusual, although this will normally be a matter for negotiation. The ability to transfer funds from many subsidiary accounts to a central account is also very efficient, which can be a major advantage in an organization with many stores or branches scattered throughout the country.

Central and local government and nationalized industries are also major users of National Girobank services and they encourage consumers to use the giro system for the payment of rent, rates, electricity, gas, water, taxation bills, etc. Debtors can either pay cash in respect of the account or make a transfer out of their giro account. This will probably be more convenient than visiting several premises and it should save stationery and postage. Incoming bank transfers can also be paid directly into a giro account if the individual is prepared to accept this form of payment; some government benefits are paid in this form.

In October 1985 the National Girobank became a public limited company and a wholly owned subsidiary of the Post Office, and it is now expected that an even wider range of services will be provided with the installation of ATMs, issue of credit cards and travellers cheques, and the provision of a limited range of international services. An increasing number of private individuals and business organizations are therefore likely to open National Girobank accounts, although in the business sector it is more !' ' to be in addition to, rather than in place of, conventional banking acc ʼunts. The Girobank is therefore no longer primarily concerned with money transfer facilities, although it does provide an excellent electronic funds transfer service from one giro account to another. We must wait and see, however, whether the Girobank will be able to persuade a large number of corporate customers to use their increasing range of bank services over and above the very popular cash lodgement and funds transfer facilities.

SOCIETY FOR WORLDWIDE INTERBANK FINANCIAL
TELECOMMUNICATION

In the late 1960s discussions took place between leading bankers in Europe and North America on the possibility of setting up an automated system to deal with the rapidly growing number of international banking transactions, many of which needed urgent attention. As a result of these discussions, the Society for Worldwide Interbank Financial Telecommunication (SWIFT) was set up in 1973 with the status of a non-profit-making co-operative organization.

SWIFT began operations as a computer-based telecommunications network in 1977 with a small number of staff, mainly located at their administrative offices in Brussels. Initially there was a membership of 239 banks from 15 different countries in Europe and North America. The volume of activity expanded very rapidly in the early 1980s and by the beginning of 1986 (see table 7.2) SWIFT was handling over 600,000 messages per working day from 1,275 member banks (38 in the UK) in nearly 50 countries. To handle this volume of activity, there are three operating centres – in Belgium, the Netherlands and the USA – each one of which is connected to regional processors with one or two in each member country. Messages can be transmitted at any time of the day or week.

Table 7.2 Recent annual statistics of the Society for Worldwide Interbank Financial Telecommunication (SWIFT)

Year	Member banks	Member countries	Operational countries	Messages per annum (nearest million)
1981	900	39	26	62
1982	1017	44	32	80
1983	1063	53	37	104
1984	1188	54	40	130
1985	1275	58	46	157

Source: Official SWIFT statistics (1986).

The services offered by SWIFT are intended to provide bankers with a cheap, secure and reliable communications network which can handle a large number of international messages. The system is therefore a means of communication between banks in account relationship with each other. Before the introduction of SWIFT, international banking transactions were arranged by a combination of telephone, telegram, telex and ordinary mail facilities. These techniques are still being used, although a substantial number of transactions have been transferred to the SWIFT system, especially those involving banking and customer funds transfers, documentary credits and foreign exchange operations. Large banks may also use their own telecommunications network or that of a large international computer agency, although SWIFT services are still very popular.

From the banks' viewpoint, the SWIFT network has provided a considerable improvement in international banking communications. National messages can also be handled, especially in large countries such as the USA. Initial bank set-up costs can be high but once these costs have been paid there should be a much improved system to offer to customers, frequently in association with local automated systems, e.g. the CHAPS service in the UK.

From the business organization's viewpoint, costs will once again be a matter for negotiation. One of the major components will be the SWIFT charge, which at the beginning of 1986 was a minimum of 18 Belgian francs (about 30p) per message. In addition, there will be local bank costs which may vary significantly depending on the services provided. There may also be currency costs for which estimates should be obtained in advance. The speed of the transfer of funds will naturally be important, as in the past substantial interest losses have often been incurred as a result of international transfers being 'lost' in the system. These losses should be substantially reduced if the paying bank is able to use the SWIFT system, although there may be a delay of one or two working days before cleared funds become available in less widely used currencies.

By the end of the 1980s the SWIFT system should be capable of dealing with at least one million messages per day largely because of the introduction of a new, more sophisticated computer installation (SWIFT II). This will provide the capability to bring in new countries and banks and possibly non-banking organizations. There are strong differences of opinion, however, as to the desirability of admitting organizations such as credit card companies, finance companies and stockbrokers and it will be interesting to see what decisions are eventually made on these matters.

The SWIFT system is therefore *not* strictly speaking part of an international funds transfer network. It does, however, provide a means by which messages can be exchanged between banks internationally and as this network grows it should be possible for funds transfer instructions to be sent to most countries where funds are urgently required. Directors, accountants and treasurers should be aware of these services, as this method of bank communication may be helpful when funds have to be transferred overseas and/or brought back to the UK at short notice.

SUMMARY AND CONCLUSIONS

The British banking community already has one highly successful funds transfer agency, BACS, as a result of electronic developments, with the prospect of another similar success story with the recently set up low-volume, high-value CHAPS service. The National Girobank also provides a highly sophisticated electronic payments network with the prospect of a much more extensive range of services in the future.

The UK is therefore well placed to move rapidly in a significant changeover from a system that is dominated by cash and paper-based settlement methods to a much greater use of electronic methods of settlement. In addition the SWIFT system provides the ability to extend these methods to international settlement practices, although much will depend on the sophistication of the methods available in the overseas country.

In the next decade more of these highly specialized electronic transfer systems will probably be set up; for example, it is extremely likely that a specialized agency will be set up to provide electronic point-of-sale facilities in the retail sector. By the end of the current century, therefore, the whole face of the UK payments system will probably have been radically changed, as banks and their customers gradually move towards a much greater use of EFT systems.

8 Direct Debit Agreements

Direct debiting has been used as a method of payment in the UK since 1967, although there has always been some opposition to the idea that the seller of goods and services should initiate payment, subject of course to the purchaser's agreement. These transactions were at one time paper-based, although in recent years the vast majority have been arranged on an automated basis through the BACS organization. As a result, direct debits have become an important part of the movement towards EFT systems, and they now make up over 40 per cent (in volume terms) of BACS payments.

Table 8.1 shows the number of automated direct debits arranged in the UK in the early 1980s. In the 1970s there was a gradual build-up of transactions from 50 million in 1972 to 100 million in 1976 and 150 million in 1979. In the 1980s the speed of expansion has been much faster, with the 200 million mark being reached in 1982 and 300 million in 1985.

Table 8.1 Automated direct debit transactions in the UK

Year	Transactions (millions)	Percentage increase
1980	173	–
1981	193	11.6
1982	220	14.0
1983	254	15.5
1984	295	16.1
1985	346	17.3

Source: Abstract of Banking Statistics, 1986.

A direct debit – unlike the credit transfer and standing order – is originated by the seller, rather than the purchaser, of goods and services. Any selling organization which wishes to use this system will have to obtain approval from its bank; private individuals are *not* allowed to originate payments in this form. The banks are very guarded about the criteria that are used in deciding general acceptability. Discussions with senior bankers suggest that genuine attempts are made to ensure that direct debit originators are 'reputable organizations'. As a result there apears to be a significant number of refusals, although it is impossible to obtain an estimate of what this figure might be.

If the seller is considered to be a suitable user of the direct debit system, detailed discussions will take place with the sponsoring bank and with BACS (it is assumed that automated methods will be used) regarding the most suitable form of computer input. These matters may be briefly discussed before an application is made to use the system, but they will obviously have to be considered in more detail at a later stage. Details regarding input methods and direct debit case studies can be obtained from BACS.

The direct debit system is normally most appropriate where there is a regular provision of goods or services. In these circumstances the seller should approach existing customers to see whether they would be prepared to authorize their bank to make payments in response to direct debit payment requests. This will not be an easy task, as many private individuals and business owners are reluctant to sign a form which authorizes their bank to pay any direct debit initiated by the seller, as long as it is within the terms of the agreement. This problem has in some respects become worse in recent years because most new originators have tried to ensure that direct debits are for a variable, rather than a fixed, amount so as to allow for the effects of inflation, although a maximum figure is sometimes specified. Dates may also be variable, although much will depend on the nature of the payment.

To overcome some of these problems and objections, the operating banks have drawn up an indemnity form which covers all direct debit originators. This document lays down the payer's rights to refund in case of error, the need for prior notice if amounts or dates are changed, and the option to cancel the agreement. All originators must agree to honour this undertaking.

When a direct debit is accepted, the instruction form will be lodged with the purchaser's bank after completion of all appropriate details by the seller. Payment requests will then be initiated by the seller, usually through the BACS organization. This will involve the same computer-input and timetable provisions that have already been described in chapter 7, e.g. input data lodged with BACS before 9 p.m. on day 1 will be arranged by the start of business on day 3, or later if required (up to 31 days into the future).

The automated direct debit system is therefore an extremely effective way for a seller to arrange payments in respect of regular transactions. It may be difficult, however, to persuade purchasers to accept a variable amount agreement in this form, largely because of the lack of control over the amount and time of payment.

PAYER VIEWPOINTS

Benefits

The following matters should be considered by any payer who has been asked to make payments under the direct debit system:

1 *Cost savings*. There is no need for the payer to take any action in respect of regular commitments, apart from the obvious (but sometimes forgotten) obligation to provide funds at the appropriate time. There should therefore be time, postage and stationery savings, especially when comparisons are made with cheque payments. Similar benefits will be received by the payer when regular payments for a set amount are made through the standing order system.

2 *Timing of payments*. All payments should be made on time as long as funds are available. This may be extremely important with payments such as insurance premiums and membership subscriptions. Standing orders should once again produce similar benefits, although there may be less certainty about the date on which the payment reaches the payee.

3 *Reduced bank charges*. In those situations where the payer is liable for bank charges, the amount paid in respect of an automated direct debit will frequently be less than that for a cheque, especially in respect of payments made by a business organization. For example, in 1986, most major businesses were paying in the region of 5p for a direct debit settlement as compared with at least 15p for a cheque. The differential for private individuals subject to charges will probably be much smaller or even non-existent, as several of the major banks have recently decided to charge the same amount for all

personal payments, presumably because of the problems involved in analysing different types of payments.

4 *Automatic revision of amounts payable.* If the amount payable changes – as has often been the case in recent years with building society payments, rent, rates, subscriptions and other regular commitments – an appropriate adjustment will be made by the payee as long as the direct debit mandate is for a variable amount. Any originator of a direct debit should, however, inform the payer of changes in the amount due. This should be an advantage from the payer's viewpoint as compared with the standing order system, under which the payer will have to arrange a visit or conduct correspondence with the paying bank to change the appropriate amount. On the other hand, some payers will obviously not be happy with the amount of freedom that the direct debit originator has in a variable mandate to adjust payment figures.

5 *Possibility of incentives.* Discounts are sometimes offered if payments are made by direct debit; the Automobile Association, for example, has recently been advertising that you can 'save £4 when you join the AA by direct debit'. Discounts of this nature do, however, appear to be the exception rather than the rule, and much will depend on how important the goods or services are to the user. Other benefits, apart from cash, could also be offered to payers, although there does not appear to have been much use of this type of incentive.

The above matters should be considered by all private and business payers. Some of the benefits may not be very significant in the large or medium-sized company, where there will almost certainly be established payment personnel and systems. It may therefore prove to be difficult to convince a business payer that payments should be made by direct debit, although attitudes may be changed by attractive discounts or other inducements.

Problem Areas

Businesses and private individuals will all need to consider potential problems that may arise on acceptance of a direct debit:

1 *Possible earlier payment.* It is possible that direct debit payments may have to be made at an earlier date than would have been the case with other methods of payment. There could therefore be interest losses for the payer, especially if payments were previously made by

cheque. In this connection it is important that comparisons should be made with the date when cheques have been paid in the past, as shown on the bank statement, rather than the date of signature or despatch. The direct debit payment date will frequently be a matter for negotiation in dealings between businesses, with the payer having to consider matters such as the strength of the seller, the importance of supplies, past payment practices and incentives offered (if any).

2 *Cash availability and control.* Slight variations in the date of payment for credit transactions have always been possible under a cash or cheque payment system, subject of course to credit terms and pressure applied by the seller. These circumstances will largely disappear if payments are made by direct debit as the agreed date cannot normally be varied. Payments on the agreed date may cause major problems when the payer is overdrawn, with the amount involved rapidly approaching the maximum acceptable level, or is facing other liquidity problems.

3 *Possibility of errors.* Many payers are concerned that mistakes can occur in direct debits for variable amounts. Users of the direct debit system have to agree that refunds will be arranged when errors are discovered. Mistakes have in the past caused financial embarrassment and extreme annoyance, and numerous stories are told of such errors. Many of these tales concern life assurance companies, which are the major users of the direct debit system. One of the best-known stories concerns the newly insured person who agreed to pay a yearly premium by direct debit. The life assurance company requested the correct amount from the payer's bank but unfortunately invoices were put through monthly, not yearly. The mistake was not discovered until four months had passed, by which time the payer had become rather worried about the state of his bank balance! Errors of this nature are believed to be rare today, but the fact that they can occur is a cause for concern.

4 *Information about non-payments.* When funds are not available to finance a direct debit, the payee will quickly become aware through the bank that payment has not been made. By contrast, under the cheque system it will be much more difficult for the payee to make a realistic assessment of the reasons for non-payment, because of the many different delays that can arise in the use of cheques.

The importance attached to the above matters varies from one payer to another. Many private payers are monthly paid salaried employees, and it may not be of great importance to them whether payments are made at the beginning or in the middle of the month. Attitudes could change, however, when funds are low or the account is overdrawn.

Business payers are more likely to be aware of the interest implications of payment by direct debit, especially if the end-result of acceptance of such a mandate could be earlier payment. The lack of flexibility and control over payment dates and amounts is also likely to be an important consideration, especially if there are liquidity problems or fears about the correctness of invoices. It seems probable, therefore, that sellers will face many problems in persuading business payers to accept direct debits, although this does not mean that the task should not be attempted.

PAYEE VIEWPOINTS

Most of the benefits obtained from use of the direct debit system are received by the seller of goods and services, i.e. the payee, but the banks should also receive benefits because of the replacement of cash or paper-based payments by automated methods. Possible advantages to the payer have already been examined, although these are not considered to be very significant amongst business payers.

Benefits

The payee should receive benefits in one or more of the following areas:

1 *Cost savings*. The reduction in paperwork that normally arises through the adoption of the direct debit system should produce printing, stationery and postage savings, in addition to which there could be some staff savings. Much will depend, however, on the methods that were being used in the organization before the introduction of the direct debit system. Savings are generally greatest when cash or paper-based methods were previously the dominant method of settlement, although there could be significant savings as compared with automated credit transfers, which are considered later in this chapter. A well organized direct debit system usually produces payments in respect of at least 95 per cent of amounts due (over 99 per cent in some cases), in which case the payee should be able to work on an exception principle using information provided by the paying banker regarding non-payment. Overall savings may be difficult to assess, as some administrative costs are relatively fixed, e.g. salaries, whilst others vary according to activity, e.g. postages. Nevertheless, practical experience would suggest that some very worthwhile savings should be achieved.

2 *Timing of payments*. The direct debit system should produce more certainty concerning the timing of receipts. This should obviously be of assistance in the budgeting and investment process, although it is important to appreciate that payment requests will not always be met. If so, the request for payment will usually be presented for a second time, although much will depend on the reason for non-payment. If payments are made on time, there will probably be interest savings, as funds could become available at an earlier date than was previously the case with other forms of payment. In this connection the direct debit transfer date, which is the same for both payer and payee, should be compared with the date when a cheque would normally be cleared. Similarly, if comparisons are made with paper-based credit transfers, it should be appreciated that under that system there are normally delays of at least two working days between transfers out of the payer's account and transfers into the payee's account.

3 *Improved credit management*. In a cheque-dominated payment system it is always difficult to decide when action should be taken on overdue accounts because of the delays that can take place in the postal system. If direct debits replace cheques, the payer and the appropriate bank know when payment should be made. If there are payment problems, the bank should inform the payee within a few days and it should be possible to take appropriate collection action within a short time of the due date. As a result, the direct debit system should produce more efficiency in collection systems and the overall credit management process.

4 *Reduced bank charges*. The payee's bank charges should generally be less than was the case with cash receipts, cheques or paper-based credit transfers. Precise figures cannot be provided to back up this statement, although practical experience suggests that charges are frequently less than one-third of the amount levied in respect of paper-based systems. Savings will be less predictable when automated standing orders were previously in use; this is a matter that should be discussed with the local bank manager.

The precise benefits obtained by payees through use of the direct debit system will naturally vary from one organization to another. BACS has, however, produced a number of leaflets based on actual business experience which the interested potential customer should examine. Users are naturally reluctant to quantify benefits, although there does seem to be general agreement that substantial savings should be achieved *if* a worthwhile number of payers can be persuaded to accept direct debit mandates.

Costs and problems

Benefits arising from the direct debit system cannot be satisfactorily assessed without consideration of additional costs. In this area much will depend on existing computer and telecommunications systems. If highly sophisticated systems are already in operation, there will probably be little or no additional capital expenditure; if not, it may be necessary to purchase additional equipment, or adapt existing systems. Preparation and verification costs must also be considered; these are often underestimated.

It should also be appreciated that one of the results of a direct debit circularization campaign could be partial or complete failure. It will generally be desirable, therefore, that some testing of responses should be arranged before a major campaign is launched, to ascertain the probable response. In assessing success (or failure) some companies set an arbitrary response target below which it would not be worthwhile setting up the system; this is most frequently laid down in the 20–40 per cent range, although much will depend on the total number of organizations or individuals that are approached.

On balance, benefits to the business payee who can produce satisfactory computer-input material should be far in excess of the attached costs, although the ultimate success or failure of the system will depend on payer reaction. Very careful thought should therefore be given to the way in which the payer is approached and the incentives, if any, that should be offered as part of this process.

CURRENT USERS AND APPLICATIONS

There are no published statistics available regarding the major users of the direct debit system, although the BACS organization has produced some data on this subject. Table 8.2 shows such data for 1984, split up into major user groups.

The table shows that the major originator of direct debits is the life assurance sector, which arranges well over 50 per cent of these transactions. Most new life assurance policies now require or encourage the use of direct debit payments, and attempts are constantly being made to persuade existing policyholders to accept this system. Over 200 life assurance companies now use the direct debit system, and it is estimated that well over one-quarter of all payments are now received by means of direct debits as compared with 2 per cent by standing order. Cash still dominates the receipts picture – over 50 per cent of all payments – although there is little doubt that the position will change very dramatically by the end of the century.

Many insurance companies are, of course, involved in both life and non-life activities. As a result, it is not surprising that the success of the direct debit system in the life sector has led to its increasing use in non-life business. Growth in this type of settlement has been extensive in recent years, although paper-based forms of settlement (cheques and credit transfers) are still the dominant method of settlement.

Table 8.2 Direct debit usage of BACS by business and government organizations

Application	Transactions (millions)
Life assurance premiums	153
Hire purchase	22
Household rates	20
Non-life insurance	17
Utility billing	15
Subscriptions	10
Loan repayments	10
TV rental	8
National insurance	6
Commercial billing	4
Budget accounting	3
Rents and leasing	3
Mortgage repayments	3
TV licences	3
Other payments	2
Total	279

Source: Bankers' Automated Clearing Services – 1984 statistics. A slightly different accounting year has been used for these purposes as compared with table 8.1.

The building society movement has many similarities to the life assurance sector, but it will be seen from the table that direct debit mortgage repayments are comparatively small with only 3 million transactions per annum. This is less than 3 per cent of the total number of building society payments. In this case, however, there is substantial use of the standing order system – over 70 per cent of all payments – most of these payments being made through BACS. The comparative merits of automated direct debits and standing orders are considered in the next section of this chapter, with particular reference to the contrasting attitudes of life assurance companies and building societies.

Local authorities now make extensive use of direct debits, especially for rates transactions. Most authorities are prepared to split up the rates account into ten or twelve equal instalments which can then be paid by direct debit or standing order. About 15 per cent of rates accounts are paid by direct debit and over 30 per cent by standing order. Cash dominates the overall situation, with over one-third of all payments. Rather surprisingly there are more than 150 rating authorities still not using direct debits, although there are now many more – over 250 – using this method of collection.

Utility billing covers accounts initiated by electricity, gas, water and other similar organizations. In some of these transactions it is difficult to predict the amount that will have to be paid in the year that lies ahead. This problem can be overcome, however, by the use of budget or other similar accounts under which an estimate is made of next year's consumption. This is then split up into monthly payments with the balance due to or from the payer being settled at the end of the year. Use of the direct debit system by utilities is, however, very limited, with only about 5 per cent of payments being made in this form. By comparison, standing orders make up over 15 per cent of payments. Cash once again dominates the payments position, with over 40 per cent of all transactions.

Professional bodies and other similar organizations are now making extensive use of direct debits, with transactions currently in excess of 10 million and growing rapidly. Most payments are still made by standing order – over 50 per cent – although the direct debit figure is rapidly approaching the 25 per cent mark. The attitude of the professional accountancy bodies towards direct debits is interesting to observe: the Institute of Chartered Accountants in England and Wales only started to make widespread use of this system in 1985, whereas the Institute of Cost and Management Accountants has been using it for many years.

Hire purchase and finance companies are also major users of direct debits. Over 20 per cent of all payments are made by direct debit and 40 per cent by standing order. Cash is still very important, with 25 per cent of all payments being made in this form.

A more detailed examination of table 8.2 shows that most of the applications are dominated by payments from private individuals rather than business organizations. In transactions between businesses there are very few sectors where there is widespread use of direct debits. Perhaps the best-known situation arises in the oil sector in dealings between petrol companies and garages. For example, it was reported in 1982 that over 90 per cent of BP Oil's retail account proceeds were settled by direct debiting.[1]

Other popular business applications arise in dealings between car

1 BACS Case Study – BP Oil Limited, *Payments flow automatically for BP Oil* (BACS, 1982).

manufacturers and distributors, and between breweries and public houses. A few other powerful suppliers, e.g. British Oxygen (now the BOC Group), have been able to persuade some customers to accept direct debits, although in most competitive situations it has proved to be extremely difficult or even impossible to obtain widespread acceptance of the system.

COMPARISON WITH STANDING ORDERS

There is obviously some disagreement about the comparative merits of receipts by means of automated direct debits and standing orders, as is shown by the figures for life assurance companies and building societies provided in table 8.3. These organizations receive a large part of their income through regular payments – usually at monthly intervals – and some similarity in payment methods might therefore be expected. The major life assurance companies have traditionally received a substantial part of their income through cash collection, but one would expect to see a similar degree of importance attached to direct debits and standing orders as both payees are in a powerful position, with the ability to put pressure on payers to use the direct debit system if this was considered to be desirable.

Table 8.3   Analysis of payments received by UK life assurance companies and building societies (percentage of total receipts)

Type of payment	Life assurance premiums	Building society mortgages
Automated direct debits	29	3
Automated standing orders	2	70
Paper-based items – cheques and credit transfers	11	17
Cash	58	10
	100	100

Source: Calculated from 1984 data produced by Bankers' Automated Clearing Services.

Table 8.3, together with other available data, suggests that life assurance companies have decided that from their viewpoint direct debit receipts are more advantageous than standing orders. On the other hand, most building societies appear to have decided that there are no major disadvantages in widespread acceptance of standing orders. Exceptions do exist – for example, the Town and Country Building Society has made major efforts to persuade payers to adopt the direct debit system, and over 50 per cent of mortgage repayments have recently been made in this form – but there appears to be very little evidence that the larger societies are convinced of the value of direct debits.

To the casual observer there are many similarities between direct debits and standing orders. From the payee's viewpoint both systems produce a regular source of income and there should be savings in internal administrative and security costs, especially when compared with payments by cash or cheque. Credit management practices should also be improved under both systems, as payments are likely to be made as long as funds are available, and there should be a reasonable degree of certainty about the period over which payments should be received. Non-payment should become known fairly quickly, unlike the cheque system where items may be delayed or lost in the post, and it should therefore be possible to take appropriate collection measures soon after the due date.

There are, however, some important differences between the two systems, especially when payments become due. Under the direct debit system, the payee has a high degree of control over the date of payment as long as funds are available and the payment demand is within the terms of the agreement with the payer. By contrast, the payee has no control over the standing order, the payment of which may be delayed by a variety of different factors, most or all of which are unlikely to be known by the payee. If funds are available, the arrival date of a standing order payment should not vary by more than three or four days between one month and another, although the payee would naturally prefer even more certainty regarding the date of payment. The speed of transfer may also be different, as the UK banks generally insist on a two-day delay between the debit and credit of standing orders. The automated direct debit system with debit and credit effected on the same day should therefore provide a higher degree of certainty regarding the date of receipt and a faster transfer of funds together with more information regarding reasons for non-payment.

It may also be extremely difficult for the payee to identify the source of standing order payments. Appropriate reference numbers should always be provided by the payer – often in a separate communication – but there will be situations where this does not happen. As a result it could be time-consuming to check bank statement receipts against amounts due. By contrast, the payee controls the direct debit reference data, and there are normally no identification problems. Payment checking procedures should therefore be much easier under the direct debit system, as the payee can operate on an exception principle based on information provided through the banking system.

Bank charges and mandate changes should also be considered as part of an overall comparison process. Business charges for automated items are generally cheaper than paper-based transactions, although it is difficult to generalize about comparative costs for direct debits and standing orders. Discussions with the local bank manager should clarify this situation. There will be direct debit advantages to the payee, however, when regular payment amounts have to be adjusted because of new interest rates, taxation changes, etc. Changes in the direct debit demand are relatively simple as long as the original mandate provides for this type of change. Adjustments to a standing order are much more difficult, as the payer must be contacted and should then visit or write to the bank to change mandate instructions. It is also possible that there may be errors by the payer or bank staff in completion of the standing order mandate or any other alterations that are made.

A detailed consideration of the points that have been raised in this section will usually lead to the conclusion that from the payee's viewpoint the direct debit is preferable to the standing order *as long as* the payer can be persuaded to accept a direct debit mandate. The building societies may consider that acceptance could be a major problem, although there is no real evidence that they have made concerted efforts to convince mortgagees that payment should be made by direct debit. Most of the major building societies have excellent computer systems, so there should be no difficulties in providing suitable computer-input material. The conclusion must therefore be that the life assurance companies have a greater awareness than the building societies of the benefits that can be obtained from an automated direct debit system, although it is possible that some of the smaller building societies may not have been able to convince banks that they should be allowed to use the system.

The larger organization that is currently being paid by standing order – over 250 million payments of this nature are made each year – should therefore consider the possibility of approaching payers to see if they would be prepared to make payments by direct debit. If letters are properly worded and followed up, there should be a reasonable response, especially from private individuals, and as a result it should be possible to make significant time and cost savings as compared with the standing order system.

FUTURE DEVELOPMENTS

The number of direct debit payments has increased by more than 15 per cent per annum over the last five years, and many specialists in this area expect the growth rate to increase to at least 20 per cent per annum over the next five years. This would mean that by the end of the 1980s there could be over 700 million direct debit transfers, and the one billion mark might well be reached in the first half of the 1990s.

The major growth in direct debit payments will almost certainly come in transactions between business organizations and private individuals, as has been the case in recent years. This situation has arisen because there is relatively little opposition to direct debit payments amongst private individuals, who generally find this method of settlement cheap and convenient.

Suppliers of services to private individuals have generally been slow to appreciate the advantages of the direct debit system. As a result, there is considerable room for growth, especially amongst local authorities and public utilities, where the direct debit usage rate, as compared with all payments, is in the region of 5 per cent. Central government has made virtually no progress in this direction, although it would seem possible that some taxes could be collected in this way. In the non-government sector there is considerable scope for increased usage, especially by building societies and professional bodies.

Those suppliers of services to private individuals who already use the direct debit system are in the vast majority of cases extremely pleased with the results. In the local authority sector, BACS case studies are now available regarding the experiences of the Coventry, Southampton and Southend councils, all of which make very extensive use of the BACS system. Amongst public utilities, similar case studies can be obtained regarding the successful use of direct debits at the Eastern Gas Board, and the Eastern and North Eastern Electricity Boards.

In the life assurance sector, major users of the direct debit system are the Prudential and Norwich Union companies. In the building society movement there is much less usage, although the Town and Country Building Society regards the direct debit system as 'the most efficient, least troublesome and at the same time cheapest method of collecting mortgage repayments'.[2]

It seems inevitable, therefore, that there will be increasing pressure on private individuals to pay for regular services by direct debit. This process will in most cases be of benefit to the individual, although some consumers still refuse to accept direct debits because of cash availability problems and the possibility of invoicing errors. Objections are, however, gradually being overcome, and the increase in numbers of people opening bank

2 BACS Case Study – Town and Country Building Society, *Building Society Success with Direct Debiting* (BACS, 1982).

accounts should help in this process, especially if the banks decide to launch a major publicity campaign to emphasize the benefits that can be obtained by using direct debits.

There are likely to be far more problems, however, in persuading businesses to accept direct debits. The possible objections have already been considered, and in the absence of incentives it will be difficult for companies in a competitive situation to persuade payers to use the direct debit system.

The increasing awareness amongst payees of the benefits that can be obtained through using direct debits may, however, persuade more payees to offer discounts or other incentives to business customers; discounts in the region of 1 per cent have been suggested.[3] Much will depend on the effect that the direct debit system has on the speed of payment as compared with savings in administrative costs, bank charges, etc.

Objections to the direct debit system amongst business payers are, however, deeply rooted, and there is little doubt that it will be extremely difficult to persuade accountants and treasurers to arrange payment in this form, even if attractive discounts are offered. In the long term the advantages of electronic payments will undoubtedly be accepted by an increasing number of payers, although this may lead to more automated credit transfers, under which system the control of payment times and amounts can be maintained, rather than direct debit acceptances.

SUMMARY AND CONCLUSIONS

Direct debiting is already well established in the UK, and the prospects for expansion look extremely good, particularly in transactions between business organizations and private individuals. This system is therefore likely to play a significant role in future EFT developments, especially if a more positive image can be attached to direct debit agreements.

The benefits that can be obtained from direct debit agreements as a replacement for cash and paper-based settlement systems are very significant, although most of the benefits tend to go to the payee. Less powerful payees may therefore have to be prepared to share benefits if they are not dealing with private individuals.

The banks should also benefit from direct debit agreements, as they should help to contain the very substantial amount of paperwork that has built up in recent years. As a result, charges to business customers should be much less than for cheques and paper-based credit transfers.

3 See, for example, P. R. A. Kirkman, Changing Payment Patterns, *Management Accounting (UK)*, June 1983, p. 25.

The major barrier towards expansion is, however, the business payer, who will always be reluctant to surrender control over the timing and the amount of payments. This may become slightly less important if interest rates fall, but there may still have to be sizeable incentives to overcome this opposition, and we may therefore see a considerable amount of experimentation with discounts and other similar concessions as payees attempt to obtain a more widespread acceptance of the direct debit system. This should eventually lead to increasing acceptance by business payers, although most of these payments will probably continue to be made by private individuals in settlement of their debts to business and government organizations.

9 Purchase Ledger Payments

The vast majority of goods and services supplied to UK business and government organizations are provided on credit. Settlement in respect of these transactions frequently takes over two months, and as a result there are considerable amounts outstanding on purchase ledgers. The settlement of purchase ledger transactions is therefore a very important part of the UK payments structure.

Table 9.1 provides an indication of the total number of UK purchase ledger payments and the way in which settlement is effected, divided up into seven market sectors. The 1984 total of over 740 million payments makes up approximately 25 per cent of all UK business and government payments. Government benefits involve a very large number of payments (see chapter 11), and if these are excluded, purchase ledger payments increase to about 45 per cent of all payments.

Table 9.1 UK purchase ledger payments by market sector

| Sector | Transactions (millions) | | | |
	Total	Paper-based	Cash	EFT systems
Central government	16	14	2	–
Local government	20	18	–	2
Public utilities	10	10	–	–
Insurance companies	7	4	3	
Financial services	13	12	–	1
Manufacturing	263	259	2	2
Service industries	412	352	59	1
Total	741	669	66	6

Source: Bankers' Automated Clearing Services, 1984 statistics.

The table shows that purchase ledger payments are dominated by paper-based methods of settlement – over 90 per cent of all payments. In most cases these payments are made by cheque, although there will be some paper-based credit transfers. Cash payments make up about 9 per cent and electronic transfers a miserable 1 per cent. There is therefore considerable scope for the increased use of EFT systems in the settlement of purchase ledger transactions.

TRADITIONAL UK PRACTICES

Cash was at one time a popular method of settling purchase ledger transactions but it is now seldom used except in the retail and service sectors, where there is usually plenty of cash available and a practice of paying for some supplies or services in cash. Settlement by cheque has traditionally been the preferred method of settlement in government and manufacturing organizations, with most cheques being sent out by second class post. Postal and bank clearing delays have in many cases produced a situation in which a total settlement delay of at least a week is available to the payer after cheque despatch. The knowledgeable payer will therefore be reluctant to abandon this built-in delay period with its important cash availability and interest implications.

In the 1950s and 1960s a small number of companies began to use paper-based credit transfers for purchase ledger settlement purposes, largely because of savings in administrative costs. The advantages attached to this method of settlement have already been considered in chapter 4. In the 1970s, however, interest rates increased significantly, and many payers abandoned credit transfers, mainly because of the feeling that the cheque system provided more flexibility and probable later payment.

In the 1980s payment by means of EFT systems – usually through BACS – has become widely available through the use of computerized accounting methods. As a result, many organizations are now using BACS for remuneration payment purposes – nearly 14,000 in 1985. There were, however, only about 850 companies using the BACS system for purchase ledger settlement purposes in 1985, which obviously indicates that many directors and accountants have strong reservations about the desirability of automated purchase ledger payments. The reasons for these reservations will be considered in more detail later in this chapter.

POTENTIAL BENEFITS

BACS, in its promotional literature on purchase ledger payments, suggests that there are five major benefits that should be obtained through the use of EFT systems:

1 *Improved cash flow management*. The BACS system should produce more certainty regarding payment dates, and as a result budgeting and planning processes should be improved. Many commercial and industrial accountants would, however, be sceptical about this argument, as most directors prefer the uncertainty of late payment by cheque to the certainty of early payment by EFT. The counter-argument is, of course, that the date of payment by EFT systems is negotiable, although there may be difficulties in arranging 'late' payment.

2 *Reduced bank charges*. In 1986 the charge to user banks for a BACS electronic transfer was 3.3p per item. In addition to this basic cost, the individual bank has to pay some associated costs, although many of these costs are fixed rather than variable. As a result, charges are unlikely to exceed 5p per item in a competitive situation. On the other hand, the total cost to the banks of clearing a cheque or paper-based credit transfer is at least 30p, of which approximately half relates to the payer. Charges are naturally subject to negotiation, although the typical charge to the business payer of at least 15p per cheque suggests that EFT transactions should only cost about one-third of the amount incurred in the processing of cheques.

3 *Reduced administrative costs*. In most applications the use of EFT systems should produce significant savings in staff time, printing, stationery, and associated costs. A large number of cheques will no longer have to be prepared, signed and despatched, although the purchase ledger will obviously have to be produced in the normal way. Time spent on bank reconciliation should also be reduced. Postage costs will, however, not necessarily be eliminated, as remittance advices may still need to be sent through the postal system. Savings will not be so great if a paper-based credit transfer is already in operation, although practical experience suggests that the benefits will still be significant.

4 *Reduced queries or errors*. Cheques are sometimes incorrectly produced, mislaid or lost, although much depends on the efficiency of the paying organization. In an EFT system the scope for errors will almost certainly decrease, but inefficient staff can still create problems. It should not necessarily be assumed that errors will be restricted to minor matters in an EFT system. It is not unknown for computerized tapes to be sent out twice to BACS or other similar organizations and this could, of course, lead to double payment. Practical experience has shown, however, that errors are generally reduced when a payer changes from a cheque to an automated payment system.

5 *Two days' money saved.* This benefit is relevant only when EFT payments are being compared with paper-based credit transfers, where the transaction debit is usually made two working days before the corresponding credit, as compared with the instantaneous debit and credit of the EFT purchase ledger system. In recent years, however, very few purchase ledger payments have been made by paper-based credit transfers.

Several case studies have been produced by BACS concerning companies that use automated methods for purchase ledger payments, e.g. Heinz, Searle and Smiths Industries. All these companies pay the majority of their suppliers by means of EFT systems. After several years' experience there is general agreement that significant administrative savings have been achieved – printing, stationery, staff time, etc. Bank charges have also been substantially reduced, e.g. Smiths Industries are paying seven times as much for a cheque entry as for a BACS transaction. Other advantages are claimed – improved cash control, fewer errors, etc. – although these points do not appear to be as important as others mentioned earlier in this section.

The rather limited practical experience to date would therefore suggest that the use of EFT systems for purchase ledger payments should at the very least produce significant administrative and bank charge savings. There will, however, be costs and problems to set against these benefits, and these will now be considered in some depth.

COSTS AND PROBLEMS

The lack of usage of the EFT system for purchase ledger payments in UK businesses suggests that there are some major costs or problems attached to this method of payment. An attempt will therefore now be made to assess the reasons for this lack of usage:

1 *Implementation costs.* The process of persuading payees to accept payment directly into a bank account can be time-consuming and expensive. This should, however, be largely a 'one-off cost' (depending on the number of new suppliers each year), and if it is properly handled a good response should be obtained.

2 *Cost and suitability of computer systems.* The EFT services provided by BACS and other funds transfer organizations cannot be used if satisfactory computer-input material is not available. In most large organizations this is unlikely to be a major problem, as long as

members of staff are available to set up the system. In the small or medium-sized company there could be more problems, although it may be possible to provide appropriate data with the assistance of a computer bureau. The processing costs could, of course, deter some small companies.

3 *Lack of knowledge and information.* Many directors and accountants have a surprising lack of knowledge about recent developments in money transfer processes, especially those involving EFT systems. There have admittedly been many areas of rapid change in cash management in recent years, but this seems to be one area that has been badly neglected in business education and literature. Some branch bankers are also not as informed as they should be on this subject. BACS personnel are, of course, very familiar with these matters, but they are supposed to work through the major banks, at least initially, and this means that it is difficult for direct approaches to be made. There is therefore considerable scope for improvement in knowledge and information concerning EFT systems, and even where this knowledge is available at management level, there may be a shortage of skilled personnel to implement systems.

4 *Availability of cash resources.* There is likely to be a much greater preparedness amongst payers to use EFT payment systems if the paying organization is normally in a cash surplus situation. Companies in a bank overdraft situation or liquidity crisis frequently attempt to delay payment for as long a period as possible in order to stay within overdraft limits or survive for a longer period. Such tactics will naturally be much easier when a cheque payment system is being used, although there is a limit to all delay tactics. Companies with liquidity problems are therefore unlikely to be prepared to use EFT payment systems, unless considerable pressure is put on them.

5 *Clearance delays.* Most business payers soon discover that a cheque sent by second class post is unlikely to be presented for payment until at least seven days after despatch because of postal, lodgement and bank clearing delays. The payer who is considering EFT payment systems should therefore examine the dates of past bank presentations to see whether it is feasible to arrange transfers on a date which does not create a significant loss in interest terms.

6 *Credit terms enforcement.* In the UK the official credit period offered by most companies is in the region of 45 days (end of month following the month of transaction). Average credit taken is, however, well over 60 days (about 70 days in the manufacturing sector). Payers may therefore be reluctant to arrange a bank transfer

at the end of the month following the month of the transaction if they have habitually been able to delay cheque payment for several days or weeks after the due date.

It is difficult to assess which of the above reasons has been the principal deterrent in possible changeover to an EFT payment system. Discussions with numerous accountants would suggest, however, that in most cases resistance is based on the feeling that EFT systems will inevitably lead to earlier settlement and a consequent loss in interest terms.

It must be stressed, however, that it is not essential that EFT payments should be initiated on the same date as previous cheque despatches. The large or powerful purchaser will in most situations be able to adjust the payment date to the approximate date of bank presentation under the cheque system. The informed seller will probably appreciate that no loss is being suffered, although there is a considerable amount of misunderstanding in the business sector regarding the operation of the bank clearing system. Less powerful purchasers may have more problems, although once again much will depend on the seller's knowledge of the clearing system. Figure 9.1 shows a draft letter which BACS suggests could serve as a basis for communications with organizations which it is proposed to

Figure 9.1 Suggested form of letter to prospective EFT payees

```
Because we are automating our payments to suppliers, we shall be
grateful if you will fill in your bank information on this form
(not shown) and return it to us.

Under our new system you will continue to receive a remittance
advice from us by post in the usual way. The remittance advice
will indicate the payment we are making direct into your bank
account by automated bank giro credit. This well-established and
proven payment system is operated by the clearing banks through
Bankers' Automated Clearing Services Limited (BACS). Payments
can be made through this system into any branch of any bank in
the United Kingdom.

For you, the payee, the BACS system removes the possibility of
cheques being delayed or lost in the post, and you are saved the
trouble of paying cheques into the bank. Bank clearing time-lags
are also eliminated as cleared funds are available in your bank
account the same day that our account is debited. Our use of
this automated system will make your accounting simpler and more
predictable all round; to include you in the system we require
the basic information asked for below and shall be grateful if
you will fill in that page and return it to us.
```

Source: Bankers' Automated Clearing Services, Edgware, Middlesex. The form provided by BACS requests information on the name and address of the company's banker together with sorting code and account number, and a signature with company stamp.

pay by EFT methods. It is noticeable that in this document there is no mention of the future date of payment, although the effect of postal and clearing delays on cash availability is stressed.

It should also be appreciated that large payments can easily be made by non-EFT methods. BACS case studies suggest that in those companies which have adopted an EFT system between 60 and 90 per cent of payments are made by electronic transfer. High-value payments are frequently made by cheque, although there are differing opinions as to whether it is advisable to impose a 'top limit' on EFT payments.

Accountants may also feel that flexibility in payment times will be lost if the cheque system is abandoned. Several payment dates during the coming month can, however, be inserted on computer data submitted to BACS, and cancellation of instructions is possible up to the final working day before payment. This may not be good enough for the accountant whose company is in a precarious liquidity position, but it should be satisfactory for organizations in a cash surplus situation.

Some accountants are also concerned about the lack of space that is available on BACS payment instructions for reference data. This matter is being thoroughly investigated by BACS and it is hoped that improvements will be arranged in the near future. In the meantime, most user companies are having to send out remittance advices through the postal system. This is currently regarded as essential if numerous queries are to be avoided.

There are, therefore, some important costs and problems attached to the introduction of an EFT purchase ledger payment system. Some of these matters will be difficult to quantify, but it should nevertheless be possible to prepare an approximate indication of costs to match against potential benefits. Discussions with BACS and existing users should help in this process, as there is now a small but increasing amount of evidence on this subject.

SUMMARY AND CONCLUSIONS

Those directors and accountants who are currently in charge of computerized purchase ledger systems should by now be seriously considering the possibility of payment by EFT systems. Cash, cheques and paper-based credit transfer systems involve many costs which frequently can be reduced through the use of electronic bank transfer systems. The two major benefits that should be obtained from a change to electronic systems are:

1 administrative cost savings – staff time, printing, stationery, etc;
2 reductions in bank charges.

Other possible benefits have been suggested, e.g. fewer errors and more precise cash management, but these are not considered to have the same overall level of importance.

It is surprising that in spite of these potential benefits only about 6 per cent of the companies that make EFT remuneration payments use the same system for purchase ledger purposes. Several possible reasons have been suggested for this state of affairs. Probably the most important in recent years has been the fear that accounts will have to be paid at an earlier date than was previously the case. It must be stressed, however, that under an EFT purchase ledger system, payers still control the date of payment and large amounts can, if necessary, still be paid by cheque.

It seems probable, therefore, that over the next decade there will be a substantial movement from cheque to EFT for purchase ledger settlement purposes. Central government and public utilities have surprisingly made very few moves in this direction, although it is in the manufacturing and service sectors, with over 90 per cent of purchase ledger transactions between them, where the principal opportunities for improved practices are available. Many of these companies have in the last decade been very short of cash, but if liquidity improves and interest rates fall there will probably be a significant changeover to EFT payment systems.

Directors and accountants should therefore pay more attention to the costs involved in traditional purchase ledger payment systems, and the savings that might be achieved by a change to EFT systems. A comparison of costs and benefits will not necessarily lead to immediate change, but there should at the very least be an awareness of the bank transfer systems that are available when the organization is capable of providing suitable computer-input material.

10 Wages and Salaries

In all developed countries wages and salaries provide an important part of personal income, although high rates of unemployment have produced a situation in which many people are having to rely on government benefits. In 1985 the official UK 'employed labour force' was over 24 million, of whom 2½ million were self-employed.[1] The number of unemployed people was about 3¼ million, many of whom were receiving unemployment or supplementary benefits. The payment of government benefits is considered in more detail in chapter 11.

This chapter will be primarily concerned with the possibilities of automation for traditional forms of remuneration, i.e. wages and salaries, although similar arguments could be put forward in respect of occupational pensions. Payment in respect of all these forms of remuneration may be made in cash or by cheque, bank transfer, or through the post office system. The method of payment will obviously be influenced by the attitudes and policies of employers, employees and various other interested parties. The subject will therefore be examined from all these viewpoints, although there will be a particular emphasis on the employer's needs. The employer should not, however, introduce new forms of payment without a proper appreciation of the employee's viewpoint and other relevant factors.

BACKGROUND SITUATION

UK employees have traditionally preferred to be paid in cash, presumably because immediate purchasing power is available. In the last twenty years, however, employers have become less prepared to pay remuneration in

1 Department of Employment, *Statistics for 1985* (HMSO, 1986).

cash, mainly because of the costs and risks attached to cash payment. The changeover process has not been easy, although there has been a reasonably good response from employees with bank current accounts.

The changing attitudes of employers and employees towards cash payment of remuneration is very effectively shown by the statistics provided in table 10.1. In 1969, 75 per cent of employees were paid in cash. By 1984 this figure had fallen to 37 per cent, and most current estimates suggest that the appropriate figure is now in the region of 35 per cent. We can therefore now think in terms of just over one-third of employed adults receiving their remuneration in cash.

Table 10.1 Percentage of UK adult employees paid in cash

1969	1976	1979	1981	1984
75	59	54	44	37

Sources: The UK High Street Banks, *Modernising Payment Methods*, May 1983, and Inter-Bank Research Organisation, *Research Brief*, October 1985.

The table does not provide a split between manual and non-manual employees. Current estimates suggest, however, that about 65 per cent of manual workers are paid in cash as opposed to 25 per cent of non-manual workers. Most manual workers are still paid weekly, although practices are changing. The importance of the distinction between manual and non-manual workers will become more apparent when the legal aspects of this subject are examined.

If a comparison is made between the UK and most other countries in Western Europe it will be seen that the UK has been extremely slow in accepting non-cash methods of remuneration. Germany has been the leader in developments of this nature, with under 5 per cent of employees now being paid in cash. In France, legislation has recently been introduced on this subject, and cash payment of remuneration is now restricted to amounts of less than 2,500 francs (about £270) per month. In the Netherlands and Sweden more than 80 per cent of employees are now paid by non-cash methods and Norway and Finland appear to be moving in this direction. Outside Europe the USA leads the way with only about 1 per cent of employees being paid in cash.

There are, however, a very few countries, such as Italy and Spain, which have a much higher proportion of employees paid in cash than is the case in the UK. UK government and employers must therefore decide whether we should be numbered with the Mediterranean countries or move in the direction of the example set by the USA, Germany and other similarly inclined countries.

LEGAL FRAMEWORK

A large part of UK legislation relating to the payment of manual employees has in the past been based on the Truck Acts of 1831 and 1887, although the original legislation on this subject goes back to the fifteenth century. The major objective of these Acts was to protect employees against payment in kind, and to clarify the position regarding the circumstances in which deductions from wages were acceptable.

The 1831 Act laid down that the entire amount of the wages earned or due to workers in certain trades had to be paid in 'current coin of the realm', subject to the exceptions laid down in the Act. Section 8 of the Act allowed workers to be paid by cheque, subject to the consent of the worker, although the bank on which the cheque was drawn had to be licensed to issue notes and be within 15 miles of the place of work. This part of the Act became meaningless in England and Wales when private banks stopped issuing their own notes. The provisions of the Truck Acts were extended in 1887 to cover all employees engaged in manual labour (except domestic servants). Two more Truck Acts were passed in 1896 and 1940, but they did not have any significant effect on the form of payment.

Further legislation was introduced in 1960 through the Payment of Wages Act. This laid down that manual workers could at their written request (or through a person authorized to act on their behalf) be paid by transfer into a bank account or by cheque, postal order or money order. The employer could refuse to change the method of payment but had to do so within fourteen days of the request being made. Both employer and employee were able to withdraw from the non-cash payment method by giving four weeks' notice in writing.

Changes in this legal framework were considered in a consultative document issued by the Department of Employment in 1983.[2] Several possible courses of action were examined:

1 amendment of the legislation;
2 repeal of the legislation with suitable replacement provisions;
3 complete repeal of the relevant legislation.

Numerous comments were received on the consultative document, as a result of which the Truck Acts and the Payment of Wages Act will be repealed and in their place there will be new legislation to protect employees against arbitrary deductions. This legislation is contained in the

2 Department of Employment, *Proposals for Updating the Law Relating to the Payment of Wages* (HMSO, 1983).

Wages Act 1986 the relevant parts of which will come into operation in January 1987.

Potential benefits

It is now widely accepted that there are substantial benefits available to employers if employees can be persuaded to accept non-cash methods of payment for remuneration purposes. If cash payment can be completely eliminated, savings should be possible in some or all of the following areas:

1 *Payroll staff and equipment*. If the payroll is produced internally, staff will obviously still be required to prepare the appropriate payroll data. It will, however, no longer be necessary to collect and count cash and put it in pay packets. In most situations there should be significant staff savings, although much will depend on the size of the employing organization and the status of the payroll staff. Cash handling facilities, if any, should no longer be necessary, although equipment may have to be purchased for the new payment processes.

2 *Transport and security costs*. Many large and medium-sized companies now use security organizations for the collection and distribution of cash for wage payment purposes. These costs can be substantial over the course of a financial year. If the company's own staff and vehicles are normally used, there will once again be savings in costs, although they may not be as large as when outside organizations are used. Storage of pay packets and the protection of staff handling cash resources present additional problems which could be largely removed if non-cash methods of payment were accepted by employees.

3 *Insurance premiums*. Most companies insure against risks involved in the collection and lodgement of cash. These costs may be very significant, although much will depend on average amounts carried and held on the premises, security arrangements, type of business, etc. Insurance may still be necessary for other cash items, but there could nevertheless be worthwhile cost savings in this area.

4 *Stationery costs*. Payroll envelopes will no longer be necessary, although details of the calculation of net emoluments will still be required. The cost of pay envelopes over a typical financial year can be surprisingly high.

5 *Employee time.* In some industrial situations, workers have to be allowed time off to collect their pay packet. This should no longer be necessary, although it may still be desirable to allow some time off for visits to the bank (or cash dispenser) if these facilities are a long way from the workplace.

6 *Bank charges.* Banks normally make a charge where cash is required by businesses. This charge is likely to be in the range of 30p to 60p per £100 collected, depending on the make-up of the cash required – notes, coins, etc. There should therefore be savings in this direction, although comparisons will obviously have to be made with the costs involved in the 'new' method of payment. Savings will be greatest if EFT methods can be used for payment purposes.

7 *Cash flow benefits.* In those organizations that make remuneration payments in cash, money often has to be drawn out of the bank one day before payment to ensure that adequate time is available for collection, counting and distribution of cash. The 'new' cash flow situation will depend on which system is used in the future. Paper-based bank transfers are generally debited at least two working days before payment, as compared with the same-day transfer of funds by electronic methods. Cheques could be beneficial from the employer's viewpoint, as there will normally be a clearance delay of two or three working days if employer and employee are not with the same bank and branch. Employees are, however, likely to object very strongly to a system under which it may not be possible to withdraw funds at the time the cheque is paid into the bank.

The benefits mentioned above may not all be realized, especially if some employees still have to be paid in cash, although it would probably be reasonable to expect that most of the suggested benefits should be at least partly achieved.

Problem areas

There are always likely to be disadvantages or problems associated with an attempted conversion to non-cash methods of remuneration. These will now be briefly considered under three headings:

1 *Negative responses from employees.* If the conversion campaign results in only a minority of employees accepting the scheme, a decision will have to be made as to whether it is worthwhile proceeding with the proposed plan. In this connection it is important to appreciate that it could be more costly to operate two payment

systems side-by-side rather than a cash system on its own. In many situations, however, a non-cash payment system will already be in operation for salaried employees.

2 *Excessive conversion costs.* The costs associated with the conversion process could cancel out most, if not all, of the benefits received in the early years following the changeover to non-cash methods. The major direct costs will probably be those relating to educational and publicity material, and much time and expertise may be required from senior members of the management team. The value of incentives will also need to be taken into account; in some recent settlements there do appear to have been some extremely generous payments. This matter is considered in more detail in the section on 'payment frequency and incentives'.

3 *Legislative problems.* It has already been pointed out that UK legislation has in the past laid down numerous safeguards in respect of payment to manual workers. Under this legislation, one of the major problems for the employer who introduced a non-cash payment system was that manual employees had the right to insist on payment in cash upon giving four weeks' notice. The Wages Act 1986 has, however, removed these rights.

In most situations the above disadvantages and problems will not outweigh the benefits that have already been considered, although the costs of the new system will have to be taken into account. All employers, except those with a very small number of employees, should therefore seriously consider non-cash methods of payment, although there will probably be objections from some employees.

EMPLOYEE VIEWPOINTS

It has been suggested by some trade unionists and employees that all of the major benefits involved in the abandonment of cash methods of remuneration accrue to the employer. Most informed observers would feel, however, that this is not always the case, although much will depend on the level of incentives or concessions, if any, provided for employees.

Potential benefits

In a properly negotiated non-cash payment scheme, some or all of the following benefits should be received by employees:

1 *Improved safety and security.* In recent years there have been many cases of assault and theft where persons have been believed to be carrying pay packets. Accidental loss can also take place, and there may be disputes regarding the amount contained in the pay packet. Non-cash methods of remuneration may therefore be advantageous to the employee, even though cash will still need to be obtained for many essential purchases. It should be possible, however, to make some payments by cheque or bank transfer.

2 *Advantages attached to a bank account.* Acceptance of non-cash payment methods may involve the opening of a bank account, expecially if the employee does not have a suitable account; in the latter case the employee should be able to obtain the normal benefits associated with a bank account. The sceptic might argue that these services are available to any reputable person; however, it is possible that bank charges will be less than is normally the case if there is a special agreement between the employer and the bank.

3 *Possibility of improved service conditions and incentives.* Many non-cash conversion schemes involve the provision of improved status and service conditions. Lump sum incentives may also be offered, although these benefits will usually be taxable. These matters will be considered in more detail later in this chapter.

The first two benefits mentioned in the preceding section may not sound very attractive to the employee who has been paid in cash for many years and has no wish to change. The incentives provided, if any, will therefore have to be carefully considered together with any disadvantages which are of particular importance to the individual employee.

Problem areas

It is always difficult to assess why employees object to non-cash payment of remuneration, although most of the major reasons will probably be found under the following headings:

1 *Cash availability.* Access to cash resources may be difficult for an employee paid by non-cash methods, especially if the employer's premises are situated some distance from the nearest bank. The bank's opening hours are also likely to be restricted, although the situation has been improved in recent years through the provision of cash dispensers and limited Saturday opening. To overcome this problem, some employers have agreed to cash cheques, although this will obviously remove some of the benefits attached to non-cash

payment methods, especially if business receipts are mainly in the form of cheques.

2 *Bank charges*. The opening of a bank account may involve the payment of bank charges or interest, especially if the employee finds it difficult to monitor bank receipts and payments. To overcome this problem, most banks that are involved with non-cash remuneration schemes offer one or two years of charge-free banking subject to certain conditions. Alternatively some employers offer an annual contribution towards bank charges, although this may be regarded as taxable income by the Inland Revenue.

3 *Loss of secrecy*. The provision of a monthly bank statement may mean that family or friends will discover the employee's net pay, especially if the envelope containing the bank statement is opened and left lying around the house. With a pay packet, on the other hand, the employee may be able to remove cash without the knowledge of the family or other beneficiaries (especially if the pay slip is destroyed). It is extremely difficult to assess the importance of this factor, although it is believed to be of great relevance in some households.

The above factors are considered to be important by many employees currently paid in cash, although discussions with employees and trade union representatives (if any) could reveal other matters that may need to be considered, e.g. fear and ignorance of bank practices and procedures. It should also be appreciated that older employees who have been paid in cash for many years may find the changeover process extremely difficult. Counselling of some employees may therefore be necessary, although bank personnel are not always as frightening as some employees imagine!

OTHER INTERESTED PARTIES

There are several sectors of the community that are extremely interested in the development of non-cash remuneration systems. Three of the most important of these are:

1 *Central and local government*. There are substantial risks involved in the collection and distribution of cash and there is little doubt that the opportunities for robbery would be significantly reduced if cash remuneration payments were largely or completely eliminated. Expenditure in respect of police forces, courts and prisons might also be significantly affected, although there is a danger that an increase

in electronic systems could lead to a great upsurge in computer fraud. Central and local government are also major employers and it must be hoped that a better example on non-cash payment will be provided in the future.

2 *Banks and other similar financial institutions.* In January 1981 the major UK banks launched a joint campaign to encourage the movement from weekly cash payment of wages to payment through a bank account. A full-time project executive was appointed to promote the campaign, and individual banks set up special task forces to approach employers and other interested organizations. The banks naturally hope that this campaign will help to produce a significant increase in the number of bank accounts together with a reduction in the amount of cash that has to be handled by the banks. Other financial institutions, e.g. building societies, are interested in the changes that are taking place, although there has been no concerted campaign to help in this process as has been the case with the banks.

3 *Trade unions and other employee representatives.* The attitude of the Trades Union Congress (TUC) towards non-cash payment of remuneration has generally been one of encouragement rather than compulsion. Decisions have therefore been left to individual unions and their members. Enlightened trade unionists are by now well aware of the benefits that this type of change can bring to the employer, and this almost inevitably leads to a demand that benefits should be shared rather than a scheme being totally rejected. Nevertheless there is usually an insistence that individual employees should be given the right to refuse change if they so decide.

ALTERNATIVES TO CASH PAYMENT

If it is decided that a non-cash payment system of remuneration should be adopted, there are several methods of payment which can be used. These will now be briefly considered under three main headings:

1 *By cheque.* Until the mid-1960s the cheque was the most popular form of non-cash remuneration payment. As with all cheque payments, there are substantial preparation costs, although the overall costs will probably be signficantly less than those incurred under a cash system, especially if it is possible to abandon all forms of cash remuneration. The employee will in the vast majority of cases

have to possess or open an account into which the cheque can be paid at a bank, post office or building society – although arrangements are sometimes made by employers for non-account holders to cash cheques at a specified bank. There may, however, be difficulties in obtaining cash on the date a cheque is paid into the bank, primarily because of the two or three-day clearing period. This problem may be avoided if employer and employee bank at the same branch of the same bank. Cheques are therefore likely to produce some problems from the employee's viewpoint, and many employers have now found that the credit transfer provides a more efficient and cheaper method of payment.

2 *By credit transfer.* The paper-based credit transfer system was for many years heavily used for remuneration payment purposes, and many small and medium-sized businesses are still using this method of payment. In recent years, however, automated credit transfer systems – usually through BACS – have been increasing in popularity, especially in those businesses which can provide satisfactory computer-input material. Both types of credit transfer should provide significant savings as compared with cash payments. Electronic transfers through BACS will nearly always be the cheapest method of payment, unless the number of employees is very small, but much will depend on the employer's existing computer equipment, which may be inadequate or non-existent. The credit transfer system has in most cases worked very well for employers, although payroll data must be finalized at least two days before the date of payment; this can be a problem with some weekly wage applications. Employees must, of course, possess a suitable account into which the credit transfer can be paid, and as long as this can be arranged, funds should be available on the due date provided that satisfactory transfer arrangements have been made.

3 *By payment at a post office.* There are several ways in which payment can be arranged at a post office. For example, postal and money orders were used for remuneration purposes at one time, although the evidence that is available suggests that it is little used today. Giro cash cheques, payable at a named post office, can also be used, although this is likely to be an expensive form of payment as compared with cheques and credit transfers. The National Girobank will also arrange transfers to an employee's giro account if the employer has a suitable type of account. If the employer does not have a National Girobank account, BACS will arrange transfers into Girobank accounts from other clearing bank accounts. The employee

should therefore be able to withdraw funds on the agreed date of payment.

Table 10.2 shows the results of a banking study of remuneration methods carried out in 1984. This survey indicated that 37 per cent of employees were paid in cash at that time. The cheque system was used for 16 per cent of payments, whereas the credit transfer system had been accepted by 43 per cent of employees. No information was provided as to the breakdown of credit transfer payments into paper and electronic methods, although unofficial estimates suggest that at least 75 per cent of credit transfers in respect of remuneration are now made by electronic methods.

Table 10.2   UK methods of remuneration payment

Details	Percentage of total number of payments	
Weekly paid employees		
Cash	37	
Cheque	8	
Credit transfer	12	
		57
Monthly paid employees		
Cheque	8	
Credit transfer	31	
		39
Not known		4
Total		100

Source: Inter-Bank Research Organisation, *Research Brief*, Exhibit 3, October 1985. Credit transfers cover both automated and paper-based transactions.

Table 10.2 also shows the difference between weekly and monthly paid employees as far as methods of payment are concerned. Weekly paid employees are still largely paid in cash, although there is now a significant acceptance of cheques and credit transfers. Monthly paid employees have virtually abandoned cash payment methods, with the credit transfer system being much more popular than cheques.

It seems inevitable, therefore, that in the next decade there will be a strong movement towards non-cash payment methods, with particular emphasis on EFT systems. As a result, we may find that by the end of the

1980s about 70 per cent of UK remuneration payments are made by non-cash methods, with most of those payments being made by electronic transfer methods.

PAYMENT FREQUENCY AND INCENTIVES

Those employers who have considered the payment of remuneration in some depth have frequently come to the conclusion that ideally a monthly electronic bank transfer system should be adopted for all employees. If numerous employees are paid weekly in cash, this may prove to be impossible to implement, although it should at the very least be seen as a long-term objective.

The benefits that should be received by the employer from a monthly, rather than a weekly, electronic bank transfer system are fairly obvious. Less staff time, processing costs and stationery should be involved in payroll preparation over the course of a financial year, in addition to which there could also be cash flow advantages, although much will depend on the date of monthly payment. Incentive payments and other concessions will naturally have to be taken into account in assessing the net benefits.

Many different types of incentives have been offered by employers in attempts to persuade employees to switch to a cashless system. The attractiveness of the incentives will probably have to be much greater if attempts are also made to adjust the frequency of payment. The possibilities that might be considered could include:

1 increased pay and/or reduced hours;
2 improved status and/or service conditions, e.g. a longer notice period, better pension rights, improved holidays, etc;
3 a large lump sum payment;
4 an interest-free loan repayable over an agreed period;
5 annual contributions towards bank charges;
6 improved staff discounts on purchases;
7 monthly payment of remuneration well in advance of the end of the month.

One of the most important matters that will have to be considered in deciding which, if any, of these benefits should be offered to employees is that a high level of acceptance is essential if the changeover scheme is to be financially successful. In some schemes the incentives offered have been linked to a high percentage acceptance by employees, although this may prove to be difficult to achieve. Obviously there might only be very limited benefits in introducing a scheme which has only been accepted by a small number of employees.

In recent employee negotiations the most popular incentive has been the lump sum payment. One of the best-known offers in recent years was the £75 lump sum payment made available for water industry workers who accepted monthly bank transfer methods. This was an important part of the peace formula which was worked out after weeks of strike action. Similar payments have been offered in many central and local government payment negotiations. In some cases these incentives have been for amounts of £100 or above. Thus non-industrial civil servants have recently been offered £100 to change over from a weekly cash system to a monthly bank transfer method. This was expected to cost £6½ million if all eligible employees took up the offer, although it was hoped that the overall saving would be significantly above this figure.

When a monthly payment scheme is being negotiated, the proposed date of payment can be very important. In the retail sector, payment around the middle of the month has been a feature of several large settlements. For example, Marks and Spencer pay all permanent retail staff at monthly intervals on the 10th of the month, and Currys have a similar arrangement with payment on the 17th. Negotiations may become rather complicated when there are existing monthly paid employees, who may well feel that they should be paid at the same time as those who are likely to change over to monthly pay.

The benefits that may become available to an employer in a switch from weekly cash pay to monthly electronic bank transfer are extremely difficult to estimate. In the early 1980s Lloyds Bank suggested that it was then costing about £32.50 per annum to pay an employee weekly in cash as opposed to £6 per annum using a monthly electronic transfer system. More recent estimates have suggested that the weekly wage packet is now 13 to 16 times more expensive over the course of a year than the monthly electronic transfer system.[3] Estimates of this nature are, of course, very difficult to produce with any precision, especially as far as internal administrative costs are concerned, although the figures quoted are the result of practical experience in large organizations.

Despite disagreements on precise figures, there seems little doubt that substantial benefits are available to the organization that can persuade its weekly paid workers to accept monthly payment by electronic transfer into a designated bank account. In the vast majority of cases a movement of this nature will not prove to be easy, although a sensible use of incentives combined with a detailed educational process should persuade a worth-while number of employees to accept such a scheme.

3 D. Balmforth, How Automated Clearing Cuts the Cost of Paying, *Accountant*, 30 May 1985, pp. 22–3.

Table 10.3 provides an indication of the movement from weekly to monthly payment in recent years. Between 1976 and 1985 the percentage of employees receiving monthly payment increased from 33 to 41 per cent, and recent surveys suggest that this figure is rapidly approaching 45 per cent. A considerable amount of progress has therefore been made in the last decade, although there is still a long way to go if monthly payment is seen as a desirable long-term objective in payment systems.

Table 10.3 Frequency of remuneration payments in the UK (%)

	1976	*1979*	*1985*
Weekly[a]	67	64	59
Monthly[b]	33	36	41
Total	100	100	100

[a] Includes employees on fortnightly pay.
[b] Includes employees on a four-weekly system.
Sources: The UK High Street Banks, *Modernising Payment Methods*, May 1983, and Inter-Bank Research Organisation, *Research Brief*, October 1985.

FUTURE DEVELOPMENTS

In the next decade it seems probable that there will be a continued movement towards non-cash remuneration methods in the UK, especially now that government has repealed the rather restrictive clauses contained in past legislation. Most employers will welcome this change, although there will still be a reluctance to accept these methods amongst elderly and low-paid workers who have traditionally been paid in cash.

Table 10.4 provides an indication *in value terms* of the acceptance of EFT systems for remuneration purposes. Weekly wages are dominated by cash payments, with less than 9 per cent being made by EFT systems. On the other hand, monthly salaries are now largely paid by means of EFT processes – over 72 per cent in total. Occupational pensions are somewhere between these two methods, with 39 per cent of the value of payments being made by EFT systems. If the three sets of figures are added together, the EFT usage rate in value terms is just over 21 per cent.

Recent developments would suggest that by the end of the current century the vast majority of salaries and occupational pension payments will be made by EFT systems. Most recipients would probably be prepared to be paid in this form, although some small and medium-sized

126   *Wages and Salaries*

Table 10.4 Forms of UK remuneration payment in value terms
(to nearest £ million)

	Total	Paper-based	Cash	EFT systems
Weekly wages	611	150	409	52
Monthly salaries	128	34	1	93
Occupational pensions	74	38	7	29
Total	813	222	417	174

Source: Bankers' Automated Clearing Services, 1984 statistics. The amounts for paper-based transactions cover both cheques and non-automated credit transfers.

employers may be unwilling to provide the necessary computer-input material or use a service bureau.

The weekly wages situation is less clear and it will probably be a considerable achievement if the 50 per cent mark (in value and number terms) is passed by the end of the century. Much will depend on government action, although the banks could still do more to improve the attractiveness and availability of their services.

The movement towards EFT methods of remuneration will probably be accompanied by an increasing use of monthly payment systems. Attractive incentives may have to be paid out to achieve these changes, and increasing awareness of the benefits that EFT systems can produce will probably play a significant part in these processes. Some employees will object to these changes, but it seems probable that by the end of the century they will be part of a minority movement.

SUMMARY AND CONCLUSIONS

The payment of remuneration was one of the first applications for which EFT systems were used, especially in the case of monthly salaries. It has proved to be much more difficult, however, to automate wage payments, but there has been some progress in this direction in recent years.

Many obstacles still remain in the process of change, although these are gradually being removed. Further action by government and the banks is still desirable, while improved telecommunications methods are gradually making EFT systems a practicable proposition for most employers with computer systems. Employee attitudes are also changing, although there are still many deeply ingrained objections to cashless payment.

The remuneration picture is therefore one of gradual change as we move towards cashless remuneration with an increasing number of employees being paid at monthly intervals. These changes may take many years to achieve, although government action (as in France) could speed up this movement. While it seems unlikely that anything will reverse this process, there will probably always be a limited number of employees who will have to be paid in cash because of poverty or the smallness of remuneration.

11 Government Benefits

Reliable figures regarding the number of government payments are difficult to obtain, although information on this subject is occasionally published by central government and other sources. Bankers' Automated Clearing Services (BACS) is one of the few organizations to have produced recent estimates of payments made by central and local government and other sectors of the economy. These figures are shown in table 11.1.

The table shows that over 1,200 million payments were made by UK central government in 1984. This figure, which represents over 42 per cent of the total number of government and business payments, rises to nearly 48 per cent if local government and public utilities are included in government payments.

Payments by government take many different forms: social security benefits, wages, salaries, occupational pensions, expenses, purchase ledger payments, grants, investments, etc. BACS has estimated that in 1984 over 1,070 million social security payments were made, which represents about 88 per cent of the total number of government payments.

Table 11.1 Payments made by UK government and business organizations

Market sector	Number of payments (millions)
Central government	1211
Local government	120
Public utilities	39
Financial institutions	115
Manufacturing and production	598
Service industries	785
Total	2868

Source: Bankers' Automated Clearing Services, 1984 statistics.

Government benefits are paid in four different ways. The most common method, 88 per cent of all payments, is by order book foils. These foils are normally converted into cash at a specified post office. Giro cheques account for about 11 per cent of all payments; these are mainly used for payments which it is hoped will be short-term, e.g. unemployment benefits. Giro cheques must be cashed at a post office or paid into a bank account. The remaining 1 per cent of payments are made by means of payable orders (0.5 per cent), which have to be paid into a bank account, and automated credit transfers (0.5 per cent), which are normally arranged through BACS or the National Girobank. These figures, together with a considerable amount of other information, were provided in a special report issued by the Comptroller and Auditor General in February 1985.[1]

The payment of government benefits is thus heavily reliant on order book foils and giro payments which will in the vast majority of cases involve the delivery, storage and distribution of cash by post office personnel. Benefit foils and giro cheques to the value of £28½ billion were encashed at post offices in 1983, representing 46 per cent by value of all post office counter business.[2] There would therefore appear to be considerable scope for the introduction of EFT systems. Numerous objections have already been made to this form of payment, and these will be considered later in this chapter.

SOCIAL SECURITY PAYMENTS

There is a very extensive range of social security payments in the UK. Table 11.2 provides an indication of the importance of these benefits split up into National Insurance and non-contributory benefits. Total expenditure on National Insurance benefits was estimated to be well over £20 billion in 1984/5 as compared with nearly £15 billion on non-contributory benefits. The overall total of £35 billion is spread over 30 different types of benefits, although 80 per cent of the total amount paid out relates to pensions (of all types), child benefits, supplementary payments and unemployment benefits.

The total number of recipients of social security benefits is difficult to estimate, as there are many people receiving more than one type of benefit. It is also important to appreciate that child benefit figures are based on the number of children for whom benefit is paid – 12½ million; the number of

---

1 Report by the Comptroller and Auditor General, *Department of Health and Social Security: Arrangements for Delivering Social Security Benefits* (HMSO, February 1985), para. 1.8.
2 Reference 1, para. 1.12.

families receiving child benefit is believed to be about 7½ million. Government estimates suggest that in 1983/4 there were over 19 million people receiving benefits.[3]

The organization of the social security benefit system is obviously a huge task, the administration of which was estimated to cost £1,328 million in 1982/3. Major components of this total were £495 million for payment

Table 11.2   Estimated UK social security payments – 1984/5

	Expenditure (£ millions)	Average number of recipients at any one time (millions)
National insurance benefits		
Retirement pensions	15435	9.3
Other pension payments – invalidity, industrial disablement, widows' benefits, etc.	3160	1.4
Lump sum payments to pensioners	104	10.1
Unemployment benefits	1538	1.0
Other payments – sickness, death grant, maternity allowances, etc.	455	1.0
Non-contributory benefits		
Supplementary pensions and allowances	6157	4.3
Child benefits	4291	12.5
Housing benefits – rent rebates and allowances	2461	4.1
Other non-contributory pensions and allowances	1998	3.5

Source: *Government Expenditure Plans (Cmnd 9143)*, HM Treasury, 1984. Recipients may be drawing more than one type of benefit.

3 Reference 1, para. 1.5.

processes, £260 million for post office and girobank encashment costs, with most of the remainder being made up of staffing and postal costs.[4] It is not surprising, therefore, that attempts are being made to reduce these costs through the more widespread use of EFT systems and other money-saving techniques.

GOVERNMENT INITIATIVES

In 1979 Sir Derek Rayner (now Lord Rayner) was asked by the UK government to lead a small team of investigation into ways in which government spending might be reduced. Numerous recommendations were made by this team and these were in turn considered by committees in the various ministries affected by the recommendations. Final decisions were, of course, made by government, although in some cases a consultative document was issued before the final decision was made.

Amongst many other things, the Rayner Committee produced recommendations that government benefits should wherever possible be paid by automated credit transfer (ACT), with a reduction in the frequency of payment (over 90 per cent of benefit payments were for one week only at the time of this statement). The Social Services Committee[5] endorsed these recommendations, although it was suggested that weekly benefit payments should continue to be provided where beneficiaries so wished. Government then sought further views by the issue of a consultative document (Cmnd 8106) in December 1980.

In May 1981 the Secretary of State for Social Services announced the government's decision based on the various recommendations and responses to the consultative document. As far as the ACT issue was concerned, it was decided that this system would be offered from 1982 onwards to most recipients of government benefits. Payment was, however, to be made in arrears at the end of each four-week period. This was against the advice of the Social Services Committee, which had recommended that payment should be made two weeks in advance and two weeks in arrears. It was also decided that *new* recipients of child benefits should be paid four weekly in arrears unless hardship could be proved. In the case of hardship and for all existing beneficiaries who did not wish to change over to the new system the weekly order foil payment system was to be retained.

As a result of these decisions, it was decided to send out letters to

4 Reference 1, para. 1.14.
5 The Social Services Committee is normally made up of nine Members of Parliament who have the task of examining the administration and policies of the Department of Health and Social Security.

recipients of specified social security benefits. The starting dates of the different campaigns were as follows:

1 October 1982: retirement and widows' pensions;
2 April 1983: mobility allowances;
3 January 1984: child benefits;
4 March 1984: war pensions;
5 April 1984: attendance allowances (where not paid with retirement or widows' pensions).

The circularization process should have been completed in 1985, but it has been delayed by staffing and computer problems which caused a temporary suspension of the programme. New claimants are, however, being approached to see if they would like to use the ACT system. It is unlikely that recipients of other benefits will be contacted, as most of these payments are short-term or on a means-tested basis.

IMPLEMENTATION POLICIES AND PROBLEMS

The attempt to persuade recipients of certain government benefits to accept ACT payments began in the latter part of 1982 with letters being sent out to the first of about 10 million pensioners. Before the despatch of the ACT letter, about 80 per cent of pensioners were paid weekly by order book foils, and 10 per cent were paid by means of four-weekly or thirteen-weekly payable orders. Most of the remainder were paid through the giro bank system.

The letter to pensioners offered payment into a designated bank or building society account at four-weekly intervals; there was no compulsion to change over to the new system. Bank transfers at weekly or monthly intervals were *not* allowed. Payment under the new system was to be made in arrears at the end of every four weeks with no attempt being made to provide the type of incentive that has been offered in many cashless remuneration schemes.

The National Federation of Sub-Postmasters, whose members are responsible for the payment of about 70 per cent of government benefits paid at post offices (the remaining 30 per cent are paid out at Crown Offices), was very alarmed by these developments, as it was felt that widespread acceptance of the government offer could take away a large part of post office business, especially in rural areas. As a result, a poster and circularization campaign was launched to emphasize the value of the local post office system, with particular stress on the importance of convenient opening hours and the problems involved in the new scheme, for example, possibility of bank charges, long distances from banks, cash availability on changeover, etc. Numerous letters were also sent out to Members of Parliament and other interested parties.

The response to the pension payment ACT campaign was disappointing from the government viewpoint, as by the end of 1985 fewer than one million people had agreed to be paid by ACT methods. All pensioners who were previously paid by means of payable orders – nearly 0.9 million – have been approached, and rather surprisingly a sizeable minority have not accepted the ACT offer. New pensioners are also showing a strong preference for cash, and only about 20 per cent have agreed to be paid through the ACT scheme.

The child benefit ACT campaign began in January 1984 and letters will eventually go out to over 7 million existing parents and all new parents. New parents had already been required to accept a four-week payment system from April 1982, although about 30 per cent of parents have been exempted on hardship grounds. By the end of 1985 about 300,000 parents were receiving payment through the ACT system, with the positive response rate being in the region of 10 per cent from existing parents and 20 per cent from new parents.

Through a variety of factors, therefore, the government initiative on the use of automated payments for benefit payment purposes has produced disappointing results, and by the end of 1985 positive responses had only come from about 1¼ million people, many of whom were already being paid at four-weekly or thirteen-weekly intervals. There are, however, numerous beneficiaries who have not yet been approached, and there will always be some people who have agreed to accept the ACT scheme but are not yet being paid in this form. Revised government estimates produced in 1985 suggested that there would be a take-up by 2.1 million for the ACT scheme by 1987/8 as compared with an original estimate of 3.5 million.[6]

The major blame for this rather negative response must lie with the government ministers who made the decision that transfers would be made at the end, rather than in the middle, of the four-week period. This decision went against all the evidence that had become available over the last decade in persuading employees to accept monthly paid bank transfer remuneration systems. Government ministers and their advisers were apparently heavily influenced by the fact that payment in the middle of the four-week cycle might cost a considerable amount in interest terms, but little effort was made to calculate the benefits that might result from an increased acceptance of EFT systems.

It is not suggested, however, that the government initiative would have

6 Reference 1, para. 2.12.

been a tremendous success if payment had been offered at an earlier stage in the four-week period. The response would certainly have been better, although there are many other personal preferences for cash payment which have already been considered in previous chapters. It is also possible that the campaign by the National Federation of Sub-Postmasters had a significant effect, as most recipients of government benefits appear to be keen to maintain the post office system.

The child benefit payment system is also complicated by the fact that most mothers regard this source of income as spending money in respect of their children's requirements, and there is a great fear that available funds will be cut down if transfers are made to a bank or building society account which may be partly or wholly controlled by the child's father.

The possession of a bank or other similar account may be another problem area. Research conducted by the Inter-Bank Research Organisation suggests that 47 per cent of pensioners and 69 per cent of parents receiving child benefits have bank current accounts.[7] It must be remembered, however, that the government ACT scheme covers transfers to national savings and building society accounts; if these are included the number of account-holders will be very much higher. Distance from a bank may also be a serious difficulty for some beneficiaries, although national savings and giro bank accounts can, of course, be opened at post offices.

It is considered, therefore, that the government scheme to introduce automated payments for social security benefits was seriously defective, especially as far as the timing of payments was concerned. It must be accepted, however, that there will always be problems in persuading a significant section of the population – especially the poor and elderly – to accept non-cash payment methods, even if incentives are offered. Government ministers must therefore consider whether the present scheme should be revised or abandoned, as it has had little success in its present form.

FUTURE DEVELOPMENTS

In recent years considerable efforts have been made by UK governments to improve the quality of financial management practices, largely as a result of recommendations from numerous committees, the most recent of which led to the Financial Management Initiative (FMI) in Government project, which was launched in May 1982. Rather surprisingly, this initiative does

---

7 Inter-Bank Research Organisation, *Research Brief*, October 1982.

not appear to have produced any detailed recommendations on overall government payment practices, apart from the action that has already been taken on government benefits.

Table 11.3 provides an indication of the extent of government use of EFT systems, from which it will be seen that only just over 3 per cent of government payments are made by EFT processes. Nearly all monthly salaries are paid by automated methods, but this movement has not been extended to weekly wages and occupational pensions, where fewer than a quarter of recipients are paid by these methods. In other applications where business organizations are beginning to make significant use of EFT systems, e.g. purchases ledger payments, there is little or no sign of movement from cheque payment systems.

Table 11.3 Annual EFT payments by UK central government (to nearest million)

Application	Total number of payments	Number of EFT payments	EFT payments as percentage of total number of payments
Social security	1072	9	1
Weekly wages	21	4	21
Monthly salaries	12	12	98
Occupational pensions	33	8	24
Purchase ledger settlements	16	I/S[a]	–
Grants	3	1	42
Investments	28	I/S	–
Expenses	4	I/S	–
Other payments	22	4	18
Total	1211	38	

[a]I/S = insignificant.
Source: Bankers' Automated Clearing Services, 1984 statistics.

In the social security sector about 1 per cent of state benefits are currently paid by EFT systems, despite an expensive and time-consuming circularization campaign. Government ministers may therefore be reluctant to spend a lot more time and energy on the automation of these processes, especially as the recent campaign proved to be politically unpopular.

It must not be forgotten, however, that significant savings are available to government if an increasing number of benefit payments can be automated; recent government estimates suggest that it costs £6 per annum for a four-weekly ACT payment as compared with £16 per annum for the weekly order book system.[8] It will probably never be possible to automate more than a small number of the payments made in respect of unemployment and supplementary benefits, largely because of the recipient's immediate need for cash and the frequent absence of a bank account. It should nevertheless be possible to persuade a substantial number of recipients of child benefits and retirement pensions to accept payment into a designated bank or building society account provided that attractive incentives are offered to those who accept payment in this form.

There are, of course, some unique factors in the automation of government benefits, one of the most important of which is the continued existence of the post office system. In the UK there are currently over 20,000 post offices, which receive over one-third of their income from charges levied for dealing with government benefits. In many rural post offices these activities represent about 75 per cent of counter business, and it is doubtful whether a majority of sub-post offices would be economic if a substantial number of benefit payments were removed from the post office system.

The Committee of Public Accounts has recently considered this matter and came to the conclusion that the role of the Department of Health & Social Security (DHSS) shoiuld be to provide the most cost-effective service, and not to concern itself with the viability of sub-post offices. The following sentence was particularly significant – 'if any financial support is necessary to maintain the viability of the Post Office network it seems to us that this should be provided by the Department of Trade and Industry as the sponsoring department'.[9] All that this recommendation achieves, however, is the transfer of responsibility from one government department to another, although it may be a comforting statement from the DHSS viewpoint.

Governments of the future will therefore have some difficult decisions to make on the automation of benefit payments. This question is inevitably intertwined with the future of the post office system, and even if this problem can be overcome there are still strong personal preferences for cash, especially amongst those who have insufficient resources to justify a bank or building society account. Governments may in the future be prepared to share out some of the advantages that can be obtained from automation – in the form of incentives of one form or another – although it seems probable that even in the twenty-first century there will still be a need for cash payment for at least a minority of government benefit payments.

8 Committee of Public Accounts (Twentieth Report), *Arrangements for Delivering Social Security Benefits*, (HMSO, June 1985), para. 12.
9 Reference 8, para. 9.

SUMMARY AND CONCLUSIONS

There are currently over 1 billion payments made by UK central government each year in respect of a wide variety of state benefits. These payments make up well over 40 per cent of the total number of payments made by business and government organizations. Decisions on the form of payment of these benefits are therefore likely to have a significant effect on the movement towards cashless methods of payment.

In 1982 the UK government launched the first of what may be several initiatives to automate the benefit payment process and reduce the frequency of payments. These initiatives have persuaded about 1¼ million beneficiaries to accept electronic transfers into a bank or building society account at four-weekly intervals. Many of these people were already being paid by means of payable orders, which are very similar to a cheque payment. The vast majority of recipients of government benefits have therefore decided that they would prefer to be paid in cash at a post office, either with an order book foil or a paper-based giro warrant.

It therefore seems probable that it will be extremely difficult to persuade a large number of recipients of government benefits to accept cashless methods of payment. Attitudes may change as increasing numbers of people open bank accounts, although government benefits are by their very nature often paid to the poorest in our society, many of whom will never have sufficient resources to justify a bank account. It should not be forgotten, however, that a large number of recipients of retirement pensions and child benefits have bank accounts, and one might therefore expect that over a long-term period a substantial number of them would accept payment into a bank account, as long as government were to offer attractive incentives to all who were prepared to be paid in this form. This could produce savings of many millions of pounds, although government might then find that the business of many small post offices was irreparably damaged. Decisions in this very controversial area are therefore likely to be strongly influenced by political considerations as well as payment savings.

12   Automated Cash Dispensing

Cash dispensing machines have been used in the UK since 1969 although it was not until the mid-1970s that automated teller machines (ATMs) became widely available. There is no generally agreed international definition of an ATM, but most writers on this subject regard the ATM as a cash dispenser with additonal services, the most popular of which are the provision of information regarding account balances and the ability to order a cheque book or bank statement. Other services that may be provided include the acceptance of deposits, transfers between accounts under the same control, arrangement of regular payments, information regarding recent bank statement items, issue of travellers cheques and handling of loan applications. It is rumoured that a recently introduced ATM in the USA can provide 125 different services!

ATMs are in most cases very sophisticated machines costing up to £25,000 but basic cash dispensers are also available – normally for in-branch purposes – costing about £10,000. Most new ATMs operate on an on-line basis with instantaneous or end-of-day account updating facilities. UK banks usually update customers' accounts after the event, whereas many building societies have instantaneous updating facilities. Some existing ATMs and cash dispensers are off-line, or have a combination of off-line and on-line facilities; these will probably be replaced by machines with full on-line capability by the end of the 1980s.

The banks are reluctant to comment about the amount of cash held in ATMs; it is believed that some dispensers are capable of holding up to £100,000, depending on the value of notes held in the machine (it would be necessary to use a large number of high-value notes to reach this amount). The average amount held in any one of these machines is probably in the region of £10,000 to £15,000, which means that in a country like the UK there could be in the region of £100 million held in machines for withdrawal purposes.

A cash card is required for ATM withdrawals. This is in effect a debit card, a card that allows approved holders to draw on their bank accounts. Cards are issued on request to customers by most major banks. At the end of 1985 there were believed to be about 300 million of these cards in circulation throughout the world, of which 18 million were held in the UK. When a withdrawal is required, the cash card is inserted into the ATM together with details of the holder's personal identification number (PIN) – usually made up of four digits in the UK – and the amount required. The cardholder should then be able to obtain the required amount subject to the balance held in the account and any withdrawal limits. Other services can also be used if these are available and required.

The modern ATM is therefore a product of the electronic banking era, and it seems probable that the range of services will become increasingly sophisticated in the future. On-line electronic facilities already provide the ability to transfer funds instantaneously or at the end of the day from the account of the cardholder to that of the bank (or other financial institution), and some machines are now providing a bill payment service under which regular commitments can be paid, provided that bank and other appropriate details have been lodged with the card issuer before-hand. ATMs could therefore eventually become an important part of a nationwide electronic funds transfer service.

INTERNATIONAL DEVELOPMENTS

Over the last twenty years approximately £3 billion has been invested in different parts of the world on ATMs and cash dispensers. This has resulted in about 160,000 installations, with a current annual increase rate in the region of 20 per cent. Table 12.1 provides an approximate indication of the worldwide situation in early 1986. End-of-1986 figures are expected to reveal total installations rapidly approaching 200,000, of which over 40 per cent will be in North America, 30 per cent in Asia and 20 per cent in Europe.

ATM developments in North America have been strongly influenced by the problems which US banks face in providing a satisfactory nationwide service; it is very difficult under current state regulations for branches to be opened in another state or sometimes in another part of the same state. It may be difficult, therefore, for account-holders to cash cheques or obtain other bank facilities when they are away from their home area. The ATM has helped to alleviate this problem, especially in situations where there are shared networks, nearly 200 of which have been set up on a regional basis and 7 on a national basis. Total US installations are now above 60,000

Table 12.1 Worldwide automated teller machine installations

Continent	Number of installations (to nearest thousand)
North America	65
Asia (mainly Japan)	48
Europe	35
Other areas	12
Total	160

Sources: Various bank agencies – January 1986. The figures are very approximate, as precise worldwide data were not available at the time of publication.

with another 3,000 machines in Canada, and trade experts are now suggesting that there could be in the region of 100,000 machines installed in North America by the end of the 1980s.

The second largest country in ATM and cash dispenser installation terms is Japan, where the total number of machines passed the 40,000 mark in 1985. Most employees receive their remuneration through the banking system by transfers to a savings account, although very few private individuals use cheques. The introduction of ATMs, mainly inside bank premises, has therefore been welcomed as a quick means of obtaining savings account funds. ATMs are also extensively used for depositing funds and making transfers to other bank accounts.

In Europe (apart from the UK) the major users of ATMs are the French with more than 8,000 installations at the beginning of 1986. Spain is the next major user – about 3,000 installations – probably because of the extensive use of cash by residents and tourists for all types of transactions. West Germany is a surprisingly small user of ATMs, with only about 2,500 installations, although new machines are rapidly being installed. Bankers from 17 major European countries are now working on a system which, it is hoped, will enable cardholders to obtain cash from ATMs when visiting most Western European countries. This scheme will initially concentrate on the Eurocheque card, although it is hoped that all major cards will eventually be accepted.

Outside North America, Western Europe and Japan the use of ATMs is not very significant, although the number of installations is growing, especially in Australia, New Zealand, South Africa, Singapore, Hong Kong, Brazil and Mexico. Installation costs can, however, be heavy in a small or developing country, especially when there is a shortage of people with installation experience. Developments over the next few years will therefore probably be in those countries that have already built up a strong ATM base, although some observers believe that a saturation point in the number of new external installations will be reached in several major countries by the end of the 1980s.

UK INSTALLATIONS

The total number of bank ATM and cash dispenser installations in the UK was in the region of 9,000 at the end of 1985, with expectations of a figure above 10,000 by 1987. Table 12.2 shows the number of machines installed by the major UK clearing banks at the end of 1985, from which it will be seen that the National Westminster and Lloyds were at that time the leaders in the number of machines installed. The figures provided in the table do not include the smaller banks and other financial institutions, which increase the number of machines in service by more than 50 per cent.

Table 12.2 Installations of automated teller machines and cash dispensers by major UK banks

Bank	Number in service	Number of cards (millions)	Number of transactions (millions)	Value of transactions (£ billions)
Barclays	887	2.61	55.8	1.84
Lloyds	1716	3.98	81.7	2.61
Midland	1081	2.95	56.0	1.54
National Westminster	2022	3.89	88.3	2.44
Total	5706	13.43	281.8	8.43

Source: Abstract of Banking Statistics, 1986. The figures are based on ATM and cash dispenser installations at the end of 1985.

Over 70 per cent of ATMs in the UK are installed on a 'through-the-wall' basis. Most of the remaining machines are in lobbies or customer areas, although a small number are on 'stand-alone' sites, e.g. outside large retailers. The current trend in new installations appears to be towards 'in-branch' cash dispensers; Barclays, Midland and National Westminster are now beginning to follow the example of Lloyds, which already has about 1,000 of its machines in lobbies or customer areas.

There have been several important ATM developments in the UK in the last two or three years. Probably the most important has been the setting up of shared networks, as a result of which there are now two major bank networks of roughly equal size. The first is made up of the Midland and National Westminster groups, whilst the second is in the process of being implemented by Barclays, Lloyds and two major Scottish banks – the Bank of Scotland and the Royal Bank of Scotland. There have proved to be numerous problems in the setting up of these networks, mainly because of the incompatibility of different equipment and systems, although most of these problems have now been overcome. This is naturally a welcome development from the users' viewpoint, as it does provide a much greater number of machines for individual cash withdrawal purposes.

Another major development has been the growth in the number of machines installed by the smaller banks and the building societies. In the banking sector the major ATM installers, apart from the clearing banks named in table 12.2, have been the Clydesdale Bank, the Royal Bank of Scotland and the Bank of Scotland, all of which have at least 250 installations, and the Trustee Savings Banks, which recently passed the 1,000 mark. The National Girobank has only recently entered this market, but rapid growth is now expected to take place.

The building society movement may also be an important future influence in the ATM market. The largest society (in asset terms), the Halifax Building Society, with over 10 million account-holders, has set up its own scheme, with about 350 machines installed by the beginning of 1986. Most of the other major building societies have joined, or are in the process of joining, shared schemes. The most popular of the shared networks has proved to be the Link Scheme, in which the major building society participants are the Abbey National and the Nationwide together with several other societies and financial institutions working through a recently formed organization called Funds Transfer Sharing Limited. There are a few non-building societies in the Link Scheme, e.g. the National Girobank and the Co-operative Bank. Over 800 ATMs will probably have been installed by members of the Link group by the end of 1986, including about 500 by building societies. Another group called Electronic Funds Transfer Limited has been set up by seven leading building societies under the name Matrix; these societies plan to install over 400 machines by the end of 1986. By the beginning of 1987, therefore, UK building societies will probably have installed more than 1,200 ATMs.

The UK ATM and cash dispenser market has thus grown rapidly since the first machines were installed in the late 1960s, and there is now about one machine for every two bank branches amongst the major clearing banks. With ATMs being installed by other cash dispensing organizations such as the building societies, there could be 12,000 machines in operation by the late 1980s. The cash dispensing business in the UK will therefore have changed very significantly between the early 1970s and the late 1980s.

The objectives behind the installation of ATMs have never been clearly laid down by the UK banks. Some of the early cash dispensers are believed to have been installed as an answer to the criticisms of Saturday morning closing, although this reason has at least partly disappeared with the recent reappearance of Saturday opening. In the last decade, however, ATMs have been installed as a result of many other influences, probably the most important of which have been a desire to contain or reduce costs and a response to competitive pressures.

In terms of cost containment ATMs have probably achieved at least a limited degree of success, as in the absence of ATMs there would almost certainly have been a need for additional buildings and staff. The substantial increase in overall banking activity over the past decade has, however, produced a situation in which there have been very few reductions in bank premises or staffing, although the banks are now handling much more business than was the case in the 1970s.

From the banks' viewpoint, ATMs and cash dispensers must obviously be regarded as investments. The cost of an installed machine can vary from £10,000 to £25,000, depending on where a machine is situated and whether it is restricted to cash dispensing or provides a wider range of services. Running costs, especially repairs and maintenance, may be substantial. A reasonable estimate of capital expenditure and running costs should be possible before machines are installed, although unexpected costs may arise, for example, planning application costs have been unexpectedly high in some external installations. The assessment of benefits will, however, be much more difficult, as is frequently the case with new electronic developments.

In any assessment of ATM benefits the probable number of transactions per machine must be carefully considered. Using the statistics in table 12.2, an average UK figure of over 4,100 transactions per machine per month emerges, which is significantly higher than the overall European figure of about 3,100 transactions per month.[1] In the USA, various

1 P. Hirsch and R. Ashworth, ATM Report – Surveying the Worldwide Scene, *Banking Technology*, November 1985, p. 31.

break-even figures have been suggested, based on comparisons between ATM and normal cashier costs; most of these estimates have been in the range of 3,000 to 5,000 transactions per month.[2] The average US figure is now well above these figures – about 5,500 transactions per month.

There are, however, strong differences of opinion regarding the way in which ATM and normal cashier costs should be calculated. In the USA a few calculations of this nature have been published. In 1983 Citibank estimated that its ATMs cost in the region of $40,000 per annum (including depreciation and overheads) for approximately 72,000 transactions. The average cost per ATM transaction was therefore less than 60 cents whereas the cost was over $1.20 (including overheads) for a transaction handled by a cashier who was able to deal with only about 36,000 transactions per annum.[3] A break-even point cannot be calculated from these figures, as there is no information regarding fixed and variable costs; it would seem probable, however, that the figure would be in the range of 3,000 to 4,000 transactions per month.

Table 12.2 also shows that the average value of a cash withdrawal is currently in the region of £30. This figure is smaller than the average cashed cheque, which is probably due to the fact that ATMs can be more conveniently used than bank premises. Many bankers regard the number and value figures for an ATM as important indicators of the success (or failure) of a particular installation, although charge income must obviously be taken into account. In most countries, however, private individuals pay very little in bank charge terms, and more attention is therefore devoted to cost-effectiveness.

Other costs and problems associated with ATM usage should ideally be considered before a purchase is embarked upon: the cost of security measures, probable levels of fraud, cash float implications, effects of machine breakdowns, employee and customer attitudes, etc. It will be extremely difficult to quantify some of these factors, although it would be dangerous to ignore such matters.

Bank marketing staff are likely to be more interested in the effect of ATM installations on market share and the reaction of customers to these installations. In the USA many banks installed ATMs in the hope that market share would be increased, but in the medium term ATM expenditure seems to have done little more than help a bank maintain its market share.[4] The UK banks have been reluctant to make any

2 A study of the way in which these calculations might be made is contained in A. H. Lipis, T. R. Marschall and J. H. Linker, *Electronic Banking* (Wiley, 1985), p. 25.
3 ATMs Are Bringing About a Revolution in US Banking, *Bankers' Magazine*, June 1983, p. 14.
4 See, for example, E. Williams, ATM Networks – Facing the Future Together, *Banking Technology*, July 1985, pp. 11–13.

pronouncement on this subject, although most commentators feel that ATM expenditure has had little effect on market share, probably due to the fact that all the major banks have invested very heavily in ATMs. Customer reactions to ATMs are also important and these will be considered in the next section of this chapter.

It is difficult, therefore, to assess the success of bank ATM operations. The major UK banks would appear to be reasonably satisfied with their ATM investments, although there are major problems involved in assessing costs and benefits. Transactions per machine, in number and value terms, have increased significantly over the last few years, and there is now some evidence, using US data, to suggest that most of the major UK banks have reached a break-even level looking at the overall number of transactions and installations. It would be helpful, however, if the UK banks published some data on this subject!

CUSTOMER VIEWPOINTS

About 40 per cent of UK bank customers use ATMs fairly regularly for cash withdrawal purposes,[5] although there still seems to be a fairly silent majority who do not use these facilities. An increasing number of customers do, however, appear to accept that the use of an ATM will be quicker and more convenient than dealing with a bank cashier, in addition to which some banks charge less for an ATM transaction than an over-the-counter withdrawal (in cases where the customer is subject to charges). It must also be remembered that the ATM is available at most, if not all, hours of the day and night for withdrawal purposes and the sharing of machines now means that in most towns and cities access to a machine should be relatively easy.

There are, however, a number of disadvantages and problems associated with ATM usage. In most cases (except at weekends) the customer's account will be debited on the day of the transaction, and there will be no clearing delay as in the case of a withdrawal at a bank other than the customer's own branch. This could cause problems for a customer who is temporarily short of funds. There may also be reliability problems, as machines inevitably break down or are out of action at some point. Most trade estimates suggest that breakdowns do not exceed 5 per cent of total operating time, although this type of problem can be extremely annoying. The loss or theft of the cash withdrawal card presents additional

5 See, for example, *Banking World*, August 1985, p. 22. This survey suggested that 44 per cent of bank customers preferred ATM cash withdrawals to over-the-counter services.

difficulties, and in some situations it will be difficult to get the card replaced at short notice, e.g. when a person is on an overseas trip or holiday.

A more recent problem, the subject of a special report by the UK National Consumer Council,[6] is the possibility of unauthorized withdrawals. This type of situation usually arises following the theft of a card, especially if the cardholder has written down the PIN on a stolen item, e.g. on a piece of paper in a wallet or handbag or even on the card. There have, however, been a small but increasing number of situations in the UK and several other countries where banks have claimed that cash withdrawals have taken place when the cardholder is convinced that the card has not left the wallet or other appropriate place. The attitude of the banks tends to vary in these circumstances, although most banks appear to be insisting that where the correct PIN has been used the owner of the card must be responsible (as is normally laid down in the conditions attached to usage of the ATM card). US banks have found this a major problem, as recent legislation appears to suggest that the onus of proof in disputed transactions will in the vast majority of cases lie in the hands of card-issuing organizations. As a result, small cameras are being installed in some ATM units, although the capital cost of these is currently in the region of $5,000.

On balance, most users of ATMs seem to be satisfied with the standard of service that they are receiving, despite occasional problems. ATM transactions are often quicker and in some cases cheaper than over-the-counter withdrawals which are, of course, restricted to traditional banking hours. Over the next decade more ATMs should become available through expansion and the sharing of networks, in addition to which there are hopes that in the not-too-distant future it will be possible to use UK cash cards in most parts of Europe (this is already happening in Spain with some UK cards). With this range of machines and services the number of UK bank customers using ATMs will probably increase very significantly.

FUTURE DEVELOPMENTS

It now seems probable that ATMs installed by major UK banks on a through-the-wall basis may be close to an optimum level, especially when recent network sharing arrangements are taken into account. Inside banks there may be room for more basic cash dispensers, especially if prices can be brought down to significantly less than £10,000. There is, however,

6 National Consumer Council, *Losing at Cards* (1985).

some staff and union resistance to these developments, since they could reduce the demand for cashiers and back-up staff. The banks may also install more ATMs in large shopping or transport centres, possibly in conjunction with major retailers.

There could also be significant growth in the number of ATMs installed in or outside the smaller banks, and by building societies and other similar financial institutions. Amongst the banks there is room for more installations at the Trustee Savings Banks, especially after the raising of funds from the general public, and also by the National Girobank, where ATM installations have only just begun. Building Society installations could also grow very rapidly from a few hundred in 1985 to several thousand by 1990.

There is currently considerable debate about the range of services that should be provided by ATMs. In the USA, transfers to the account of another customer are available on some ATMs, and about 4 per cent of ATM transactions are believed to be transfers of this nature.[7] This is a development that many UK cardholders would like to see, although it would bring with it more security and fraud problems for the banks and building societies. The Halifax Building Society has already made this facility available to customers – provided that account details have been lodged with the Society beforehand – but the UK banks appear to be rather reluctant to introduce this type of service (the Scottish Trustee Savings Bank bill paying service is one exception). These transfers are, however, not yet arranged on an electronic basis.

Most future ATM installations are expected to be on-line, although a fully operational 24-hour service does mean that back-up computer services will have to be constantly available. Security and control systems should be much better in an on-line, rather than an off-line, system, but the additional costs involved must be carefully considered. The reliability of on-line systems will always be extremely important, as was shown by the Lloyds Bank ATM breakdown in May 1985 when there was a five-hour gap in service.[8] This incident showed very clearly the importance of adequate back-up services when on-line systems are being used.

The battle against fraud will also continue with many of the measures that have already been described in respect of credit card services (chapter 5). The fraudulent users of plastic cards will almost inevitably become more sophisticated in the future, but there are signs that the level of fraud as related to turnover or withdrawals is being contained and in some cases reduced. Customer co-operation is essential in this sector, and it must be

7 J. Revell, *Banking and Electronic Fund Developments* (OECD, 1983), p. 44.
8 T. Huggins, ATMs – the Need for Systems Reliability, *Computing*, 23 May 1985, p. 16.

hoped that in the future there will be an increased appreciation of the risks involved in plastic card use.

The ATM business will therefore almost inevitably continue to grow in the late 1980s as more financial institutions install machines. In the 1990s we may reach saturation level in new installations in some countries; much will depend on the range of services that can be obtained from these machines. The relationship, if any, between ATMs and electronic point-of-sale systems (see chapter 13) will be very important, as both systems may eventually be capable of transferring funds between different accounts. We must all wait, however, to see how these matters are resolved in the late 1980s and early 1990s.

SUMMARY AND CONCLUSIONS

ATMs and cash dispensers have been a remarkable success story since the first very basic machines were introduced in the late 1960s. In the following decade the sophistication of ATMs gradually increased, and there are now over 160,000 ATMs installed throughout the world, many of which provide a wide range of banking services.

In the UK, ATM installations have gradually become a major source of cash withdrawals and in 1986 there are expected to be more than 500 million transactions most of which will be arranged by electronic transfer methods. Similar developments have taken place in most parts of Western Europe, although the speed of development has been nothing like that of the USA and Japan, which each now have well over a quarter of world installations.

Bank and customer attitudes towards ATMs are now mainly favourable, although the banks would ideally like to reduce the amount of cash circulating in banking systems, mainly because of the cost involved in control and security systems. This change will come about only if the debit card that is used for cash withdrawal purposes can also be used for retail and service point-of-sale transactions. This development is only just getting off the ground in Europe and North America. By the end of the 1990s, however, the popularity of the ATM may have waned as we move into an era in which consumers settle an increasing number of retail transactions by electronic transfer methods.

13 Point-of-Sale Transactions

For a large part of the present century, retailers have used mechanized point-of-sale systems, the most popular aid being the cash register. These machines have over the years been updated from simple electro-mechanical devices to the complex electronic units that are available today. Cash registers still fulfil an important role in most retail organizations, although by the end of the current century point-of-sale systems will probably be very different from what they are today.

Electronic point-of-sale (EPOS) services were defined in the early 1980s as systems 'which record sales data at the point of payment on to cassette tape or computer file'.[1] A distinction was therefore made between conventional cash register services, which had not traditionally had any direct connection with centralized computer services, and the new range of EPOS facilities; this distinction has become increasingly blurred in recent years. The range of EPOS services has also advanced, with the introduction of new techniques such as laser scanning,[2] which could over the next decade have a dramatic effect on point-of-sale efficiency and stock management.

At the beginning of 1986 about 50,000 EPOS terminals had been installed by UK retailers, although only about 5 per cent of these installations had laser scanning facilities. A rapid increase to 250,000 EPOS terminals is expected to take place by the beginning of the 1990s. In expenditure terms this is expected to involve over £800 million in 1990 as

1 Distributive Trades EDC, *Technology – the Issues for the Distributive Trades* (National Economic Development Office, April 1982), p. 46.
2 Laser scanning provides the ability to 'read' bar codes by passing suitably marked goods over a low-powered laser scanner installed below a 'window' at the point-of-sale. For information regarding current and possible future developments see, for example, D. Churchill, A Revolution at the Supermarket Checkout, *Financial Times*, 30 March 1983.

opposed to £100 million in 1985.[3] The most advanced of these units can now provide sales figures analysed into programmed categories, pricing data, automatic till roll printing, up-to-date stock levels, credit card authorization and numerous other facilities, although much will depend on the size of the store and the services required.

The range and availability of point-of-sale services is therefore changing rapidly, although the finance and expertise required may initially limit adoption of the full range of new facilities to the larger store. Advocates of electronic funds transfers at the point-of-sale (EFTPOS) must therefore appreciate that retailers will have many difficult decisions to make over the next few years as to the time at which existing services should be replaced and the range of services that should be installed. The development of EFTPOS is therefore likely to be heavily influenced by the whole range of changes that is taking place at the point-of-sale. In the long term there is little doubt that EFTPOS systems will be of interest to many retailers, provided that consumers are prepared to make extensive use of these services.

SCOPE AND OPERATION

There are believed to be over 300,000 retail stores in the UK, although many of these stores are extremely small. There are, however, in the region of 700,000 point-of-sale units – mainly cash registers – installed in these organizations; this provides some indication of the potential of the EFTPOS market. The new range of facilities may also be of interest to companies which provide services, although most installations will be in large and medium-sized retail stores.

No precise figures are available as to the way in which UK retail payments are split up. It has already been suggested (chapter 1) that there are in the region of 60 billion cash payments each year, of which the vast majority are for retail transactions. In addition, the retail sector receives over 1 billion cheques and initiates more than 0.4 billion credit card transactions. Some or all of these payments could eventually be replaced by EFTPOS debit card transactions, although the very limited amount of experience to date suggests that, at least initially, substitution will be mainly in respect of cheques. In the long term it is hoped that many cash deals – especially those for amounts over £10 – will be replaced by electronic transfers.

EFTPOS services may cover a wide range of transactions. At one time

3 International Computers Limited, *Retailing Tomorrow – the Impact of Technology in Retailing* (1985), pp. 4, 5.

these systems were thought of in terms of transfers between bank current accounts – from customer to retailer – at the time of sale, although it has now been accepted that the actual transfer can be made at the end of the day or even several days later if this is considered desirable. It has also become accepted that transfers need not be restricted to bank current accounts. Savings or deposit accounts could be used, although some of these accounts are based on set notice periods. Other financial institutions such as building societies could also be interested, provided that adequate funds are available to set up such a system. Similarly, customers might deposit funds in a special interest-bearing retail account, in which case there would be no reason why a transfer should not be arranged from that account to the retailer's main account.

It has also been suggested that EFTPOS systems could cover automated credit card transactions, as electronic transfers could easily be made to a credit card account. It is debatable, however, whether the term 'funds transfer' should cover credit transactions, although the mechanics of these transfers would be virtually the same as those for bank account transfers. For the purposes of this book a distinction between bank transfers and credit card transactions is considered to be desirable, and this chapter will therefore be primarily concerned with the transfer of cash resources, while credit card and other plastic card developments will be examined in more detail in chapter 14.

EFTPOS transactions will in the vast majority of cases be based on the use of a plastic card and personal identification number (PIN). In the case of non-credit transactions, the plastic card will be a debit card, which will probably be the same card that is used for cash withdrawals (ATM card). Alternatively, there could eventually be a multi-purpose card which might be used for cash, credit and cheque guarantee purposes as well as point-of-sale systems.

Funds transfer processes will commence towards the end of normal check-out procedures, after the total of goods purchased has been agreed. Where there is an integrated point-of-sale unit, it will probably not be necessary to enter the total amount on a separate terminal, although this type of installation may not be widely available until the early 1990s. The EFTPOS card is an essential part of the funds transfer process, and the cashier will pass this card through the authorization terminal. The customer will then enter the appropriate PIN on a special key pad, which should preferably be shielded from the view of other customers. Various electronic checks will then be carried out on card validity and available funds, and if all is well a transfer will be made from the customer's account to that of the retailer. Alternatively, this information might be stored until a transfer takes place at a later time or date.

Electronic processes at the point-of-sale may sound complex, but in most cases it is hoped that the whole EFTPOS process will be completed in under 30 seconds, provided that the cashier and customer are familiar with the system. Electronic security checks will vary according to whether the system is on-line or off-line. Under an on-line system, it should be possible with the aid of an appropriate telecommunications system to compare card details with centralized computer lists of stolen or missing cards, check on availability of funds and ultimately make the transfer. Under an off-line system, comparisons will be made with the data stored on the card to check the PIN, spending limits, etc., but the transaction data will probably not be transmitted or despatched until the end of the day or other appropriate time.

It is difficult, therefore, to generalize about the operation of an EFTPOS system. In the UK the national scheme that will probably be implemented in the late 1980s will almost certainly be an on-line magnetic stripe system, although this type of approach is inevitably more expensive than the off-line system being experimented with in several European countries. The on-line system should, however, provide a better security system in the case of stolen or missing cards. In the USA, most EFTPOS systems are on-line. Ideas may change if it eventually proves possible to use memory cards on an extensive national or international basis (see chapter 14).

RETAIL VIEWPOINTS

Retail attitudes towards EFTPOS systems are at this stage of development in a rather confused state, probably because of the lack of detailed practical experience regarding the operation of these services. A recent survey carried out by the UK computer company ICL suggested that a large majority (77 per cent) of retailers believed that the introduction of EFTPOS was inevitable, although there was considerable scepticism as to whether consumers really wanted such a system.[4]

Discussons with retailers would also suggest that there is a considerable amount of ill-feeling towards the banks, which are seen to be trying to introduce EFTPOS systems without proper consultative processes. The banks have, however, now accepted the need for discussions with retailers, and a joint liaison committee has been set up. Retailers will be represented by members of the Retail Consortium, although it is extremely difficult to represent the interests of all retailers.

One of the problems in any retail assessment of EFTPOS systems is the

4 *Ibid.*, p. 17.

lack of information about costs. Bankers hope that the vast majority of capital expenditure costs within individual stores will be borne by retailers; there is considerable opposition to this idea, especially amongst those retailers who consider that most of the major benefits will be obtained by the banks. Costs may be substantial initially, for terminals, computer hardware and software, telecommunications systems, possible store rewiring, etc. This could all add up to a total of between £1,500 and £3,000 per check-out point. Stores may also be concerned with other EPOS developments, e.g. laser scanning, which could have a considerable influence on the preparedness of management to invest further funds and change point-of-sale systems.

If a national scheme is to be implemented in the UK, there will probably have to be some guidelines on the way in which costs should be shared. Initially, there may have to be subsidies or incentives from banks or other promoters to get systems 'off the ground', with most of these schemes probably being based on leasing or rental agreements. Rental costs will presumably have an influence on bank transaction charges, which may be another source of controversy in talks between banks and retailers.

Benefits

The major potential benefits for retailers in an EFTPOS system will probably lie in the following areas:

1 *Increased speed through the check-out point.* Recent trials in the UK and overseas suggest that an EFTPOS transaction should take between 15 and 30 seconds (after adequate familiarization) as compared with about 30 seconds for cash, 75 seconds for a credit card and 90 seconds for a cheque.[5] There could therefore be some significant time savings at the point-of-sale. The extent of these savings will be influenced by the way in which the increased time availability is used – for additional sales, other check-out duties, reduction in number of cashiers or simply standing around doing nothing! A careful study of other check-out services, e.g. packing of goods, may also be desirable.

2 *Reduced bank charges.* EFTPOS transactions are expected to cost the banks significantly less than cash or paper-based transactions, and these benefits should at the very least be partly passed on to

5 For example, the Granada group has estimated that the average EFTPOS transaction takes about 22 seconds. See J. Cockroft, Electronic Games, *Banking World*, August 1985, p. 26.

. retailers in the form of reduced bank charges. There will obviously be protracted negotiations on this subject. In the USA, Mastercard and Visa have been attempting to charge the same percentage rate as for credit card transactions, although there is considerable opposition to this idea. In France, initial charges varied from 0.5 to 1.25 per cent of turnover, but recent protests from retailers seem to have produced a situation in which most banks are finding it difficult to charge more than 1 per cent. Set transaction charges that do not vary according to the value of the sale are favoured by some card issuers and retailers, and this approach is now gaining in popularity. When tariffs are eventually negotiated, most retailers hope that there will be significant savings in bank charges as compared with present systems. Much will depend on the type of transaction that is being displaced; BP, which is the major retailer in the Clydesdale Bank experiment in Scotland, has indicated that EFTPOS sales are costing about 6p per transaction in bank charges as compared with 15p to 18p for a cheque.[6]

3 *Earlier availability of funds.* If funds are transferred to the account of the retailer on the day of the transaction, there could be improved availability of funds, although much will depend on existing banking practices and systems. For example, with cash receipts, only a limited proportion of cash received during a day is likely to be banked on that day. With cheques, the savings should be greater, depending on the arrangements that have been made with the bank regarding assumed speed of clearance. Opposition from consumer groups could lead to a delay of one or two days in the speed of crediting of EFTPOS transactions to the retailer's account. This could remove most, if not all, of these benefits, although there should still be other types of savings.

4 *Reduction in paperwork and processing costs.* The volume of paperwork that has to be handled in connection with cash and paper-based payments may be substantial and EFTPOS systems could reduce processing costs very significantly. With cash transactions, there are many associated costs that could be eliminated, although it is unlikely that there will be a large reduction in cash receipts, especially in the early years of implementation. Cheque receipts are more likely to be replaced by EFTPOS transactions, in which case there should be worthwhile savings in clerical and administrative costs; it is unlikely, however, that the need for a daily visit to the bank (if banking is carried out this way) will be rendered

6 M. Cash, Cashless Society is on the Doorstep, *Account*, 18 July 1985, p. 19.

unnecessary. It should also be appreciated that there will probably be a need for some paperwork in EFTPOS systems, e.g. receipts for customers.

5 *Guaranteed payment*. Bad debts, fraud and theft may all have an influence on retail income. Under an EFTPOS system, payment will almost certainly be guaranteed, provided that all proper card checking processes have been carried out. Once again, the level of savings will be strongly influenced by existing systems. If receipts have traditionally been in the form of cash, immediate savings may be small, although notes and coins can be counterfeit. The risk of theft by staff, customers or other parties should, however, be significantly reduced. If cheques were previously used, savings could be quite large, but much will depend on the size of transactions, as sales under £50 will frequently be covered by a cheque guarantee card.

The benefits received by retailers through the adoption of EFTPOS systems could therefore be substantial, although it may take some time for these benefits to materialize as consumers become familiar with new payment methods. It is also possible that in the long term EFTPOS cardholders may spend more than people who use other methods of payment, but it will always be difficult to assess what would have been spent in the absence of EFTPOS cards.

Problem areas

If agreement can be reached with the banks on the sharing of costs, several important matters must be considered by retailers. First of all, there is the phasing in of new developments, which should be properly planned well in advance. Many major retailers will be introducing laser scanning systems in the late 1980s, and if it is not possible to install EFTPOS systems at the same time, there may be reluctance to arrange another point-of-sale reorganization for at least five years. There may also be a fear of 'cluttering up' the point-of-sale with too much equipment, and there could therefore be a tendency to wait for smaller integrated point-of-sale units, which might combine cash register, sales analysis, laser scanning, funds transfer and other appropriate check-out facilities.

Reliability and security will be additional areas of major concern. EFTPOS systems have many similar characteristics to ATM units, and in most ATM installations there has not been 100 per cent reliability. With EFTPOS systems, reliability will be extremely important, and retailers will obviously be reluctant to embark on projects where there are doubts concerning reliability. Security will also have to be carefully studied to try and ensure that all transfers to and from accounts are properly made. Bank consultation on this subject will be extremely important, and retailers will obviously try to ensure that customers are not upset by unnecessary delays or errors.

If these problems can be overcome, there should ultimately be worthwhile savings for the retailer who installs an EFTPOS system. For example, past surveys would suggest that under current conditions the average cost of an EFTPOS transaction – taking into account staff time, bank charges and other associated costs – will probably be about 10p as compared with at least 25p for cash and cheque transactions.[7] These figures will, of course, be strongly influenced by current and possible future levels of bank transaction charges, which may vary significantly from one organization to another. Retailers should, of course, make their own assessment of costs and benefits, but the figures already quoted ought at the very least to provide a rough indication of the size of savings that might be expected under an EFTPOS system.

CUSTOMER VIEWPOINTS

Very few attempts have been made by banks and other providers of EFTPOS services to ascertain consumer knowledge and opinions on this subject. A recent Gallup Survey for ICL did, however, suggest that 88 per cent of consumers had never heard of EFTPOS and most of the remaining 12 per cent were not very clear about the overall objective of the system.[8] An educational programme may therefore be necessary before a national system is launched.

The Consumers' Association has conducted two more detailed surveys in which those involved were provided with a detailed description of the EFTPOS system. They were then asked whether they would use this system. In 1982 only 16 per cent said that they would consider using this service. By 1985, however, this percentage had gone up to 23 per cent with an additional 17 per cent prepared to think about it if it speeded up

7 Several cost surveys have been carried out on EFTPOS systems but these have been hindered by lack of information on rental and transaction costs. See, for example, E. Foster, EFTS and the EPOS Market in Europe, *Retail and Distribution Management*, November/ December 1982, p. 48. Costs have, of course, increased significantly since this article was published, and the figures quoted in the text have been revised in line with 1986 cost standards.
8 *Retailing Tomorrow*, p. 7.

payment.[9] Reactions may therefore have changed with the increasing use of plastic cards for credit and cash withdrawal purposes.

Benefits

Very few real benefits become available for consumers as a result of the provision of EFTPOS services. The following benefits may, however be of importance to some consumers:

1 *Increased speed through the check-out point.* There is little doubt that major retailers will obtain real benefits through increased speed of service at the check-out point, but there are considerable doubts as to whether this will lead to reductions in staffing levels or improved service for customers. It is also debatable whether increased speed of service is an important matter for consumers. In the UK, Debenhams attempted to ascertain customer opinion on this subject, and came to the conclusion that 'the public does not seem to be generally very concerned about the time spent on completing a transaction at the point-of-sale'.[10] It is questionable, therefore, whether many consumers will change their shopping habits as a result of slightly improved speed at the check-out point, although the Consumers' Association survey, mentioned earlier in this section, seemed to indicate that this could be an important matter for some shoppers. Perhaps this conflict is due to the considerably varying efficiency of existing practices from one store to another.

2 *Ability to buy goods when cash is not available.* In the past some shoppers have experienced difficulties in purchasing goods or services because of problems in obtaining cash from the bank or other sources. With the advent of ATMs and cash dispensers, this has become less important, and in any case cheques and credit cards are now widely accepted. EFTPOS cards may help in acquiring goods or services in some circumstances, but this is probably a much less important consideration than it was a few years ago.

3 *Better protection against theft.* If comparisons are made with cash settlement, EFTPOS cards should provide improved security, although problems are also likely to arise if debit cards are stolen. This may therefore be a marginal advantage: much will depend on levels of security and the availability of other forms of payment.

9 Electronic Banking, *Which?* December 1985, p. 570.
10 P. Carr, The New Payment Systems Environment, *Retail Control*, November 1984, p. 20.

4 *Reduced bank charges.* In recent years, many banks have offered reduced bank charges for automated transactions, although most of these differentials were removed in the new charges structure for personal customers announced in December 1985. In the long term, it would seem to be inevitable that EFTPOS payments will be charged out at a cheaper rate than paper-based transactions for those consumers who are subject to bank charges. Under current conditions, therefore, this is not an important point, but it could be an important matter in the future.

5 *Possibility of discounts.* It has been suggested that some retailers will offer discounts on EFTPOS settlement to encourage use of this method of payment. This would seem to be a logical development, especially if there is a transfer of funds to the retailer's account on the day of sale; it is possible, however, that card issuers may try to discourage or prohibit discounts.

Most consumers are therefore unlikely to find this list of benefits very attractive, especially if the retailer already accepts credit cards. If the retailer does *not* accept credit cards – as with many food stores – there may be more attractions; much will depend on the availability of special discounts and the speed of bank transfer.

Problem areas

It is by no means certain under what conditions future EFTPOS cards will be issued. The following matters should, however, be carefully considered by card issuers and users:

1 *Legal aspects.* It is important that the regulations relating to loss, theft or unauthorized use of the EFTPOS card should be properly explained and understood. Government legislation may eventually be necessary to provide proper safeguards for consumers (see chapter 17).

2 *Funds availability.* Facilities should ideally be provided by retailers to enable customers to ascertain bank account statement data on entry to the store, so that rejection at the point-of-sale can be avoided. Much will depend, however, on the cost of this service to the retailer. Consumer organizations also hope that the banks will agree to provide short-term overdrafts up to, say, £50 for holders of EFTPOS cards. Funds transfers would therefore not be rejected if the overdraft as a result of the EFTPOS transaction was less than £50.

3 *Confidentiality.* Provision should ideally be made for the customer's insertion of the PIN to be made in some degree of secrecy, as it is not inconceivable that a criminal may take a note of the number before stealing the associated debit card.

4 *Authorization.* Cardholders may have difficulties in remembering their PIN. Many cardholders write down their number on the card or other nearby document. This can obviously be extremely dangerous if the card is stolen.

5 *Record of transactions.* It is unlikely that there will be any compulsion for card issuers to provide receipts, although it is obviously desirable from the consumer's viewpoint that proper receipts should be made available as evidence that payment has been made. Absence of adequate records could also produce account updating problems.

It is obvious, therefore, that there will be major difficulties in persuading consumers to use EFTPOS facilities. To some consumers the convenience of using plastic cards for all types of transactions will be paramount, especially if there is an appropriate bank account and regular weekly or monthly source of income. In many other cases consumers will prefer to use cash, cheques or credit cards for settlement purposes, although the provision of attractive incentives to users of EFTPOS cards could overcome the objections of some bank account-holders.

INTERNATIONAL DEVELOPMENTS

The USA has been the leader in many electronic banking developments, but it is doubtful whether it will ever be possible to introduce a national EFTPOS scheme, largely because of the fragmented nature of the banking system. Numerous experimental projects, usually based on magnetic stripe technology, have been launched since the early 1970s, but many of these have had to be abandoned because of inadequate support. In the last few years, however, conditions for introducing EFTPOS systems have improved, with the creation of a large number of shared ATM networks which may be able to provide the basis for point-of-sale systems.

Leaders in recent EFTPOS installations have been the oil companies and major retail groups. Most of the major oil companies, such as Amoco, Exxon, Gulf, Marathon, Mobil, Shell, Standard and Texaco, are providing debit and credit card facilities in co-operation with banks and other financial institutions, with discounts frequently being offered for payment by debit card.

In the retail sector, a small but growing number of supermarkets and grocery stores offer EFTPOS systems, with Publix Supermarkets of Florida being one of the best known. Departmental stores do not appear to be heavily involved in this type of activity, although credit card transaction telephones are extensively used.

Shared point-of-sale networks are also becoming more popular with a small number of groups having more than 4 million cardholders, e.g. the Interlink network organized by five major Californian banks. Bankers are therefore interested in EFT developments, although it seems probable that in both the USA and Canada the oil companies will, at least for the time being, be the main providers of EFTPOS services.

In Europe, France has been one of the major pioneers of EFTPOS systems with experimental schemes being set up from 1979 onwards. Most of the early schemes were set up by banks, with the Crédit Agricole installing numerous off-line terminals following its initial scheme in Limoges and Clermont Ferrand in 1980. The first on-line scheme was set up in St Etienne in 1983 by a group of 12 banks headed by the Société Générale. This has proved a successful venture with about 400 terminals installed in numerous shops, hotels and restaurants. Installations have also been arranged by card issuers, oil companies and large retailers, e.g. Carte Bleue, Total and Carréfour.

Strong support was provided by the French government for EFTPOS projects in the early 1980s, most of them based on magnetic stripe technology. In 1983, however, it was decided that extensive trials of memory cards should be arranged to assist in the decisions that had to be made as to which card should be used in the proposed national system. At the end of these trials, the government decided that a new card should be used in the national system, incorporating a magnetic stripe on the back of a memory card. The French have therefore decided to base their national system on the memory card, which is considered in more detail in chapter 14. It is hoped that the national scheme will be in full operation by the late 1980s or early 1990s.

In Belgium, electronic transfer systems based on magnetic stripe technology have been in operation since 1980. Most of the early installations were in petrol stations, where there are now over one thousand on-line terminals. These systems have in most cases been installed by major banks such as Bancontact and Mr Cash, although retailers have been extremely annoyed by the lack of an integrated system. As a result, the country's largest retailer, GB-INNO-BM(GIB), set up its own system in 1983, and this system now provides debit and credit card facilities for all holders of Maxi store cards and some bank cards. One of the most interesting aspects of this scheme is the integrated point-of-sale terminal which combines cash register, funds transfer and other relevant facilities. The banks are now moving towards a national system after many years of discussion, and this could mean that there will be a full EFTPOS service in operation by the late 1980s.

In Germany and the Netherlands, there have surprisingly been very few EFTPOS installations. A few local experiments are, however, taking place, e.g. in Munich and Eindhoven. There are hopes that it will be possible to set up a national system in Germany in a few years. In Austria the situation is very similar, although a small experiment in Salzburg involving the Sparkasse bank has attracted a lot of publicity. This installation, which was set up in 1980, is located in the Interspar supermarket where 4 of the 14 check-out points have on-line EFT terminals. The system is claimed to be successful, but there have not been any further installations in recent years.

In Scandinavia and surrounding countries there have been some interesting developments. In Norway there have been numerous small installations, the first of which was set up in 1981. Most of these installations have been in petrol stations – over 200 nationwide – although a few have been in supermarkets. Memory cards are being used in an experimental project in the Oslo area, but magnetic stripe systems are still the most popular form of installation. In Sweden and Finland the level of activity has been much lower, although point-of-sale systems have been used in petrol stations for several years. On the other hand, a national scheme is being planned in Denmark, with existing installations in Copenhagen and Jutland; this could well become the first or second fully comprehensive national scheme in Europe. While initial experiments took place at a much later date than was the case in Norway, there appears to be a great determination to set up a national system based on multi-purpose payment cards. There have unfortunately been some strong differences of opinion between promoters and retailers on charges and other related matters; there are signs, however, that these problems are gradually being overcome.

Elsewhere in Europe there have been some installations in Spain and Switzerland. In Spain, several hundred on-line terminals have been installed in Madrid and Pamplona, mainly through the initiative of the savings banks. Most of these installations have been in retailers, although the oil companies are now beginning to show interest. In Switzerland, there is an off-line system 'Tankomat' which is based on cards issued by petrol stations. A national system is being considered, and it is hoped that an experimental scheme will be launched in the next year or two.

In Asia, the first EFTPOS installations were expected to be in Japan, but government restrictions have slowed down developments, although a

few small experimental schemes have recently been set up. The first major
EFTPOS system in Asia was launched in Thailand in May 1985 by the
Bangkok and Siam Commercial Banks. These banks have installed over
100 terminals, mainly in leading retailers. Experimental projects were set
up in Hong Kong and Singapore in June and July 1985 and these have now
become fully operational. The Hong Kong scheme is probably the only
system to date which involves all the leading national banks – about 30 in
total. The Singapore scheme is organized by five leading banks, but the
number of terminals installed is still relatively small. Asia has therefore
made a promising start in the setting up of EFTPOS systems.

There have been important recent EFTPOS developments in both
Australia and New Zealand. In Australia it has proved difficult to reach
agreement on a national scheme, and individual banks have set up their
own systems. The leader in this respect has been the Westpac Banking
Corporation, which has installed about 2,000 terminals, mainly in leading
retailers and petrol stations. Westpac is now co-operating with the
Commonwealth Bank to set up shared networks, and eight other leading
banks have recently announced their intention to set up a joint nationwide
scheme. In New Zealand, experimental schemes have been in operation
since December 1984 arranged by both the trading and trustee savings
banks. Most of these schemes have involved groups of banks combining on
joint ventures. It is hoped that it will ultimately be possible to set up a
national scheme, provided that agreement can be reached between banks
and retailers and there is a good consumer response to the existing
experimental projects.

There is worldwide interest, therefore, in EFTPOS systems, although
most countries are still in a period of experimentation. Developments will
be influenced by many different factors – size and population of country,
nature of banking system, retailer attitudes, state of technology, existing
payment systems, etc. – but the most important factor may well be the
reaction of consumers, who have the power to make or break any proposed
system. No clear consensus is likely to emerge from consumers until the
1990s, by which time there will probably be a much wider range of
terminals and plastic cards.

UK INSTALLATIONS

Most of the early UK EFTPOS experiments were carried out by the
Barclays and Clydesdale Banks, and these organizations still have schemes
in operation. Other banks, e.g. Midland and National Westminster, are
now joining in as part of pilot projects launched in 1985/6. In the building

society sector, the Anglia Building Society has been the major pioneer with numerous other societies watching its activities with great interest. There is no evidence so far of retailers launching their own schemes, as in the USA and Belgium, although several of the major oil companies have co-operated with the banks in recent experimental schemes.

Barclays set up the first UK EFTPOS experiment in June 1980 in co-operation with four major oil companies. The terminals were sited at six petrol stations in and around Norwich. This was primarily an off-line system, although data could be transmitted to the appropriate head office computer at a specified time each working day (excluding Sunday). The average transaction took about 30 seconds, and was not debited to the customer's account until two working days after the day of sale. The experiment lasted just over a year and appeared to receive a good response from the oil companies and customers. Barclays has set up further experiments in recent years and is currently involved in extensive trials in the south of England, but there is a heavy concentration on credit card transactions.

The first on-line EFTPOS system in the UK was set up by the Clydesdale Bank (a subsidiary of the Midland Bank) and British Petroleum in February 1982, under the name 'Counterplus', at two petrol stations in the Aberdeen area. In February 1983 the scheme was extended to a total of 26 petrol stations in North and West Scotland, and in May 1984 terminals were installed in a large Northern Co-operative Society (NORCO) superstore in Aberdeen. Customers can use debit or credit cards for petrol and associated items, although credit cards are not accepted for food purchases. Bank accounts are debited three working days after the transaction. In all other ways the Clydesdale system follows normal on-line principles with PINs being used for authorization purposes.

Retailers appear to be pleased with the Clydesdale system, and there has been a good customer response. In the NORCO store, the EFTPOS system is available at 3 of the 22 check-out points, and about 5 per cent of customers appear to be using this method of payment. NORCO has estimated that an EFTPOS transaction costs in the region of 6p for bank charges as opposed to 15p under the cheque system.[11] Similar results have been reported by BP in respect of its petrol stations, although in this case over 10 per cent of customers are using the system. Rather surprisingly, debit cards have proved to be more popular than credit cards, possibly due to the low level of credit card use in this part of Scotland. A typical check-out point equipped with a Clydesdale terminal is depicted in figure 13.1.

11 Coop installs UK's first EFTPOS system, *Retail and Distribution Management*, July/August 1984, p. 61.

Figure 13.1   Clydesdale Bank EFTPOS equipment installed at a Scottish retail store

The Anglia Building Society EFTPOS scheme, 'Paypoint', was launched in the Northampton area in October 1985. The Anglia is the UK's seventh largest building society with assets in excess of £4 billion. £1 million has been spent on the scheme by the Anglia and the computer company ICL. About 40,000 cards have been issued, and these can be used at more than 120 stores operating well over 200 terminals. Both national and local retailers are involved in the scheme; national retailers include British Home Stores, C & A, Thomas Cook and Laskys. The installation is based on an on-line system with the account-holder's account being debited at the time of sale. The retailer's account will be credited, however, only if the organization has an Anglia account. In other circumstances, companies are paid by cheque, usually within four days, although it is hoped that it will eventually be possible to use the automated clearing house system for this purpose.

One of the controversial aspects of most EFTPOS schemes will be the retail charging structure. Under the Anglia scheme, terminals are usually acquired on rental. Initial contracts are for one year, of which the first six months are rent-free. After this introductory period, rentals are £30 per terminal per quarter. Transaction charges vary between 0.5 and 1.5 per cent of turnover, depending on volume and value of trading activity. It will be very interesting to see the response of retailers to this scheme after the first year of trading activity, as agreements can be terminated at three months' notice.

The Midland Bank EFTPOS experiment, 'Speedline', was launched in the Milton Keynes area in February 1986, with about 30 on-line terminals being installed in both retail stores and petrol stations. The scheme will be operated in a similar way to that of the Clydesdale Bank, with several different debit and credit cards being accepted. PINs will be used for debit card payments, although customer signatures will also be accepted in the case of credit card transactions. Terminal costs have fallen significantly in the last two or three years, and the Midland is believed to be providing machines at about £1,000 each, with rental charges in the region of £350 per annum. Transaction costs are subject to negotiation, with initial charges being set at about 6p per transfer.

The National Westminster Bank EFTPOS experiment, 'Streamline', also launched in the early part of 1986, has involved the installation of 24 terminals at retail stores and petrol stations in several different parts of the country. This scheme is based on the PISCES (Petrol Industry Services for the Clearance Electronically of Sales) system, which had previously been extensively used by the National Westminster group for credit card purposes. On this occasion it will also accept debit cards and the use of PINs, although there will probably be more emphasis on credit card transactions, especially at petrol stations. No details of charges have been announced.

There should, therefore, be some valuable evidence available regarding the operation of EFTPOS schemes if a national scheme is to be launched in 1988. This date could, of course, be delayed, but there does now appear to be a definite commitment to launch a national scheme in that year. There will, however, be many negotiations and decisions to make before that date, especially in respect of the equipment that will be used and the charges that will be levied on retailers.

FUTURE DEVELOPMENTS

There is little doubt that the technology is now available to set up EFTPOS systems, although there are still many issues to settle before national or regional services can be introduced. In some small countries, e.g. Hong Kong, most of these issues have now been settled, although there is still considerable uncertainty as to how consumers will react to these new methods of payment.

Government interest or involvement in EFTPOS systems has in some countries, e.g. France, been a key factor. Grants, subsidies and loans from government sources can obviously be of considerable assistance, although some bankers have a great aversion to any form of government assistance or interference. In the long term, some element of government involvement may be essential in order to provide a proper legal framework, but there are strong differences of opinion regarding more active participation.

Existing payment systems and charges may also be an important factor in any process of change. For example, in those countries where credit card use is very popular, e.g. the USA, transaction telephone systems may be extended to provide electronic data capture and communication services. On the other hand, some countries, e.g. Belgium, have adapted ATM networks to provide EFTPOS services which are very similar to those used in the more advanced ATM systems. Charges may also be an influential factor, as some countries have found when they have attempted to replace a charge-free cheque system.

The state of technology must also be carefully considered. For most of the 1970s and early 1980s it was assumed that magnetic stripe technology would be used for the vast majority of EFTPOS systems. This meant that expensive on-line communication systems had to be installed if high levels of security were required. Alternative card technologies are, however, now emerging, which could lead to a situation in which memory card systems will be extensively used in the 1990s.

It seems extremely likely, therefore, that the EFTPOS systems of the late 1980s and 1990s will vary considerably from one country or continent to another. In the USA the fragmented nature of the banking system and the large area that has to be covered will probably mean that systems will develop on a local or industry basis rather than in the form of a national system. In Europe, Asia and Australasia, major attempts will probably be made to develop nationwide systems which could develop into schemes covering several countries as networks become more sophisticated.

In the UK there are still doubts as to whether the proposed national system will get off the ground in 1988 and, if so, whether it will be supported by retailers and consumers. The banks are, however, proceeding with plans for such a system, and British Telecom and IBM have agreed to supply the initial network and software requirements. Initial developments are expected to cost £20 million, although the total bill in respect of capital expenditure for banks and retail stores could rise to over £200 million if the 250,000 terminals forecast by the banks are eventually installed.

The future of the EFTPOS service is therefore surrounded with uncertainty in the UK and many other parts of the world. We may have to wait until the early 1990s to assess whether these services have been successful, as by then several national systems will have been introduced. Reactions will not be the same in all countries, but at the very least there should be a reasonable idea of the factors which have contributed towards success or failure. The 1990s should therefore be an exciting decade for the advocates of EFTPOS systems.

SUMMARY AND CONCLUSIONS

Retail transactions have traditionally been settled by cash or cheque, with the credit card facility added for most non-food stores in recent years. These methods of settlement can be time-consuming and expensive, and it is not surprising that bankers and retailers are interested in the introduction of EFTPOS services which will allow accounts to be settled by means of a bank or other electronic transfer arranged at the time of sale.

The overall costs attached to the introduction of a national EFTPOS are, however, enormous, bearing in mind the terminals and associated equipment, services and expertise that will be required. Banks and other promoters are unlikely to be willing to bear all these costs, and there will inevitably be long negotiations with retailers and other interested parties before agreements are reached on the sharing of costs.

If these capital costs are to be justified, substantial benefits must be available in terms of cost savings, time and paperwork. These benefits will materialize, however, only if consumers find this an attractive method of payment. It is by no means certain that EFTPOS will be extensively used, and it may be necessary to share out some of the savings in discounts or other inducements to persuade consumers to adopt this 'new' method of settlement.

The EFTPOS system is therefore unlikely to provide an easy route to success for the progressive bank, building society or retail organization. Optimists hope that the long-term result of the introduction of these services will be a decrease in the number of cheques and cash receipts, and a reduction in paperwork, fraud and costs. Pessimists fear that the substantial costs involved will never produce a satisfactory return because of consumer preferences for long-established methods of payment. Any assessment as to which viewpoint is correct will probably have to wait until the mid-1990s, by which time there will have been extensive experimentation with many different types of EFTPOS systems in the UK and most other developed countries.

14 Plastic Card Developments

Users of plastic cards for cash, credit or funds transfer purposes often imagine that all cards of this nature are based on similar principles. Over the last twenty years, however, the plastic card has changed considerably from being a simple means of identification for making a paper-based transaction to a very different current situation under which personal details, usually held on a small magnetic stripe on the back of the card, have been made 'machine-readable' for identification and transmission purposes. The updated card will undoubtedly become more useful in the future, especially if debit and credit cards are extensively used for electronic point-of-sale transactions.

Credit card business, already considered in chapter 5, has grown very rapidly in recent years, but it has brought with it a considerable amount of paperwork, which has proved extremely expensive to process and store, and numerous fraud problems. In the late 1980s, therefore, much time and expertise is likely to be devoted to computer and telecommunications links under which it should be possible for sales data to be transmitted to the processing centre of the card company at the moment of sale or other appropriate time. Special electronic communication systems are already being installed in many large and medium-sized retailers to check the validity and limits of credit card transactions, and these could eventually be extended (or even replaced) to incorporate the capture and transmission of credit data. Introduction of such facilities should reduce staff involvement, paperwork, errors and fraud, although the cost of acquiring and servicing the new equipment will obviously have to be carefully considered.

It is by no means certain, however, that plastic card issuers of the future will concentrate on magnetic stripe technology. Memory cards with an inbuilt microprocessor are being used in France and experimented with in several other countries, and it is already being claimed that these cards have important advantages over those which are based on magnetic stripe systems. In this chapter, therefore, memory cards and other possible future developments will be considered in some detail, although most of the major card issuers still appear to be determined to retain the magnetic stripe card.

MAGNETIC STRIPE CARD SYSTEMS

In the vast majority of cases credit card transactions in the UK and other parts of Europe still involve the completion of a paper voucher by retailer and customer, with copies being obtained by carbon paper processes. Copies are retained by the retailer and the customer, and one copy is paid in or despatched to the payee's bank, which sends relevant information on to the processing centre of the credit card company. The transaction documents are then sorted and processed by card company employees, who eventually prepare material for posting by computer processes on customer statements. This type of operation is expensive and time-consuming, especially from the credit card company's viewpoint, and there is little doubt that over the next few years all the major credit card companies will attempt to introduce electronic data capture and transmission processes, probably with the aid of magnetic stripe technology. The personal information encoded on the magnetic stripe section of the card will therefore become a key element in the authorization and transmission processes.

Operating processes

Electronic communication systems based on magnetic stripe technology are already being used in credit card installations, mainly by large retailers. The vast majority of these applications are primarily or completely concerned with the authorization of card transactions. These systems, which normally involve the use of special transaction telephones, should ensure that the card has not been reported as lost or stolen, and the credit limit has not been exceeded (see chapter 5 for more information on this subject). If electronic data capture and transmission facilities can be added to these processes, information regarding the amount involved and other essential details could be entered on a terminal and this, together with the personal data obtained by inserting the magnetic stripe card in the terminal, could be transmitted instantaneously or at another appropriate time to the processing centre of the credit card company.

Credit card systems of the late 1980s, especially those in large stores and garages, could be heavily reliant on transaction telephones, some of which may be capable of transmitting data as well as checking the validity of cards. In many of the latter systems, personal identification numbers (PINs) will be used in place of card signature. This will allow a comparison to be made between the number held on the magnetic stripe and the PIN entered on the terminal by the cardholder. Credit card transactions could therefore become part of an EFTPOS system, possibly under another name. Much will depend, however, on the preparedness of interested parties to meet the costs of upgraded equipment and services.

The systems and technology for electronic credit authorization and data transmission are now available, but there have been a number of implementation problems. From the credit card company's viewpoint, there should be significant reductions in processing costs and fraudulent activity as compared with present systems, but there is a strong feeling that retailers must make a contribution towards the cost of terminals and other associated services. Amongst retailers there is considerable resistance towards the sharing of costs, especially if a capital contribution is required. The compromise solution will probably be a leasing or rental charge, in addition to which a reduced transaction charge may be negotiated. Retailers will have to assess whether reduced check-out time and operating costs together with less fraudulent activity justify the additional expenditure involved.

Most customers are already familiar with credit card transactions, and there should be little apparent change from the present situation, apart from the possible use of PINs in place of signatures and a different form of receipt. Speed through the check-out point, especially for large transactions, could also be quicker. There does not seem to be any reason, therefore, why the honest customer should resist the automation of credit card transactions, although it is possible that the changed transmission process could speed up the billing of some items towards the end of the invoice period. The dishonest customer will not, however, welcome these developments, as there is likely to be a much speedier detection of fraudulent transactions.

International developments

In Western Europe and North America large numbers of magnetic stripe cards have been issued in recent years. In the credit card sector, the magnetic stripe that is now on the vast majority of cards has not yet been used very extensively, although systems are gradually changing. Most new developments have been based on transaction telephones, especially in the USA, where there are large numbers of these terminals. It is by no means clear, however, whether these installations will eventually be converted into full-scale point-of-sale systems, as many retailers appear to be satisfied with the cheaper authorization process. In Europe, transaction telephones are not as heavily used as in the USA, although several countries, e.g. Belgium and the Scandinavian countries, have made considerable progress in automating credit card sales at petrol stations. There has been little progress, however, in setting up data transmission systems in retail stores, although this situation is expected to change rapidly in the late 1980s and early 1990s.

In the UK, electronic communication systems for checking card ownership and credit limits have been in use since the early 1980s, but growth has been relatively slow, largely because of retailer resistance towards the costs involved – currently from £300 upwards, with rental agreements available at about £10 per month. These systems are, however, being heavily promoted by the major credit card companies, through their Cardlink scheme, and a small number of other organizations, and it is hoped that installations will grow to more than 10,000 by the end of 1987. The range and price of these systems is changing rapidly, and several companies are now marketing terminals which will process transactions as well as checking ownership and credit limits. For example, in September 1985, British Telecom and Cresta Communications announced the introduction of a new electronic terminal system, Teletran, to provide credit authorization and data transmission facilities. Under such systems, transaction data are entered into the terminal after insertion of the magnetic stripe card, and details are then transmitted to the relevant credit card company via the British Telecom computer. A receipt is issued if required, and the customer is billed in the normal way. These systems can therefore provide a limited electronic point-of-sale service, although initial installations have been restricted to credit card acceptance.

The major UK banks and credit card companies have been involved in electronic point-of-sale experiments going back to 1980 when Barclays set up an initial experiment in Norwich. Since then, Barclaycard has set up several schemes under the title 'Pinpoint' and most of the other major credit card companies have conducted similar trials. Access and Barclaycard are taking a major part in the UK EFT experimental scheme launched in 1985/6, Barclaycard being involved in the installation of over 1,000 electronic terminals at high-activity locations in London and the south-east of England. This scheme, which is being described as DARTS (Data Capture and Authorisation Retail Transaction Service), is based on terminals which cost about £1,000, although rental agreements can be arranged from £30 per month upwards. The Midland and National Westminster Banks are involved in similar experiments; in both of these schemes debit cards are accepted as well as credit cards (see chapter 13).

There seems little doubt, therefore, that major electronic developments will take place in the international plastic card business over the next few years. The speed of change will, however, be strongly influenced by the preparedness of retailers to share in installation costs in return for a potential reduction in processing costs and credit card company charges together with a slightly increased speed through the check-out point. Bargaining processes regarding the sharing of costs could be a time-consuming process, but if agreement can be reached there should be much improved transmission and processing systems.

MEMORY CARDS

The idea of a plastic card with one or more microprocessors incorporated into it for memory and processing purposes was put forward by a Frenchman, Roland Moreno, in the mid-1970s. Initially there was little enthusiasm for this card, although there has been increasing interest over the last five years. Most writers on the subject describe this card as a memory or chip card, although it is also referred to as a microcircuit or smart card.

The memory card is likely to be about the same size as any other plastic card for credit or payment purposes. This card will, however, have surface contacts which will enable readers attached to electronic equipment, e.g. cash registers, authorization terminals and automated teller machines, to access the microprocessor system contained in the card. The unusual feature of this card is its ability to store and process large amounts of data in secure conditions: most cards will have two or three 'zones', one of which will be classified as highly confidential or secret. A magnetic stripe can be provided on the back of the memory card if it is considered that a card accepting both types of systems is desirable.

Operating processes

The user of a memory card will be provided with a PIN in a similar way to the number provided for cash card transactions. When the total amount payable for a sale is agreed, the memory card will be passed through a slot on the side of the authorization terminal, after which the cardholder enters the appropriate PIN on a key pad, preferably shielded from the view of other people. If the PIN agrees with the number stored in the card, the transaction will be allowed to proceed. The amount and brief details of the transaction are then entered on the terminal and into the card memory, after which balances and other relevant information are updated.

The memory card may be used rather like an electronic bank account; in this case the card would probably be issued by a bank with an agreed amount stored in the card memory. Funds for this purpose could be provided by a lodgement of cash, a withdrawal from an existing account, or a loan or overdraft. Alternatively, the spending limit might represent a prepaid amount in respect of gas, electricity or telephone usage. Expenditure arranged with the memory card would be set against the balance stored in the card. When the balance stored in the card was exhausted – this would probably be shown on a liquid crystal display – the cardholder would visit the bank for the card to be updated or a new card issued. On-line access to central computer facilities could provide increased security, although cost considerations might rule this out in the case of small transactions.

The memory card could also be used as a credit card, with the amount stored in the card representing the cardholder's credit limit. Deductions would then be made from the credit limit as transactions took place. This type of card could be issued by bank, credit card company, finance company, retailer or other similar organization. Arrangements could be made for the credit limit to be restored at the beginning of each month.

The card issuer would probably be provided with information regarding transactions at the end of each working day; more frequent updating could be arranged if this was desirable. The amount and details of each transaction would be calculated at the authorization terminal, and these would be held until required by the card issuer. Data could then be delivered to the card issuer on a storage cassette or transmitted electronically over telephone lines.

Costs and benefits

The production cost of a memory card will be considerably above the cost of a magnetic stripe card. UK estimates suggest that the purchase price of a memory card could initially be well over £3, as compared with about 25p for a modern magnetic stripe card, assuming in both cases that acceptable quantities are ordered. Much will depend, however, on the total size of the order. If the number of cards ordered were over a million, as has recently been the case in France, costs might fall to £2 per card or less, with a good prospect of price decreases in later years. Distribution costs could be in the region of £1 per card, in addition to which memory cards might have to be issued more frequently than has been the case with magnetic stripe cards, largely because of a limit to the number of times that these cards can be used – probably in the region of 100 transactions in the case of currently available cards. These problems may well be alleviated by the provision of increased memory capacity and the production of reusable cards.

The major benefit of the memory card as compared with the magnetic stripe card will probably be centred on increased security. Anyone stealing a memory card will find it extremely difficult to discover the PIN by trial and error, especially if several unsuccessful efforts trigger a device which automatically stops effective card operation. The memory card should therefore provide a high degree of security as long as the cardholder's identification number remains secret.

It is also believed that it will be extremely difficult to reproduce or manipulate a memory card. Any person attempting such an operation will probably require detailed information regarding the structure of the card and the microprocessor, and the amount of time and skill required would make this extremely unlikely. On the other hand, magnetic stripe data can be read or changed using relatively inexpensive reading devices; this type of activity is now taking place on an increased scale, especially in the USA. Prevention measures have, however, become much more sophisticated in recent years, although there has inevitably been a heavy cost attached to these processes.

There should also be considerable operating cost advantages attached to the memory card, as this type of card will normally operate perfectly satisfactorily on an off-line basis as long as all the required data are stored on the memory card. On the other hand, magnetic stripe systems will generally require on-line telecommunications links because of the importance of establishing account balances and other relevant information. The memory card need not be heavily dependent on telecommunications services with their heavy attached costs, although there will obviously be dangers in any off-line system when cards are lost or stolen together with information about the cardholder's identification number.

Benefits could therefore be very significant in a memory card system, although there are several problems with this type of card that still have to be resolved. Card issuers have already spent large sums of money on magnetic stripe terminals, cards and research, and there is likely to be considerable resistance to the idea that magnetic stripe terminals should be partly or wholly replaced by new terminals and associated equipment. This problem might be at least partly overcome by producing cards which could be used on both systems, as in France. There are, however, substantial cost and design problems attached to this dual approach; there are also doubts about the durability of memory cards, which could be damaged by rough use, bending or dirt. It is hoped that trials over the next two or three years will establish whether these are likely to be major problems.

At this stage of development, therefore, it is extremely difficult to assess the costs and benefits attached to memory cards. The number of trials and experiments is, however, beginning to increase, and by the end of the 1980s there should be much more evidence available regarding actual memory card use. This should help prospective purchasers decide whether the additional benefits obtained from this type of installation justify the expenditure involved.

International developments

France has so far led the way in memory card experiments and card issue, with the French government, through various ministries and state-owned organizations, providing considerable financial support, mainly in the form of grants and low-interest loans. EFTPOS trials involving the use of memory cards were held in Blois, Caen and Lyon in the early 1980s involving the issue of 100,000 cards, the installation of 600 terminals, and the co-operation of about 50 banks. At the same time, similar trials with magnetic stripe cards were taking place in Aix-en-Provence and St Etienne. As a result of these experiments, it was decided that the memory card was the preferred type of card, largely because of the high degree of security that is provided and the many potential applications.[1] It was recommended, however, that a *carte mixte* should be issued, at least initially, incorporating a magnetic stripe on the back of a memory card. The magnetic stripe will be retained for use in connection with existing ATM installations, whilst memory card techniques will be used for new point-of-sale systems, home banking installations and telephone booths.

The French banks are now heavily involved in the setting up of the memory card system, and orders have already been placed for over 16 million cards, most of which will be supplied by the state-owned Bull computer group. Current plans suggest that 3 million cards could be in use by 1987, with most of the remainder being in circulation by the end of the 1980s. Terminals and associated equipment will also have to be acquired. It is expected that memory card terminals will cost significantly less than those for magnetic stripe cards; total capital expenditure is, however, expected to be over one billion francs.

The success of the French memory card initiative will depend very heavily on the reaction of retailers and consumers. Major retailers seem to be prepared to pay installation or hiring costs, but there has been considerable dissatisfaction with the level of transaction charges. Recent negotiations have, however, produced a situation in which banks seem to be prepared to negotiate charges at about 1 per cent of selling price.

1 D. Jones, Smart Card – Smart Banking, *Banking World*, April 1984, pp. 13–16.

Consumers have had less complaints, and have in most cases responded enthusiastically to these new methods of settlement, perhaps in part because at this stage debits are not being made to the customer's account until the month following the transaction. It remains to be seen whether the delayed debit concept is maintained after the experimental period.

Memory card experiments have not been restricted to France, although it is from that country that most support has come for this type of card. In Europe, trials are taking place in West Germany, Italy and Norway, and there is particular interest in the use of the memory card for coinless telephone booths. In the UK no official trials have been carried out, but the chief executive of the EFTPOS implementation scheme has recently accepted that memory cards could eventually have a part to play in the UK system, although the initial system will be based on magnetic stripe technology.[2]

In North America, there was little interest in memory cards until the mid-1980s when several large organizations announced trials and studies of these cards. One of the most interesting of these schemes is the one arranged by Mastercard, the international credit card group, which in early 1985 announced that it would be purchasing 100,000 memory cards for issue in selected parts of the USA; 50,000 of these cards were obtained from French sources (the US subsidiary of the Bull group) for issue in Maryland, and 50,000 from Japan (the Casio group) for issue in Florida. Tests are also being carried out by Visa International, the Bank of America and Carte Bleue in a co-operative research venture. Canadian banks too are showing interest in this type of card, and the Royal Bank of Canada has recently announced a small experimental project.

Outside Western Europe and North America the major interest in memory cards has been in Japan, where the Casio company has developed a card which has some important variations from the French card, such as differences in the number and positioning of contact points and the processing and memory facilities. The first retail test of the Japanese card began in 1984, when the electronics company Toshiba and the Mitsui Bank set up a small point-of-sale experiment in Tokyo. The scale of the experiment will be extended if the trials prove successful. The differences between the French and Japanese cards have produced considerable confusion, as a result of which an industry standards group has been set up by the International Association for Microcircuit Cards. It is hoped that this will assist the International Standards Organization in publishing one or more international standards on some of the more controversial aspects of memory card design and technology.

2 UK Could Get Smart Card for EFTPOS, *Banking Technology*, January 1986, p. 10.

It is, therefore, much too early to assess the likelihood of the memory card becoming an important part of the plastic card business. There is little doubt that if the memory card had been developed at the same time as the magnetic stripe card it would have stood a high chance of success as the most popular type of card for credit and payment purposes. Unfortunately for memory card manufacturers and equipment specialists, there have been many millions of pounds invested throughout the world in magnetic stripe terminals and cards, and it is highly unlikely that there will be a rapid changeover to memory card systems. It should not be forgotten, however, that the memory card has many possible uses outside the payments sector, for example, as a security card and medical record, and if these other applications are developed there seems little doubt that the memory card will be increasingly used over the next decade, with the possibility of greatly increased use for credit and payment purposes in the 1990s.

FUTURE DEVELOPMENTS

The plastic card industry is changing rapidly and it is extremely difficult to predict developments in the late 1980s and 1990s. Growth will almost certainly take place in the number of card issuers and holders, although the total number of cards in circulation could be reduced if it eventually proves possible to issue multi-purpose cards. This idea may, however, be restricted to a small number of well known card issuers, especially if the card business becomes highly diversified through the entry of large numbers of non-banking financial institutions and retailers.

Technology will have a great influence on future plastic card developments. Electronic communication systems have changed very significantly in recent years, and it now seems probable that over the next five years most large retailers and providers of services will purchase or lease electronic data capture and communication systems that will provide credit authorization and transmission facilities. Acquisition costs will have to be set at a low enough level to persuade retailers to use this service, in addition to which other incentives may have to be provided, e.g. transaction charges could be reduced for all retailers who use electronic transmission facilities.

It is by no means certain, however, that magnetic stripe cards will retain their present tight grip on the international plastic card market. Memory cards will present a major challenge and other cards will probably be developed which will have to be seriously considered. In the last five years several 'new' cards have been developed. For example, the Visa group has pioneered two cards, the 'Electron' card which provides optical character and bar code reading facilities as well as a magnetic stripe, and a more recently announced 'Super Smart' memory card which will incorporate magnetic stripe facilities, a calculator-type keyboard and a small horizontal display screen. The Electron card has not been very successful, but there are great hopes for the Super Smart card, which will be extensively tested in 1987.

A small but increasing range of cheap 'stored value' cards is also being developed, based on several different technological systems. For example, in the UK a card is being marketed by British Telecom for use in telephone booths. These cards, which are based on holographic technology, can be purchased in several different denominations, and after each conversation value units are destroyed as a result of metering techniques. The cards are relatively cheap to produce and are intended to be thrown away when the amount stored on the card is reduced to zero.

Laser cards are also beginning to be used, mainly in the USA, with the Drexler Technology Corporation probably being the current leader in this field. These cards, which have very large storage capacity, have many potential applications including payment processes, although they are more likely to be used for medical records and other large storage applications.

In the 1990s we may therefore have a large number of multi-purpose plastic cards in circulation fulfilling the role of both debit and credit card, some of them combining the benefits of magnetic stripe and memory card technologies. These cards will not just be used for credit or funds transfer purposes, although the settlement of retail and service transactions will probably be their major use. Consumers may have to pay more for card services than they do at the present time, but the overall service should be more convenient and secure, and will probably be widely used for payments (or prepayments) in respect of certain essential or highly desirable services, such as, electricity, gas and telephone supplies. Payment systems of the 1990s are therefore likely to be heavily reliant on plastic cards backed up by increasingly sophisticated methods of technology.

SUMMARY AND CONCLUSIONS

The plastic card industry is a relatively youthful part of the payments business and over the past twenty years it has generated far more business than anyone imagined in the early 1970s. This great success has brought with it numerous problems, the most important of which have been the vast amount of paperwork generated for processing purposes and the high level of fraud.

The development of electronic communication systems with instantaneous or end-of-day account transmission facilities could help to make significant inroads into the paper mountain, although customers are still likely to require evidence of transactions. There may also be a substantial increase in the overall number of plastic card transactions, with two or three times the number of today's transactions probably being handled by the end of the century. This could mean that even if electronic transmission is extensively used the total amount of paperwork could remain at a similar level for several years.

The most suitable type of card for use in electronic transmission systems is currently the magnetic stripe card, although this card, as at present developed, is not completely satisfactory from the fraud prevention viewpoint. The memory card with its in-built microprocessor and memory facilities could provide issuers and users with better protection against fraud with less reliance on telecommunications systems. These cards are, however, at an experimental stage, and they will certainly cost more to produce than magnetic stripe cards, although there are rumours that the Japanese intend to produce memory cards in very large numbers. Costs and benefits will, therefore, have to be carefully weighed, bearing in mind that the memory card has several potential applications outside the payments sector.

In this process of change, all plastic card issuers will have to consider the viewpoints of retailers and consumers. Retailers are naturally unwilling to make any sizeable contribution towards the installation costs of new terminals and associated equipment, as most of the benefits are likely to go to the card issuers. Consumers already pay for their cards in many parts of the world, but in the UK there has been a reluctance by the major issuers to make a charge on issue or renewal of cards. As a result, UK card issuers are likely to face considerable problems in obtaining major contributions towards new technology from both retailers and consumers.

The future for the plastic card business is therefore rather uncertain. The memory card may eventually prove to have some important advantages over the magnetic stripe system, but where there is change from existing systems, cards could be issued combining the major memory card features with the provision of a magnetic stripe. This will be more expensive for the issuer, although there should be long-term fraud prevention and telecommunications savings. The prime condition for extensive movement in this direction is likely to be development of technology to bridge the gulf between memory cards and magnetic stripe systems, e.g. a dual-system card reader. This is still the subject of research and development, although there are many hopes amongst memory card advocates that this technology will become available in the late 1980s. Whether these hopes are just pipe-dreams we shall have to wait and see.

15 Home and Office Banking

Banking from the home or office has been available for bank account-holders for many years: private individuals and businesses, for example, receive bank statements at home or office and frequently despatch cheques from the same address. The telephone system has developed matters even further, and in recent years many business managers have been able to obtain bank statement data over the telephone. This type of communication will normally be followed by written confirmation, although the frequency of bank statements can vary depending on agreements between bank and customer.

Home and office banking is therefore not a new development, although in future years electronic systems are likely to be increasingly used by householders and businesses to receive bank account information and despatch payment instructions. The major equipment for this purpose is likely to be a relatively cheap computer or television set, with links to the bank being arranged by telecommunications systems.

Telecommunications networks for home and office banking installations are likely over the next few years to be based on telephone services. These systems will almost inevitably become increasingly sophisticated and may be extensively used in the 1990s. In some countries, e.g. the USA and Japan, voice recognition systems have already been developed under which it is possible for payment instructions to be given to banks over the telephone following use of agreed security numbers. The telephone will be increasingly used for the transmission of computerized data initiated by businesses and private individuals, and this will probably be the way in which the home banking service will develop, at least initially. At a later stage, cable and satellite systems will be used, especially in the USA, although there have been numerous implementation problems in Europe.

The material that is likely to be provided by banks under home and office banking systems will probably include account balances, recent transactions, standing order instructions and a limited range of other information from bank sources, such as types of accounts, interest rates, foreign exchange data, etc. In turn the account-holder will probably be able to give instructions for the transfer of funds to another type of account under the same name or control, request statements or cheque books and arrange regular payments.

The home and office banking system of the future could therefore be attractive from a bank account-holder's viewpoint, especially if the desired information is provided more speedily than at present and at virtually any hour of the day or night. Cost, security and computer reliability could, however, produce major problems, and it will be extremely interesting to see how the banks and other similar operating companies tackle these matters.

COMMUNICATION SYSTEMS

There are strong differences of opinion as to whether the home banking systems of the 1990s will be centred on home computers, television sets or entirely new methods. In the USA, most of the early experiments were based on the use of home computers, for example the Pronto system as provided by the Chemical Bank of New York. The advantage of the home computer approach – assuming that the interested party has a suitable computer, telephone and television set – is that very little additional capital expenditure need be incurred by the account-holder, apart from the acquisition of a modem for communication purposes. It has been estimated that fewer than 10 per cent of personal computer owners in the UK possess modems, although the cheapest models now cost less than £100. The major problem is, however, that many potential home banking users do not own home computers. Over two million home computers have been purchased in the UK, but many of these may not now be in use. In offices the availability of a computer will probably be less of a problem, although many small businesses still do not have computers.

In Europe most of the early experimental systems have been based on viewdata systems, e.g. the Nottingham Building Society and Bank of Scotland projects in the UK, and the Verbraucherbank operation in Germany. Viewdata is the name most commonly used for systems that link the user's television receiver to a central computer by telecommunications methods (some writers use the term 'videotex', which covers a rather wider range of facilities). Two-way communication is possible under the viewdata system, which is *not* the case with teletext systems such as Ceefax and Oracle. Viewdata computer output is displayed in the user's home or office on a television set or visual display unit (VDU).

The public viewdata service in the UK is provided by British Telecom under the trade name Prestel. The initial objective of this system, which was launched in 1979, was to provide an information service for the general public. Most private individuals decided, however, that this service was not of great interest to them. There are strong differences of opinion regarding the precise reasons for this reaction. Capital and revenue expenditure costs were obviously contributory factors, and there also appeared to be a great suspicion and mistrust of these new ideas and systems. As a result, Prestel concentrated its sales efforts on the business sector, where there was much greater interest.

One of the reasons for increasing business interest has been the provision of a 'gateway' facility for Prestel users. This enables all approved users to obtain access to information stored in an external private computer, following the use of an agreed password or number. For home banking the external computer would naturally be that of the sponsoring bank.

Prestel is therefore extensively used for applications in which business or personal subscribers wish to obtain information from one or more sources, after which it may be possible for messages or instructions to be sent back through the normal communication system. Prestel data are provided by over 1,200 independent sources; this material is normally available for all subscribers. In addition, facilities are provided for closed user groups through the gateway facility.

A Prestel viewdata set will cost at least £500, although it may be possible to reduce this figure to about £200 (for an adaptor) if a suitable television set is already in use. A modem and software may also be required, in addition to which the purchase of a printer may have to be considered. Quarterly standing charges for Prestel services at the beginning of 1986 were £18 for business organizations and £6.50 for home users, with a time charge of 6p per minute in office hours (8 a.m. to 6 p.m. Monday to Friday and 8 a.m. to 1 p.m. on Saturday). There is no charge at other times. Telephone calls must also be paid for, although local rates are nearly always applicable.

There were more than 63,000 terminals attached to the Prestel network at the beginning of 1986, as compared with 38,000 at the beginning of 1984 and 14,000 in 1982. This is still well below the original Post Office launching estimate of 100,000 users by the end of 1980, but applications are now coming in at a rapid rate, believed to be in the region of 1,500 per month. The majority of applications are from business organizations, which make up about 54 per cent of terminal users. There is a growing interest, however, amongst private individuals. There has also been considerable success in persuading overseas countries, e.g. Denmark, the

Netherlands and Singapore, to use Prestel or associated systems, although local adjustments often prove to be necessary.

Private viewdata systems can also be acquired from both British Telecom and other sources. This type of arrangement may be appropriate only in the case of a relatively large user of these services. Some of the best-known of these applications are in the holiday trade; thus Thomson Holidays provides information and accepts bookings from travel agents in this form, whilst in the motor trade the Rover group (previously BL) has a stock locator system for its distributors and agents. In the banking sector the Midland Bank has decided to use this approach in its initial home banking experiments, possibly because of the flexibility which this approach allows in the operation of the system and the setting of charges.

Outside the UK there are several major national viewdata systems, e.g. Teletel in France, Telidon in Canada and Captain in Japan. In France there has been considerable government support for viewdata systems, and Minitel terminals are now being installed in private homes without charge to replace telephone directories, with a target of 8 million in operation by 1992. There was therefore some embarrassment in mid-1985 when the data communication network broke down, largely because of the volume of business from the 800,000 households and businesses equipped with Minitel terminals at that time; this is a problem that few other countries are likely to have in the 1980s!

In the USA there are many types of viewdata system, but there is at this stage little prospect of a national network, largely because of the size of the country and the incompatibility of different systems. Cable television, which has been installed in about 35 per cent of homes, might provide an alternative communication service, and experiments are currently taking place with two-way systems. In Europe and most other parts of the world there has been little significant development in this direction, and the telephone system is in most cases regarded as the only viable means of transmitting home banking information. This situation could change, however, in the 1990s.

INTERNATIONAL DEVELOPMENTS

In the USA the modern home banking era probably began with the introduction of telephone bill payment (TBP) in the 1970s. TBP is a funds transfer system that allows consumers to pay bills by contacting their bank by telephone and arranging for funds to be transferred to one or more payees' accounts. Details of payees (and their banks) to whom payments are likely to be made usually have to be submitted to the bank beforehand.

By the early 1980s over 400 financial institutions were offering this type of service, which now tends to be at least partly automated through the use of keyboard (touch-tone) telephones. Security obviously has to be carefully maintained, and numerous safeguards are used, including the use of coded systems, often based on social security numbers.

More highly automated home banking systems were introduced in the early 1980s. The most successful of these early projects was set up by the Chemical Bank of New York in September 1983. This system is based on home computer use, with particular emphasis on Atari machines (other computers can now be used). Services offered include balance and statement data, transfers between various accounts, bill paying and numerous other banking and information services. The Pronto monthly service charge in 1986 was $12 for individuals and $30 for small businesses. A modem can be provided, if required, for $75, or loan facilities can be arranged. By June 1986 the number of users had reached 25,000, made up of 22,000 household users and 3,000 small business users.[1]

Numerous other banks from the very large to the relatively small are experimenting with home banking projects, and recent estimates suggest that about 50 banks are involved in projects of this nature, of which over 20 have set up full commercial operations. The only scheme that has so far approached the Pronto numbers is that the Bank of America in the San Francisco area, where the number of users is about 23,000. Most of the other schemes had less than 2,000 subscribers at the beginning of 1986.

The USA was therefore fertile ground for home banking experiments in the early 1980s, although there are still strong differences of opinion as to whether home banking can be made viable on its own (there were probably about 60,000 home banking users at the beginning of 1986) or whether it must become part of an extensive information service. The overall balance of opinion now appears to be moving towards the latter viewpoint, as is shown by the recent decision of the Chemical Bank, Bank of America and several other non-banking organizations, including the telecommunications group AT&T, to join together in a venture to offer electronic services to households, including banking, stock brokerage and merchandized shopping.[2] This is not necessarily the death knell for home banking as a separate service, but it does seem to be a strong indication that the future of home banking in the USA will be closely tied up with other information services.

---

1 Home Banking Grips Yuppies, *Banking World*, June 1986, p. 33.
2 Chemical and Bank of America Join Forces, *Banking Technology*, July 1985, p. 5.

In Japan, the Captain viewdata service has been operating for over three years, and this system is being used by several large banks for pilot home banking projects. Development may take place at a rapid rate if the trial projects prove successful.

In Europe (apart from the UK) the major interest in home banking has been in West Germany and France. In Germany the most interesting developments have in the past come from the Verbraucherbank, a relatively small bank centred in Hamburg. This bank mounted a major expansion programme with the aid of home banking services, largely made available through the German viewdata network Bildschirmtext. The latter service had 40,000 users at the beginning of 1986 and there are great hopes of rapid expansion in the late 1980s.

In France, numerous developments are taking place as part of the government-sponsored viewdata system, and it is expected that over 3 million Minitel terminals will be installed by 1987. About 30 banks have started to offer home banking services in the last two or three years and it has been suggested that there will be more than 250,000 users of these services by 1986/7. Home banking services should therefore be an important part of the French banking system by the end of the 1980s.

Elsewhere in Europe some of the most interesting experiments are taking place in Finland, where the Union Bank of Finland has introduced a system under which customers can obtain balance data and provide payment instructions by telephoning the bank's computer centre. Customers have to tap in their personal identification number (PIN) followed by a four-figure security code. This service is provided on the telephone – no television set is used – with the computer asking questions by means of a voice synthesis system which is able to communicate with customers. The Finnish language is apparently relatively easy to use for this purpose as there are no ambiguities in speech or spelling as in the English language.

There are, therefore, some exciting worldwide developments taking place in home banking systems. Most of these systems are experimental, although there are some indications that home banking services could be extensively used by the early 1990s, especially in those countries such as France and Germany where there has been active government involvement in the setting up of viewdata and electronic banking systems. In the USA there has been little government involvement, although the private sector does seem to be prepared to invest considerable sums of money to develop satisfactory home banking processes. The fragmented nature of the banking system will probably mean, however, that it will be much more difficult to develop a satisfactory national network than in Western Europe. As a result, US home banking systems may develop as part of electronic information networks rather than independent units.

In the early 1980s there was considerable speculation as to which UK bank would be the first to offer home banking services to its customers. Rather surprisingly, the first project to be announced was by the Nottingham Building Society in November 1982 (the scheme was operative from mid-1983) in conjunction with the Bank of Scotland and the Prestel viewdata service. At the time of the announcement, the Nottingham Building Society was only a medium-sized society with assets of about £170 million, although the society obviously hoped that a home banking facility would considerably increase the rate of growth in the number of customers and the amount of funds invested, without the usual investment in branch premises. Capital expenditure on the scheme is believed to have been in the region of £2 million.

The Nottingham Building Society scheme – usually described as Homelink – is based on the Prestel system, and all users must become subscribers to the Prestel network. Terms have varied since the Homelink scheme was introduced; at the beginning of 1986 users had to arrange an initial investment of £1,000, after which the account balance could not fall below £250. Normal ordinary account interest rates are paid. A special keyboard and adaptor may be purchased or borrowed. A purchase deal is available for £150, although borrowing facilities can be arranged at £3 per month. In addition, normal Prestel charges have to be paid.

The services provided under the Homelink scheme include the provision of balance and statement data, and mortgage account details. Payment of regular commitments can be arranged; for this service appropriate details must be lodged with the Society beforehand. Funds can be transferred to and from the Bank of Scotland (users are encouraged but not compelled to have an account with this bank). There is also access to a wide range of home shopping and information facilities, and stockbroking transactions can now be arranged. Access to most of these facilities is available at any time of the day or night on any day of the week.

Very little information has been published regarding the number of customers attracted by the Nottingham Building Society scheme. Most estimates suggest that there are 'several thousand' subscribers, but there has been no official comment on these suggestions. This has, however, been a brave pioneering effort, which the leading UK banks and building societies have been watching with great interest.

In September 1983 the Midland became the first of the major UK banks to set up an experimental home banking project. Users of the system – volunteer employees and customers – have to obtain their own equipment, although the bank is prepared to provide advice on this subject. All customers able to receive Prestel can use the system, although the method of achieving this can be in several forms, e.g. a specially adapted television set or home computer package. The scheme is not run on the general Prestel network, but on a private viewdata system operated on a mini-computer.

By the beginning of 1986 there were over 1,200 customers taking part in the Midland Bank scheme, which provides information about account balances, entries since the last statement, standing orders and a variety of bank services. Funds can be transferred between the customer's various accounts, and cheque books and statements can be ordered. There is no facility at this stage for the settlement of accounts. The major cost to the customer, apart from the acquisition of the relevant equipment, is the charge for the telephone call on connection to the viewdata service. No announcement has been made about bank charges.

A recent interview with the head of electronic banking at the Midland Bank suggested that 'the most likely markets in the short term are the small/medium business sector and the professional upmarket customer'.[3] It was also stressed that the impact on banking was expected to be slow, although there have recently been rumours that a more widespread scheme will soon be launched.

The most ambitious home banking scheme to date was launched by the Bank of Scotland in January 1985, backed up by extensive advertising. The Bank of Scotland had, of course, been involved with the Nottingham Building Society in its home banking scheme, and the new venture appeared to be an attempt to expand the banking activities of the group beyond traditional boundaries in Scotland without the heavy expenditure involved in the acquisition of numerous bank premises.

The Bank of Scotland system is organized in a similar way to the Midland system, although the national Prestel service is used rather than a private viewdata system. All users should be Prestel subscribers, and relevant equipment must therefore be acquired, in addition to which Prestel subscription fees, time charges and telephone costs must be paid. To assist in capital expenditure costs the Bank of Scotland has made available a limited supply of Prestel adaptors at £95 each. The bank also levies transaction charges and a monthly subscription fee of £2.50 for personal customers and £5 for business organizations (1986 rates). Computers may be used for access purposes provided that an appropriate modem has been purchased. An illustration of a typical Bank of Scotland terminal is provided in figure 15.1.

3 Midland Bank's Softly-Softly Approach, *Banking World*, July 1985, p. 29. This edition included several articles on home banking.

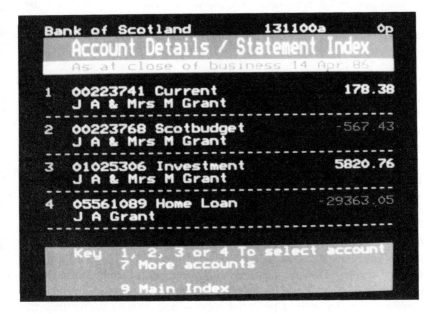

Figure 15.1 Bank of Scotland terminal display

Services provided on the Bank of Scotland system include balance information, recent statement data, standing order and direct debit details, cheque book or statement ordering, and transfers between customer's accounts including an attractive high-interest investment account. A bill payment service is also provided – up to 30 days in advance – as long as the payee's agreement has been obtained and a mandate has been completed with details of the payee's bank account and other relevant data. Home shopping facilities will also be available together with the normal services provided by Prestel.

The Bank of Scotland service can be used for business as well as home purposes, and a cash management module can be made available for an additional charge – £5 per month in 1986. This service will provide details of cleared balances together with information regarding funds that are expected to be cleared over the next three working days.

Apart from the Midland and the Bank of Scotland, several other banks have set up teams to look at the prospects for home banking. Barclays, Lloyds, National Westminster and the Trustee Savings Bank are all reported to be considering the introduction of pilot projects, with the most popular form of initial experimentation being the provision of equipment for managers in bank branches and homes. Barclays set up an 'in-house' trial in 1985 and Lloyds is planning to install terminals in branches for staff use. Most of the major UK banks could therefore have home banking systems in operation by the end of the 1980s.

BUSINESS CONSIDERATIONS

Many commercial organizations will be interested in home and office banking systems, both as promoters and users of these services. The promoters will not necessarily come from the banking sector, as has already been shown by the Nottingham Building Society in the UK and numerous non-banking organizations in the USA. There will, however, normally be banking involvement, sometimes at a secondary stage.

The attitude of the banks towards home and office banking services tends to be one of cautious interest. The technology to launch such systems is now available, although new developments could render existing systems obsolete over the next few years. Security presents another major problem which will not be easy to resolve. The biggest problem is, however, the response of potential users – both private individuals and businesses – at a price that will be economic from the banks' viewpoint.

In private households and the business sector many individuals and small firms have in the past received free banking services as a result of their current account balance situation, and there will obviously be resistance to the idea that home banking services should be charged out at what the banks describe as an economic cost. In fixing charging structures, one of the most difficult matters for the banks to estimate will be the savings as compared with present systems through possible reduced demands for buildings, staff, paperwork etc. On the other hand the banks may lose out on non-interest-bearing current account balances if a tendency develops to transfer funds out of these accounts as quickly as possible. Competition will also have to be carefully considered, as home banking services may be offered by overseas banks and other financial institutions.

From the business user's viewpoint, there will be certain attractions in office banking systems. In particular, the provision on a VDU of statement data relating to the end of the previous business day together with information regarding uncleared funds should be extremely useful. Many small firms receive bank statements only once or twice a month, and these are often delayed for several days by postal difficulties. At the other extreme, most large businesses have been receiving bank statement data daily over the telephone for some time, although there could still be a significant future demand for the provision of such data in electronic form.

Business users will also welcome the opportunity to transfer funds instantaneously to and from interest-bearing accounts, and to arrange payments on specified future dates. Transfers to and from deposit accounts have in some cases been accepted by telephone in the past, although UK banks have always been reluctant to accept instructions in this form.

It is extremely difficult to assess which types of business will be most interested in office banking services. Many large corporations, especially those with extensive international interests, are now using the electronic cash management services provided by major banks; these will be considered in chapter 16. It may therefore be the expanding medium-sized business that will be most interested in the range of services provided by office banking systems. Much will depend on existing electronic equipment, although a business with a small computer should not need to spend very much to set up a suitable system.

Amongst private individuals the level of interest in home banking has so far been rather disappointing. This may be partly due to the level of costs, although it has been suggested that most individuals regard their television set as an entertainment medium rather than an electronic information processor. The rapid expansion in personal computer ownership may change these attitudes, although this may take some time, as many computer users are teenagers who do not yet have bank accounts.

In the long term it seems probable that home banking systems will be welcomed by a significant number of private individuals, some of whom may see these services as an extension of home shopping rather than a service on its own. In the UK several companies are already offering a home shopping service (e.g. Littlewoods has recently announced a 'teleshopping' experiment), and there seems little doubt that in the late 1980s there will be a considerable expansion in these activities. Over the next few years, therefore, the banks will have to decide whether home banking should be offered on its own, or whether it should become part of a large range of home information and shopping services.

SUMMARY AND CONCLUSIONS

Home and office banking services are at present in an early stage of development in Europe and North America, although there seems little doubt that these systems will be extensively marketed in the 1990s, possibly as part of extensive electronic information networks.

In the USA there are numerous banks involved in home banking experiments and projects, and a recent consultancy report has suggested that 'by the mid-1990s as many as 22 million households in the USA (a fifth of the total) will be doing their banking and bill paying as part of an integrated information service.'[4] The US banking sector is, however, very different from that in Western Europe, where most countries have a relatively small number of banks dominating the system; developments in Europe may therefore be rather different. In the USA the competitive atmosphere has already produced considerable interest in home information systems.

In Europe most experimental projects have been based on viewdata systems, which have been heavily promoted by government agencies in France and Germany, with the eventual aim of having these systems installed in most households by the 1990s. This type of development may well mean that these two countries will become the leaders in home information systems in Europe, although there is considerable interest in the private sector in the UK.

Over the next five years many decisions will have to be made by government departments and business organizations regarding the shape and operation of home and office banking systems. The reaction of consumers – both private individuals and business organizations – will, of course, be vital in this process, and nobody is really sure at this stage whether there will be a favourable reaction to home banking or the possible future range of information services – news, shopping, insurance, investment, travel, education, games, etc.

The reaction to the home banking experiments of the mid-1980s suggests, however, that home and office banking as a separate service may not produce sufficient response to be an economic proposition, especially in the case of private individuals, who do not seem to be prepared to pay very much, if anything, for their banking services. It is suggested, therefore, that home banking will in most developed countries become part of a large range of home information services to which the individual will have access on payment of appropriate fees. The business sector may be more interested in a separate banking package, but this may not be sufficient to justify a large-scale service. Bankers must therefore prepare for a brave new world in which their services will be sold, and in some cases delivered, on television sets side-by-side with a large range of other goods and services. This vision will not appeal to many traditional bankers, but if the banks do not respond to this challenge they may find that they lose numerous customers to other banks and financial institutions which decide that home banking and other information services are the future route to success.

4 W. W. Wyman and C. Batt, Home Information Systems – the Wide Road to Home Banking, *Retail Banker*, 5 September 1983, p. 5.

16 Electronic Cash Management Services

Accountants and financial managers have been involved in the management of cash resources for many years, but it was not until the 1960s that separate departments or sections began to be set up for this and other related activities. In large companies the person responsible for this function is frequently described as the corporate treasurer, although the directors of most small and medium-sized companies regard this type of activity as an accounting responsibility.

Information regarding cash balances on different accounts and the ability to transfer funds quickly are most important elements of the cash management process, and it is not surprising that electronic systems to provide these services have proved popular, especially in large international organizations. These systems first became available in the USA in the late 1960s and early 1970s, largely because of the difficulty which most large companies were experiencing at that time in bringing together information concerning numerous domestic bank accounts which had to be opened because of the fragmented nature of the US banking system.

In Europe, where the banking system is frequently dominated by a small number of powerful banks, the treasury function did not become of any great significance (with a few major exceptions) until the 1970s. Clearing systems therefore tended to be faster and more efficient than in the USA and information regarding domestic bank balances could generally be obtained reasonably quickly. Rapidly fluctuating interest and exchange rates did, however, produce a need for cash management specialists, particularly during the highly inflationary conditions of the 1970s and early 1980s.

In the mid-1970s US banks began to offer electronic cash management services to European companies, some of which showed considerable interest. European banks did not at that time have much expertise in this area, but over the next decade most of the major banks decided to provide facilities of this nature, largely because of the fear of losing business to overseas banks. In the UK all four major clearing banks are now providing electronic cash management services, and some of the smaller banks are also engaged in the type of activity.

The range of services provided in an electronic cash management package can vary significantly from one bank to another. Initially these services concentrated on information regarding bank balances and recent transaction data together with the transfer of funds between different accounts under the same control. In recent years, however, it has become possible to initiate electronic funds transfers to most type of domestic bank accounts, and in addition there has been growing interest in international transfers. Workstation facilities have also become available as part of a move from passive information services to management planning processes. The services that can be provided by a workstation are considered in more detail later in this chapter.

Electronic cash management services are therefore gradually becoming an important feature of bank services for large companies, although there are considerable doubts as to whether these services will prove beneficial to all sizeable trading organizations. In this connection there must obviously be a relationship between the provision of these services and home banking facilities (see chapter 15). In most banks the latter services are still being marketed by different departments from those which are responsible for electronic cash management, although it would seem logical that over the next decade the business element of home banking should become part of a comprehensive range of cash management services. The reaction of small and medium-sized businesses to these developments will be very interesting to observe over the next few years.

SYSTEMS AND APPLICATIONS

The input for an electronic corporate cash management system is usually arranged with the aid of a desk-top terminal or microcomputer. The attitude of the major banks on input systems has in the past shown some variations. Some banks have recommended the use of a special teletype terminal and this may be attractive if the potential user is already using terminals and electronic communication links. Other banks prefer an appropriately programmed microcomputer, although most of the major banks are now moving towards a system with few, if any, restrictions on generally accepted input systems.

Communication networks are normally used to transmit information to and from bank computers. In some cases these networks are part of the bank's international communications system, as with the Bank of America. In other cases, networks are owned by outside organizations, e.g. computer service corporations such as Automated Data Processing (ADP) and the General Electric Information Services Company (GEISCO). Most of the UK banks use the facilities of these large international computer bureaux.

The output system is likely to be strongly influenced by input techniques. In some cases users may be satisfied with visual presentation, especially bearing in mind that paper-based statements for a large company will probably arrive in the next day or two. Most users will, however, prefer a permanent copy of the data provided, and in these circumstances a terminal printer will be highly desirable.

The quality of the information provided by electronic cash management systems frequently depends on the ability and preparedness of other banks to pass on information to the bank providing the electronic service. Very few large companies now rely on one bank for domestic and foreign transactions, and the multi-national organization may have many different banks, both in the UK and overseas. Most of the major banks will, on request from the account-holder, pass on required account data to the collecting bank, although some will not, either because of the policy of the bank or a general inability to provide information quickly enough. These matters should be investigated before a decision is made to introduce an electronic cash management system.

The information provided as part of an electronic cash management system generally includes one or more of the following facilities:

1 *Balance reporting.* This facility was at one time restricted to the closing balance at the end of the previous working day, although in the last two or three years most banks have begun to provide current-day data based on the balance at the beginning of the day together with adjustments in respect of automated debits and credits already in the system and amounts cleared in respect of that particular day. Figures are usually made available from 9 a.m. or before on all working days. Updated figures may be provided at certain times during the day, and there is also a small but growing movement, mainly by the US banks, towards real time updating facilities. Ledger and cleared balances are generally provided as a standard part of the balance reporting system, and overseas balances may be made available if time differences and communication problems can be overcome. Summarized statements may also be provided, and this could involve a 'netting' process if it has been agreed that one balance can be offset against another for bank charges and other relevant purposes.

2 *Transaction reporting*. Information concerning debits and credits for the previous working day is normally provided, although practices vary regarding the availability of data for earlier days. Cash and credit management systems should benefit considerably from this service. Some banks are able to provide only five days' data on electronic links, whilst other banks can go back 60 or even 90 days. The corporate treasurer will obviously have to decide how important this facility is, bearing in mind the extra charges involved and the fact that paper statements may already have been received in respect of most recent transactions.

3 *Cash forecasting*. Banks generally have stored information available regarding cheques already paid into the payee's own branch which should be cleared in the next two or three working days. In addition, figures regarding pre-authorized electronic transfers for the next few days should be readily available. It should be possible, therefore, for the bank to provide a skeleton cash forecast for the next three days, which the corporate treasurer can adjust internally after taking into account information not yet known to the bank. The cash forecasting service has become widely available over the last two or three years as a development of the uncleared effects report (this can generally be provided as a separate report if so desired) and other relevant data.

4 *Ability to send or receive messages or payment instructions*. At its simplest this service can be used for enquiries or transfers between accounts under the same name or control. In the UK, EFT payments can now be arranged, although some systems require that transfer account details should be lodged beforehand. In this connection the setting up of the CHAPS system has been of considerable assistance, and it is now possible for corporate treasurers to link in directly to this service through most of the clearing banks. A similar service can be provided for overseas transactions through the SWIFT network. The sophistication and integration of bank telecommunications networks varies considerably, although this may not be readily apparent to the casual user. The comparative efficiency of different systems becomes more apparent, however, when attempts are made to effect a payment towards the end of the working day.

5 *Foreign currency information and transfers*. To many treasurers of multi-national companies one of the most important elements of an electronic cash management system is the ability to inspect exchange rates and overseas account information at any time of the working day, and to transfer funds from one currency to another at very short notice. This is naturally of considerable assistance in currency and

investment management, and is a key element in the decision-making strategy of most large international treasury departments.

6 *Workstation facilities*. This is the most recent development in the provision of electronic cash management services, and it is still only provided as a commercial product by a small number of banks. The idea behind the workstation is that information transmitted can be transferred on to an electronic spreadsheet to enable interested persons to manipulate data so that a variety of different possibilities can be taken into account. The simplest application is probably that of cash forecasting, although workstations are now beginning to be used for financial modelling and other similar business applications.

A wide range of facilities can therefore be provided on electronic cash management systems and these will inevitably become more sophisticated in the future. Many organizations will not be able to justify the full list of applications that has just been considered. What often happens, however, is that companies start off using some of the more simple or obvious applications and then graduate to more complex processes. At all stages it is essential that there should be a proper cost–benefit analysis, although it will always be difficult to appraise the value of speedier information for decision-making processes.

BENEFITS AND PROBLEMS

Potential benefits

In a successful electronic cash management system there may be numerous benefits. Probably the most important of these are:

1 *Faster access to information regarding bank statement figures, interest rates and foreign exchange dealings.* The importance of these matters is naturally related to the speed of availability under existing systems. Most of the information already mentioned can be obtained by means of phone calls, telex and other methods of communication, although this can be a time-consuming process, in addition to which it is unlikely to be possible to remain in constant communication with the supplier of information. Electronic systems should therefore provide quicker access to relevant information.

2 *Improved material for decision-making, especially in respect of sources and uses of funds.* If appropriate information becomes available more quickly and in more detail, it should be possible to make better decisions, although much will depend on existing systems and

potential applications. Improvements are more likely to be possible in overseas bank data and transfers than domestic transactions, and as a result many decisions regarding sources and uses of overseas funds should be made in a more efficient way.

3 *Ability to make payments at very short notice.* It is not essential that a bank customer should have electronic cash management services to obtain access through the bank to CHAPS, SWIFT and other methods of rapid payment. It should be quicker and more economical, however, to transmit payment instructions electronically to bank processing centres, rather than use manual processes. The bank can in turn use electronic communication links to provide information about large incoming items, thus ensuring that maximum use is made of available funds.

4 *Reduction of exchange risks and administrative costs.* In businesses with numerous overseas interests, there may be substantial foreign exchange risks, especially if there is a failure to match overseas assets and liabilities. These risks will not be eliminated by bringing together overseas account details and obtaining more up-to-date foreign exchange information, although the people involved with these matters should be in a better position to make informed decisions. In addition, less time and effort will be required to obtain appropriate data, and this should make more time available for decision-making processes.

5 *Ability to plan ahead more effectively.* An electronic information system should be of considerable assistance in preparing plans for the future as well as monitoring the present performance. In this connection, banks can provide details of uncleared cheques that will be credited to accounts over the next 2 or 3 days, as well as future automated credit transfers and other similar payments. It should therefore be possible to make more effective projections of cash receipts, payments, balances and other related financial data.

Taking all these points together, an electronic cash management system should enable the corporate treasurer or accountant to have more effective global financial control, and the ability to make improved decisions regarding the most effective sources and uses of funds. Planning procedures should also be improved, although much will depend on the type of business in which the account-holder operates.

Problem areas

As with most improvements in existing systems, there are costs and problems involved and these will now be briefly examined:

1 *Capital and revenue expenditure may be substantial.* The costs involved in an electronic cash management system can be significant if little expenditure has previously been incurred on computers and telecommunications links. At the other extreme, the well equipped organization may have very little additional capital expenditure, as most, if not all, of the required equipment may already have been purchased. Computer and communication costs are often underestimated, and it is important that realistic estimates should be made of these costs before any final decisions on usage are made.

2 *The overall level of bank charges will probably increase.* The UK banks are very secretive about charges for corporate cash management services which are nearly always stated to be 'subject to negotiation'. Comments by UK bankers would appear to suggest that these services have been generated as a response to competitive pressures rather than being a major revenue-earning exercise. Information and transmission services are, of course, already available in a paper-based format and in many cases the information charges appear to be relatively cheap or even non-existent, although in the latter case it is probable that these matters will be taken into account in the overall charges negotiation process. Charges for electronic services should therefore not be set at too high a level if there is to be a real incentive for the business organization to move from paper-based to electronic systems. Average monthly costs for electronic cash management services are believed to vary from £250 for a small number of accounts to £5,000 or more for a wide range of services. Increased costs may, however, be justified by the improved quality of service and information.

3 *Security risks may increase.* All banks are very conscious of the security risks attached to electronic communication systems. Password systems are used in virtually all applications, and access is frequently limited to specified individuals, with one, two or even three levels of authorization, especially with transactions involving large sums of money. Encryption techniques are also being extensively used to prevent the deciphering of transmitted data. Despite all these precautions, unauthorized messages are sometimes sent out, and these could involve the transfer of large amounts to overseas accounts. The UK banks are reluctant to comment on these matters, but there have been rumours of some large unauthorized transfers from corporate cash management terminals.

4 *Inability to absorb additional information.* It will in most cases be beneficial to have a substantial amount of information for management decision-making purposes, although situations will arise where additional data cannot be effectively absorbed or used. The board of directors should therefore ensure that there is sufficient manpower and expertise available to make effective use of the additional information that should become available from an electronic cash management system.

5 *Computer failure may create major problems.* As with all electronic systems there is a danger of computer failure, and adequate stand-by systems should therefore be made available. Inadequate attention is often given to these matters, which can cause considerable problems where no emergency plan exists.

Weighing these costs and problems against the attached benefits will not be easy. This is not a new situation, however, as many computer projects involve a comparison of improved information systems with substantial capital and revenue expenditure costs. On balance, the most benefits would appear to arise when there are numerous bank accounts, both in the UK and overseas, although situations will arise where local financial directors have considerable discretion regarding the use of cash resources. It is also possible that a solely domestic application may be worthwhile when there are numerous bank accounts and frequent investment and payment decisions, as in some national retail stores. In all these circumstances much will depend on existing systems, which could be extremely efficient, especially if there are good personal links between company personnel and local bankers.

BANK VIEWPOINTS

The four major UK clearing banks all provide electronic cash management services, although this has been a relatively new development. The Midland was the first bank to offer these services to corporate customers in September 1982,[1] and over the next two years National Westminster (Network), Barclays (Barcam) and Lloyds (Cashcall) began to offer similar services.

The systems provided by the UK banks are largely based on computer

1 A most interesting account of the development of the Midland Bank cash management service has recently been provided in an article by K. Haaroff, An Exercise in Product Development for the 1980s, *International Journal of Bank Marketing*, Issue 1/3, 1984, pp. 56–68.

networks and software provided by US computer service corporations, e.g. ADP and GEISCO. This reflects the fact that some of the UK banks entered this market rather hastily, largely as a result of several US providers of these services entering the UK market in the late 1970s and early 1980s, e.g. Bank of America (Bamtrac), Chemical Bank (Chemlink), Chase Manhatten (Infocash), Citibank (Citicash) and Morgan Guarantee (Mars). It has also been suggested that some of the UK banks would have preferred not to offer this type of service, mainly because of the long-term effects of these systems on interest-free current account balances.[2] If, however, electronic cash management services were required by users, the UK banks probably had very little alternative to entry if they wished to remain competitive, in addition to which there were great hopes that new customers would be acquired and additional revenue-earning opportunities created.

There has also been much debate amongst bankers concerning the range of electronic cash management services that should ultimately be provided. Some of the US banks (e.g. Bank of America and Citibank) have already started to offer real-time accounting services, although this may not be as advantageous as would appear because of differences concerning the time of entry of statement data. Updating of data at several times of the day will probably become more popular, and the UK banks are already beginning to move in this direction. Corporate customers will obviously have to assess how important this type of service could be to them.

The provision of workstation input material will be another area of interest that will have to be carefully considered by the UK banks. Most of the major US banks now provide this service, but the UK banks are not yet convinced that there is a local demand for this facility. Attempts are being made, however, to assess whether customer demand is changing and, if so, whether this type of service can be provided at a reasonable price.

The banks will therefore have some important marketing decisions to make on electronic cash management systems over the next few years. If security and reliability can be maintained, there should be a ready market for these services amongst major companies, and the market will be extremely competitive. Amongst smaller companies, the more limited range of services provided as part of a home and office banking package is likely to be of greater interest, although all of these services will probably be integrated in the late 1980s and early 1990s to provide a comprehensive range of electronic services.

2 See, for example, Cash Management – the Electronic Treasurer, *Banker*, March 1983, p. 77.

SUMMARY AND CONCLUSIONS

Electronic cash management services have developed rapidly in the UK since their introduction in the late 1970s and early 1980s. Initially these services were largely confined to balance and transaction reporting for domestic accounts and a few overseas situations, but we have now reached a situation in which these facilities are being increasingly used for funds transfers, foreign exchange management, and various forecasting and planning processes.

Competition amongst the banks for the provision of cash management services is very intense, with about a dozen UK and overseas banks competing for a limited amount of business. Major corporations often use the electronic cash management services of two or three banks, although the US banks still appear to be providing a more advanced and comprehensive range of services than most European banks. For example, Citibank recently came top in a poll of over 300 international treasurers as the outstanding provider of electronic banking services.[3] The quality and range of the services provided by the major UK banks is, however, improving rapidly.

There must be some doubts, however, as to whether there will be sufficient business available in the UK to satisfy the aspirations of the banks involved in marketing processes. Nobody really knows the number of UK companies that will be interested in full electronic cash management services over the next five years, taking into account capital and revenue costs, security problems, familiarization, etc. Target companies over the next few years will probably be those with fairly extensive international interests accompanied by numerous bank accounts and a centralized treasury or finance function. This will probably limit the market to significantly fewer than 1,000 companies, which could mean that the banks will have done well if 600 or 700 companies can be persuaded to use electronic cash management services by the end of the 1980s.

In the midst of these marketing problems, bankers will be looking closely at their own charges and those of competitors. A leading UK banker has recently suggested that banks must be prepared to pay the going rate for customers' funds, especially bearing in mind increased opportunities for transfers to interest-bearing accounts, but customers must in turn be prepared to remunerate bankers more fairly for services received.[4] This seems a fair comment, although there will naturally be a

3 Treasurers' Top Team, *Euromoney Corporate Finance*, March 1985.
4 M. Rowe, Electronic Management Cuts Costs, *Accountant*, 30 May 1985, p. 25.

reluctance to pay for electronic information services when there has in the past been little or no apparent cost for similar non-electronic services.

By the 1990s, therefore, it will probably be quite usual for major companies to receive and despatch bank information and payment instructions by electronic means, and to use the same data for planning purposes. It is much more difficult, however, to predict how far these services will be of interest to smaller companies, although an integration of electronic cash management and home banking services could produce a package that should be of interest to many medium-sized businesses. Bank charges and communication costs will be an important element in this equation, although there will still be many business directors and managers around who will want to cling to old and familiar methods of paper-based bank statements and payment systems. The convenience of examining statement data and arranging payments by electronic methods will probably triumph eventually, although we may have to wait until the twenty-first century for widespread business acceptance of these methods.

17 Major Effects and Implications

The long-term replacement of a substantial number of cash and paper-based payments by electronic transfers will create both benefits and problems for the providers and users of these services. If the replacement process is gradual, as seems extremely likely, the problems will not be so great as they would be with sudden and dramatic change. It would be dangerous, however, to wait for the arrival of new EFT systems before thinking about the possible effects and implications.

In this process of change there will be many important factors for interested parties to consider. In this chapter four major areas of concern will be considered: consumer interests, legal regulations, computer fraud and employment opportunities. It is not suggested that these are the only areas of concern, but most of the other possible effects and implications have been considered in previous chapters or are briefly considered under these four major headings. A brief section is also provided on government involvement, as there are strong differences of opinion as to whether government should become involved, either directly or indirectly, in the process of change.

CONSUMER INTERESTS

Consumer groups in several different parts of the world have in recent years been considering the effects and implications of the widespread use of electronic banking systems. Some of these concerns have already been examined in the chapter on EFTPOS services, but there are a number of more general considerations that apply to most, if not all, EFT systems. Businesses may, of course, be consumers of EFT services, but it is private individuals who are more likely to require protection and representation.

One of the major consumer concerns about all computer applications is the effect this type of system might have on privacy and confidentiality. These fears are probably centred on the fact that governments and business organizations are now collecting large amounts of information about private individuals on computerized records. EFT systems do not therefore create an extensive range of new problems, but they do add to consumer concerns about the way in which these records might be used.

Consumers are also likely to be concerned that any personal material held on computerized records should be accurate. In the case of EFT records, the data built up may be purely factual, e.g. name, address, date and amount of transaction, and such data could be used simply as a guide to granting of credit or loans. What is much more controversial, however, is the possible release of this material to external parties, such as central or local government authorities, police, taxation officials, etc. In certain situations, e.g. serious police enquiries, it may be desirable that regulatory agencies should have access to these data, but there are doubts in other circumstances as to whether details about a private individual's movements and location on a particular day should be built up from an examination of debit and credit card activity.

Retailers may also be able to obtain a limited amount of confidential information about the state of an individual's bank account as a result of the card issuer's refusal of an EFTPOS transaction. This situation already exists in a rather different way with credit card transactions, although in this case refusal is only likely to indicate that the credit limit has been exceeded rather than that funds are not available. This situation may be made worse by the fact that bank posting procedures often take place at the end of the day and not at the time of the transaction, and current-day lodgements may therefore be ignored. Consumer groups will obviously want to be sure that all refusals are justified, and are not the cause of considerable embarrassment to the potential purchaser.

Choice of payment methods is another emotive subject. Consumer groups naturally have fears that private purchasers may be compelled to use certain payment methods; some life assurance companies, for example, insist that premiums are paid by direct debit. It also seems likely that over the next few years discounts will be offered if purchasers use electronic payment methods; thus some US petrol suppliers offer discounts for payment through the EFTPOS system. In the UK and several other countries, consumer groups have in the past opposed discounts for shoppers who use cash rather than credit cards on the grounds that this might increase prices for credit transactions. The logic of this argument is rather suspect, however, as it can just as easily be argued that the use of cheaper payment methods should benefit both payer and payee. An additional complicating factor is, of course, the fact that many individuals do not have bank accounts, and a discount for debit card use could mean that the poorer unbanked members of the community have to pay more than wealthy people with bank accounts.

In the UK the Office of Fair Trading has taken an active interest in EFT systems and has produced several helpful publications on the subject.[1] This organization is naturally concerned with the level of competition in the provision of payment services, and senior staff hope that the end-result of the widespread use of EFT systems will be more, rather than less, competition. This does appear to be happening in the USA, although there is some doubt in the rest of the developed world as to whether retailers, building societies and other providers of financial services will be able to break down the traditional dominance of banking corporations in the payments business.

The Consumers' Association and the National Consumer Council are also becoming increasingly interested in this subject, and the banks now appear to have accepted that there will be consultation before new services are introduced. An important role of these organizations may be in the provision of non-technical publications explaining the way in which EFT systems operate, as the banks have traditionally not been very good at explaining technical services in readily understandable language.

It is important, therefore, that the providers of EFT services should consider consumer interests before introducing EFT systems. In the past, banks and retail organizations have often introduced new systems without proper consumer consultation. Ideas are now changing with the growth in power and influence of the consumer movement, and it must be hoped that discussions between interested parties will ensure that most, if not all, adverse consumer reactions are satisfactorily met. Some protection for consumers does already exist in consumer credit, data protection and other legislation but more will be needed if debit cards are extensively used.

LEGAL REGULATIONS

In most developed countries the law relating to payments is based on rather ancient legislation enacted when cash and cheques were virtually the only forms of payment. In the UK, the Bills of Exchange Act dates back to 1882 and there has been little relevant legislation in recent years apart from the Cheques Act 1957, although the Consumer Credit Act 1974, the Unfair Contract Terms Act 1977 and the Data Protection Act 1984 may be of relevance in some specialized situations.

1 See, for example, *Micro-Electronics and Retailing* (Office of Fair Trading, 1982).

The only major country that has introduced detailed legislation on EFT systems is the USA, where the Electronic Funds Transfer Act was passed in 1978. The purpose of this legislation was to 'provide a basic framework establishing the rights, liabilities and responsibilities of participants in electronic funds transfer systems'. Opinions vary in the UK as to whether this type of legislation is desirable. The US banking situation is admittedly very different from that in the UK and most other Western European countries, but there is a growing feeling, especially amongst bank customers, that legislation will eventually be essential to clarify and protect the interests of EFT users.

Legal problems that arise in EFT transactions[2] can probably be most conveniently examined under four main headings:

1 *Authorization.* The customer's signature has traditionally provided authority for a payment to be made. In the future, however, codewords and personal identification numbers (PINs) will become increasingly important as forms of authorization. In these circumstances there is obviously a danger that unauthorized persons who have been able to obtain access to data will give instructions for payment to be made. This is not a new problem, as signatures have, of course, been obtained by fraud in the past, but the dangers could now be much greater, especially if instantaneous transfers can be made. Unauthorized use of PINs has already produced disputes in ATM withdrawals (see chapter 12) and it seems probable that the number of disputes will increase significantly if there is widespread acceptance of EFTPOS systems. Under present legislation in the UK and most other Western European countries, the customer who cannot provide evidence of negligence will almost certainly be bound by the conditions of use attached to the debit card or other method of authorization. This will usually mean that the customer will have to meet the cost of any unauthorized transaction, although there may be exceptions when loss or other suspicious circumstances are reported to the bank or card issuer. Statutory guidelines would therefore be helpful on this important subject.

2 *Cancellation of instructions.* With a non-guaranteed cheque the authority to pay can be cancelled at any time before presentation. On the other hand, it is by no means clear whether, and if so when, an EFT instruction can be cancelled or reversed. Problems have already arisen with electronic direct debits, although originators have to sign

---

2 A more detailed examination of this subject is contained in R. M. Goode (ed.), *Electronic Banking: The Legal Implications* (Institute of Bankers, 1985).

an undertaking that refunds will be arranged in the case of unauthorized transfers. This type of situation could produce even more problems under an EFTPOS system. For example, what should happen if a customer decides not to proceed with a transaction immediately after a funds transfer has been initiated? Large retailers might arrange a refund to maintain goodwill but could they be compelled to do so? In the USA (*Delbrueck* v. *Manufacturers Hanover Trust*, 1979) it has been held that an instantaneous funds transfer cannot be reversed, even when instructions to cancel the transfer are received within minutes of the payment being made. In the UK (*Momm* v. *Barclays Bank International*, 1977) a slightly different set of circumstances produced the judgement that an overnight computer transfer cannot be reversed the following morning when it is discovered that funds are not available to pay for the transfer. This has produced major problems for the UK banks, which are in most cases not using real-time accounting systems. Clarification as to the precise time when an electronic transfer is considered to be completed would therefore be of great assistance.

3 *Evidence of transactions.* In the past, banks have generally been able to refer to paid cheques as evidence that a transaction has taken place. In the future, however, the provision of evidence will become much more difficult, especially if the courts are reluctant to accept the use of computerized data as satisfactory evidence. Users may also require evidence that a transaction has taken place, and it is interesting to note that the US Electronic Funds Transfer Act has laid down that a proper receipt must be provided for every EFTPOS transaction. It is hoped that all UK customers will be similarly provided, although there will be no legal obligation, at least initially, to supply such a receipt. Providers and users of EFTPOS and other similar systems may therefore face difficulties in providing satisfactory evidence if disputes lead to legal action.

4 *Responsibility for errors.* Existing electronic systems have already shown that payments can be made in excess of the correct amount or transferred to the wrong account. In most situations these matters are settled amicably, especially if there has been an obvious error. There may be situations, however, where it is difficult or impossible to recover a wrongly paid amount. Clarification is also needed regarding liability in respect of loss caused by computer malfunction, interference with data and employee negligence, even though conditions of use frequently attempt to rule out any liability in such situations.

It does seem to be highly desirable, therefore, that payments legislation covering all non-paper transactions should be introduced over the next few years. The United Nations Commission on International Trade Law and many national organizations, e.g. the Office of Fair Trading in the UK, have already expressed concern on this subject, but very little action has been taken by individual governments. The appointment of a bank ombudsman may help in this respect, but it would be much better to have comprehensive legislation, even though it might have to be revised in a few years time. Business and personal users of EFT services should therefore check on the conditions of use attached to these systems as it is by no means impossible that large unauthorized payments might be made, in which case it could be difficult under current legislation to recover anything from the provider of these services.

COMPUTER FRAUD AND SECURITY

One of the great fears of any installer of EFT equipment must be that the introduction of such a system for payment purposes could lead to a substantial increase in computer fraud. In the past, several days have often been available to stop fraudulent cheque payments because of the operation of the clearing system. In the future, however, EFT transactions will be initiated and completed in a very short period, thus leaving far less time for the discovery or cancellation of payments.

Most estimates of the amount of UK computer fraud are in the region of £500 million per annum, of which the banks are believed to bear about £100 million. Insurance policies may cover some of these losses: Lloyd's of London are now prepared to cover electronic and computer crime losses, although premiums can be very high. Unfortunately, most business losses are not reported to the police or other relevant authorities, probably because it is felt that publicity would be damaging. It is also possible that the directors and managers of some businesses may not be certain how a particular fraud occurred and may have fears of it happening again. Non-disclosure appears to be a worldwide problem, although US financial institutions are required to file details of large fraudulent transactions with the Securities and Exchange Commission.

EFT fraud is, of course, only one of many computer fraud possibilities. It could, however, be one of the most dangerous if the system provides the capability to transfer large amounts to domestic or overseas accounts. Very few people have any real idea as to the scale of EFT fraud. It has, however, recently been rumoured that one large UK bank lost £6 million as the result of a data processing employee intercepting and changing EFT messages.[3] These rumours may not be entirely accurate, but they have been widely reported in the UK press.

Television programmes often suggest that the major dangers to computer systems arise from the activities of 'hackers' or other external parties. Practical experience would suggest, however, that most computer fraud arises from the activities of employees – present or past – motivated by greed, anger or revenge. EFT users must therefore try to ensure that proper steps are taken to eliminate or at least reduce the possibilities of internal or external systems interference.

Unauthorized use of EFT systems has been a major problem in recent years for the banks and other financial institutions. This has been particularly evident in ATM transactions,[4] and it could become much worse if EFTPOS systems are eventually extensively used. Most ATM and EFTPOS transactions will, however, be well under £100, although numerous transactions may take place before the fraudulent use of a card is discovered. With business transactions, the dangers may be much greater, as one or two individuals using a terminal may have the power under a corporate cash management system to transfer thousands or even millions of pounds to another account at very short notice. Business organizations are naturally unwilling to reveal fraud of this nature, although it has undoubtedly taken place.

Recognition systems such as finger, hand or voice prints, are available to reduce the possibilities of unauthorized access but these may not yet be completely satisfactory and could be expensive to install. Banks and other business organizations are often reluctant to install expensive security systems because there is very little evidence of widespread fraudulent activity. This evidence may be difficult to put together, however, if fraud is not reported, and in many cases not even discovered. Most businesses are therefore using cheaper and more traditional fraud prevention techniques such as division of responsibilities, use of passwords, identification numbers, etc. There are, however, growing doubts as to whether these measures will be adequate in the case of determined and skilful dishonest employees.

Management must therefore ensure that security receives a high level of priority in EFT installations. The most important aspects of security in these situations can probably be most conveniently examined under three main headings:

---

3 See, for example, R. Adair and S. Jewell, Computer Fraud: Is there Cause for Concern? *Public Finance and Accountancy*, April 1985, p. 27.
4 An interesting study of this subject is contained in *Losing at Cards* (National Consumer Council, 1985).

1 *Physical security*. The aim of this aspect of security must be to minimize, and if possible eliminate, damage to the system by intentional, accidental or natural events. It is essential, therefore, that access to the hardware controlling the system and the terminals used to initiate transactions should be properly controlled. Security measures will probably be in existence before the introduction of EFT systems, but a new consideration of this subject may be desirable if large amounts are likely to be transferred as a result of the use of terminals. In particular, password systems should be examined in depth to ensure that access is restricted to authorized users, whose precise powers and responsibilities should be laid down in some detail.

2 *Staff security*. Unsatisfactory staff can ruin a computer system through carelessness or more deliberate damage. The objective of the personnel security programme should therefore be to restrict or prevent theft, fraud, vandalism or even accidental damage. Recruitment and training are obviously important elements of this process, but there are many influences at work that can turn a satisfactory employee into a computer criminal. Ideally, no one individual should have access to all phases of the data processing operation. The possibility of collusion must not, however, be ruled out. EFT security measures may therefore be very similar to previous computer security measures and individual integrity will become even more important when there is an ability to transfer large sums of money to another account in a matter of seconds.

3 *Communications security*. EFT messages will generally be originated by human action, and it is essential, therefore, that proper message control systems should be installed. This will normally mean that detailed procedures should be laid down for authorization and validation processes, in addition to which precise instructions should be provided regarding message release and delivery. Involvement of a second person in these procedures will generally be highly desirable. The possibility of message interception must also be considered, which could mean that encryption techniques will have to be used. It should be appreciated, however, that these techniques may be of little value in the case of past or present employees unless occasional changes are made in communications security. This will not necessarily defeat present employees, but it could be a deterrent in the case of external parties.

EFT systems will therefore require similar security measures to other computer systems, although more time and money may have to be devoted to these measures when large funds transfers are being made. In these circumstances, particular attention must be devoted to terminal users and security, as it is in this area that the most significant risks are likely to be present.

Audit involvement – internal or external – in EFT systems must also be considered. Sceptics of the value of computer audits often point out that most computer fraud is discovered by accident, for example, through excessive spending or the actions of conspirators, rather than through audit work. The fact that there is an occasional audit may, however, act as a deterrent, in addition to which the more advanced audit firms are now devoting a considerable amount of attention to security systems. The issue of fraud is also of great topical interest, as UK government ministers have recently been considering the possibility of compelling auditors to disclose more information about fraud in major financial institutions.

All types and sizes of organization, as well as private individuals, may therefore be subject to EFT fraud. The dangers are probably greatest in the banking sector, and the Bank of England has recently produced a guide to security and control in computer and telecommunications systems which has been sent to all recognized banks and deposit takers. This document, together with a recent manual produced by the Bank for International Settlements,[5] is intended to alert bank directors and managers to the risks involved in the use of electronic payment systems. In turn, the banks should attempt to provide all EFT users – business and personal – with a clear non-technical statement of the risks incurred in these transactions, as there is little doubt that there is considerable misunderstanding regarding responsibilities if fraud takes place.

EMPLOYMENT OPPORTUNITIES

The long-term effects of EFT systems on employment opportunities are extremely difficult to predict. The major effects will almost certainly be in the banking sector, although it is virtually impossible to separate the influences of EFT systems from other technological developments, e.g. improved paper-based systems, office and counter terminals, word processors, telecommunications services, etc. The retail sector will also be affected by the use of EFT systems, although staffing could be more heavily influenced by other point-of-sale developments such as laser scanning. Outside banking and retailing, there will be some subsidiary

5 *Security and Reliability in Electronic Systems for Payment* (Bank for International Settlements, 1982).

effects, but it may be only in the computer and telecommunications sectors that there is any significant improvement in employment prospects.

Computers have been used in UK banks for over 20 years. In employment terms there has over this period been an increase, rather than a decrease, in the number of staff employed. For example, staff employed on banking duties by the four major clearing banks increased from about 173,000 in 1972 to 231,000 at the end of 1984. In the same period the number of items cleared by the London Clearing Banks increased from 1.5 billion to 3.3 billion. It might therefore be claimed that computers have been major contributory factors in enabling the banks to handle 120 per cent more work over the last 12 years with an increase of only 33 per cent in extra staff. It would be dangerous, however, to attach too much importance to these statistics, as there have been so many different influences affecting the banking sector over the last decade.

Most recent EFT developments have had signficant effects on banking operations. ATMs have probably been among the major influences, as many of the 400 million transactions carried out in 1985 would previously have been dealt with at bank counters. The effect of automated clearing is less obvious, although the CHAPS system could have an effect on future employment with the possible displacement of the 8,000 messengers who are heavily involved with town clearing transactions. EFTPOS and home banking could, however, be even more important influences, although it is extremely difficult to predict the extent of cash and cheque displacement.

The two major UK bank unions, the Banking, Insurance and Finance Union (BIFU) and the Clearing Bank Union (CBU) have over 200,000 members in the banking sector. One of the major concerns of these unions in recent years has been the effect of technology on employment, and several booklets have been published on this subject. In one recent publication,[6] a report by a leading firm of management consultants is quoted which suggests that there is likely to be a reduction of 10 per cent in banking staff in Europe in the second half of the 1980s. There are strong differences of opinion, however, as to whether staff numbers will be reduced over the next few years, and many bankers believe that change will be restricted by growth in the number of customers, shortages of computer skills, resistance by employees and customer inertia.

In Western Europe the banking sector probably employs about 2 million people, with over 500,000 in Germany, nearly 400,000 in France and about 300,000 in Italy and in the UK. In all of these countries there is considerable concern about the effects on EFT systems on employment. In

6 *Microtechnology – a Programme for Action* (Banking, Insurance and Finance Union, 1984), p. 4.

some countries, e.g. Germany, there has been strong union resistance, and as a result several banks have agreed that there will be no compulsory redundancies. It may become increasingly difficult, however, to provide these pledges, as is shown by the recent French suggestion that 10 per cent of bank employees may have to retire or move elsewhere over the next three of four years.[7]

In the retail sector there is less unionization, with many part-time staff employed in shops. The Union of Shop, Distributive and Allied Workers (USDAW), which has about 400,000 members of the 2.2 million employed in the retail sector, has set up a technology working party, and once again several publications have been produced. With such a scattered work force and many different employers, it is difficult to take any concerted action, although the growth enjoyed by many large retailers and the constant turnover of staff has meant that there have, so far, been very few demands for reductions in check-out or other retail staff. The combined effect of laser scanning and funds transfer systems could, however, have a significant effect in the 1990s.

If jobs are eventually lost in banking and retailing as a result of EFT systems, new jobs should be created because of the need for computer staff in the banks and also in manufacturing, distribution and servicing. It has recently been suggested, however, that banks are holding back on computer projects because they cannot find adequately qualified computer personnel.[8] These shortages are mainly in respect of systems analysts and programmers but there is also a shortage of data entry staff in some parts of the country. Ideally, more computer courses and conversion programmes should be provided by educational organizations, although government cutbacks have unfortunately restricted the availability of finance for this type of activity.

It is difficult, therefore, to predict how many jobs will be lost or gained if there is a widespread adoption of EFT systems in the UK and other developed countries over the next decade. Many routine banking and retail jobs will probably be lost, but in their place there should be a substantial demand for computer hardware and software specialists. Anyone with compassion cannot help but be concerned about increasing levels of unemployment, but this problem cannot be solved by ignoring new technology. Banks and retailers must therefore persevere with their EFT plans, although proper employee consultation and in some cases retraining should always be a feature of these programmes.

7 DP Jobs Clash in French Banks, *Banking Technology*, April 1986, p. 11.
8 See, for example, B. Crew, Staffing the Electronic Bank, *Banking Technology*, August 1984, p. 38.

GOVERNMENT INVOLVEMENT

It is very interesting to compare the different approaches of the UK and French governments on technological change, especially in relation to banking services. In the UK there has been little government involvement, with most of the capital being provided by private sources. In France, attitudes have been completely different, with large grants and loans being provided by various government ministries and state-owned organizations. The private sector is also involved, although much of the stimulus, encouragement and finance for change has come from government sources.

The results of these very different policies will probably be best seen in the late 1980s and early 1990s, when at least some of the current plans should have materialized. In France it is expected that by 1990 EFTPOS and home banking systems will be extensively used; these systems will be backed up by large numbers of computer terminals, many of which will have been supplied free of charge, together with a highly sophisticated telecommunications network. On the other hand, the UK will have to rely on private organizations, which may face great difficulties in finding the necessary finance and expertise to set up nationwide systems. Nevertheless, a limited number of EFTPOS and home banking systems are expected to be in operation by 1990, although there may be several highly diversified networks using different types of cards and technological systems.

Large amounts of government assistance do not, however, automatically lead to commercial success, as has been discovered on numerous occasions in the past. These funds can, of course, stimulate new ideas, inventions and systems, but there must be a demand for the product provided. In the early 1990s there seems little doubt that the French will be among the world leaders in the provision of EFT services, but there will have to be a substantial demand in France, and in countries to which these systems have been exported, to justify the costs involved. In the UK there is considerable scepticism about the potential demand for EFTPOS services, and this, reinforced by typical banking conservatism, has delayed developments.

In these circumstances there does seem to be room for more interest and involvement in technological change by the UK government. The present government does, however, appear to be determined to leave most of these matters to the private sector, although grants are available, usually linked to the geographical area in which the company is situated. These have provided assistance for some organizations, but they have not provided the scale and speed of change that French ministers would say is urgently required.

Government assistance should not, however, be restricted to finance. The education and training of personnel with the expertise to play an active part in the manufacture, servicing and administration of EFT systems will be extremely important over the next decade. More electronic engineers and computer specialists will undoubtedly be required, but it will also be essential that accountants, bankers and other management personnel should be able to understand the operation and capabilities of these systems. A joint educational and training initiative by government and the professions is therefore desirable, and this should ideally be accompanied by extensive retraining programmes, which if all goes well will reduce the harmful employment implications contained in the new systems.

Government will also have to consider the need for new legislation covering EFT and other associated systems. The Americans have had legislation of this nature since 1978 and it seems very likely that similar legislation will be required in the UK in the late 1980s. The UK government is determined to restrict unnecessary legislation, but there is little doubt that intervention will eventually be necessary to provide proper protection for business and private users of EFT systems.

It is suggested, therefore, that governments in all developed countries should not stand aside and allow the private sector to bear all the burden of EFT developments, especially those related to finance, tax incentives, education and training, and legal protection. These are, of course, very complex matters in which very few government ministers and civil servants have experience or expertise, but there must at the very least be an interest and involvement with these matters to provide the encouragement and incentives that are so desperately needed.

SUMMARY AND CONCLUSIONS

In the past, far too many technological changes have been embarked upon without a proper consideration of the effects and implications involved in the installation of the appropriate machinery and services. In many respects, EFT systems are typical of other technological changes in that there are important employment and social implications in the adoption of these systems. Banks and other similar interested organizations are, however, in a rather different position from manufacturers in that they are providers of services rather than goods, and it seems probable that EFT systems will be offered, at least initially, as additional rather than replacement services. Consumers will therefore have the ability to make or break the provision of these services; until recently, however, there has been little preparedness to discuss these matters with consumer organizations.

Employees will also have considerable power to hinder progress. Government and business organizations are now beginning to realize the power that programmers, systems analysts and other computer personnel have in the development and operation of computer services. The employment implications of EFT systems will therefore have to be handled very sensitively, especially in the banking sector where there is strong union representation.

Providers of EFT services will also have to pay careful attention to the possibilities of computer fraud. Improved security systems may therefore have to be installed, especially in those situations where large funds transfers are likely to be made. A detailed study should also be made of the appropriate legal regulations and conditions of use, as there is considerable confusion regarding the responsibilities of the parties involved in EFT transactions.

Actual and potential providers and users of EFT services must therefore consider the side-effects of the widespread use of electronic banking systems. Working parties are gradually being set up by interested organizations to consider some of these issues, but there is always a danger that these matters will be pushed into the background until systems are operational. This would be extremely dangerous, as there is little doubt that there could be considerable inconvenience and disruption for interested parties if proper safeguards are not incorporated into planning processes.

18 Payment Systems in the 1990s

In most major trading nations there have been periods in history when very important changes in payment practices have taken place. Probably the most important of these changes in the past have been the provision of coins and bank notes and the introduction of cheques, giro transfers and credit cards. At the time these new methods of settlement were introduced, they may not have seemed to be particularly significant, although over the years they have become an important part of the payment structure of most countries.

It should not be imagined, however, that all new payment methods have proved successful. For example, in the UK the postal giro system has not been as successful as many of its founders hoped, and in Germany and the Netherlands there has not been widespread use of credit cards. It is by no means certain, therefore, that electronic payment methods will be extensively used in the future, although many leading bankers feel that these systems will completely change the whole nature of the payments business over the next 20 years.

This final chapter will be concerned with payment changes that might well materialize before or during the 1990s. It is not expected that all of these predictions will be fulfilled, but at the very least they should provide the reader with a feeling of the changes that are currently conceivable. Revolutionary developments could, of course, take place over the next decade, and these could completely change existing ideas, but the conservative nature of the providers and users of payment systems will probably restrict the possibilities of rapid change. Judgement must, of course, be deferred until the twenty-first century, by which time it is extremely likely that the backward thoughts of 1986 will have been completely forgotten!

There seems little doubt that over the next decade the banking sector will become much more diversified, with the provision of an increasing range of financial services. In the USA, deregulation of the banking sector will almost certainly lead to a substantial decrease in the number of operating banks, as a result of which the major banks will probably become much larger and more powerful. American influences will also be felt in Western Europe, where banking power has traditionally been concentrated in the hands of a small number of large national banks. Government action could maintain this situation, although it seems likely that banking will become increasingly international, with the ability to transfer funds quickly and effectively to most parts of the world. Banking is therefore likely to become a much more competitive business in the 1990s, especially in those countries where there is little or no protection for the domestic banking sector.

It may also be found that an increasing number of organizations which have not traditionally provided banking facilities will begin to offer a limited range of payment services. In the UK, building societies will probably provide an increasing range of services; these facilities, together with the provision of attractive interest rates on all types of accounts, could damage the traditional providers of money transfer services. Some retailers may also begin to provide limited banking services, although it seems unlikely that their presence will be felt as much in Europe as in the USA, where the fragmented banking system has enabled a few powerful retailers and oil companies to gain a significant part of the payments business, especially in the plastic card sector.

Increasing competition over the next few years will almost inevitably lead to a review of many traditional banking practices. More current accounts will be provided with interest payment facilities, and in those cases where interest is not paid, current account balances may fall to very low levels. Margins on bank lending are therefore likely to fall, and this will obviously put pressure on the bank charging structure, which has traditionally been heavily subsidized by non-interest-bearing funds. The banks may, however, find it difficult to impose higher charges because of greater competition, although differential charges are likely to be introduced to encourage movement from expensive paper-based systems to cheaper electronic transactions.

The move towards interest-bearing accounts will probably be accompanied by more readily available information concerning bank balances and recent transactions. On-line counter terminals will be installed in most branches, with cashiers and customers being able to obtain immediate account information, and real-time accounting processes could be introduced if there is sufficient customer demand. Instantaneous transfers to the accounts of other businesses or individuals should become widely available, although there will almost inevitably be extra charges for this type of service. The whole money transfer process should therefore be speeded up, provided that customers are prepared to pay the appropriate charges.

Banking may also become much less reliant on the branch system, with an increasing number of businesses and private individuals receiving bank data and giving payment instructions at the home or office. By the mid-1990s the number of computer terminals in the home will have increased very dramatically, and some of the major banks will probably decide to enter the home information business. As a result, we may have to accept that a wide range of banking services will be 'sold' on television, although there will be some resistance to these developments from those who prefer traditional banking practices.

Bank customers and employees must therefore prepare for a decade of change in which many long-accepted banking ideas will be cast aside. Personal service will still be available at a cost, but customers may have to travel longer distances to obtain this type of service. Many existing branches will be closed or converted into self-service establishments, and the buildings that are no longer required for payment services could be used for marketing a much more extensive range of bank facilities, e.g. insurance, share purchase and sale, property transactions, etc. The computer-oriented customer who is prepared to initiate transactions from the home or office may not be disturbed by these developments, but there is little doubt that those who prefer personal service will find it difficult to obtain the standard of service that was available in the 1970s. It should not be imagined, however, that banking will be the only area of change in the 1990s, as by then many of us will be working at home with the aid of the latest telecommunications devices. It remains to be seen whether this is regarded as an exciting or frightening prospect!

UK DEVELOPMENTS

It has already been suggested that the cashless society is a long way off, but it does seem probable that by the mid-1990s the number of cash transactions will have been significantly reduced from the 1985 figure of approximately 60 billion. In the UK this may mean that the number of cash payments will fall from well over 90 per cent to less than 80 per cent of all transactions, although cash will still be extensively used for small purchases. In addition, the 'black economy' may still be flourishing, especially if tax rates are increased to compensate for the effects of lost oil revenue.

The major hope for a substantial reduction in cash transactions will probably rest on the memory card or an equivalent electronic store of value. These cards have already been adopted for use in some telephone booths and they could be extensively used in the future for prepayments in respect of electricity and gas supplies, parking charges, bus and train fares, and even retail purchases. Many problems will have to be overcome before there is widespread acceptance of those cards (cost of cards and terminals, life, durability, etc.) but there are real prospects of a breakthrough in this direction.

Cheque usage will probably continue to increase in the late 1980s, largely because of growth in the number of personal and business customers. The rate of growth may, however, slow down to less than 3 per cent per annum. During the early 1990s, usage may stabilize or even fall as private customers settle an increasing number of retail and service accounts by electronic transfer methods. Central and local government, nationalized industries, and commercial and industrial organizations will also make much greater use of electronic methods for payment purposes.

The preparedness of business organizations and some private individuals to move away from cheques as a form of settlement will almost inevitably be influenced by the built-in delay period that is available to payers through the bank clearing process. By the late 1990s, truncation methods under which cheque data are captured at the paying-in point and transmitted electronically may be in widespread use, and this, together with the use of various electronic communication processes, could reduce bank clearing periods very significantly. Reduction of the traditional two- or three-day clearing period could remove some of the inherent objections to electronic settlement methods, but postal delays will still be important, together with the rates of interest that can be earned from surplus funds or reduced overdrafts.

The BACS and CHAPS organizations will have a major part to play in the growth of EFT transactions in the UK in the 1990s. BACS services will be used for the vast majority of credit transfers, standing orders and direct debits, and great pressure will be put on private individuals to pay regular commitments by direct debit. Business and government organizations may still be reluctant to pay by direct debit, although the use of automated credit transfers will be much more widespread than it is today. This will also apply to government benefits, although there may be considerable resistance from the poor and elderly to non-cash methods of payment.

CHAPS services will be extensively used for large payments made at short notice, and the labour-intensive town clearing system will probably be closed down.

Credit card growth will continue into the 1990s, with retail cards becoming a much more important part of the card market. Banks may attempt to impose charges on credit card issue or renewal, and this could lead to a significant fall in the number of bank cards in circulation. This should not, however, lead to any substantial loss in the overall amount of business, although much will depend on the charge that is levied. The most important changes in this sector will probably be in card authorization and processing, which will be largely handled by electronic communication processes. This should lead to a reduction in paperwork and fraud, although the more sophisticated criminal will almost inevitably continue to create major problems.

The biggest change in payment practices over the next decade could, of course, be provided by EFTPOS transactions. It is extremely difficult, however, to predict how retailers and consumers will react to these new methods of payment. EFTPOS pioneers have received encouragement through the widespread acceptance of ATM transactions – about 40 per cent of UK personal account-holders now make regular use of cash dispensing machines – although these machines perpetuate the use of cash which many bankers wish to discourage. By the early 1990s, ATM expenditure will probably be largely restricted to replacement machines, as the number of installations reaches saturation point. Substantial expenditure will, however, be required if the EFTPOS system appeals to the general public.

Official bank estimates produced in 1985 suggested that EFTPOS transactions should reach 500 million in 1991. This figure does, however, include automated credit card transfers, which are likely to be more popular than debit card payments. Preparedness to pay by means of an instantaneous or end-of-day bank transfer may be strongly influenced by the discounts, if any, offered for settlement in this form. Bank estimates could therefore turn out to be fairly accurate if discounts are offered, although opposition to this policy could mean that an overall total of 300 million transactions will be more realistic, perhaps made up of about 240 million credit card transfers and 60 million debit card payments. By the end of the 1990s these figures could be doubled or even trebled, especially if arguments about the comparative merits of magnetic stripe and memory card technology are statisfactorily resolved.

The prospects for home and office banking are even more problematical, as growth will depend on the preparedness of private individuals and business personnel to use computers and electronic communication processes. Developments could therefore be disappointingly slow initially, and the banks might well decide to sell these services to customers as part of an extensive range of home information facilities. In the business sector, the demand for office banking and corporate cash management services may be largely restricted to large and medium-sized organizations, although this type of activity could generate a substantial volume of business. By the end of the 1990s, however, far more individuals will be 'computer-literate', and one might expect a rapidly increasing demand for these services from 1995 onwards, especially if cable and satellite links are extensively used.

By the mid and late 1990s, therefore, a table showing methods of payment will look very different from the position that existed in the mid-1980s (see table 1.2, p. 5). The overall number of transactions will probably not have increased very significantly, but there will almost certainly have been a large increase in electronic transfers, with the possibility of a total approaching 10 billion transactions by the end of the century as compared with less than 5 billion cheques and other paper-based transactions. This would still leave about 50 billion cash payments with plenty of room for progress towards a 'less-cash' society in the twenty-first century.

HARDWARE AND SOFTWARE PROBLEMS

Estimates of UK capital expenditure on EFT systems over the next decade tend to vary between £200 million and £500 million, which is obviously good news for the providers of computer terminals, telecommunications systems and associated equipment. It seems probable, however, that many orders will go to American and Japanese businesses, which have the finance, production and marketing expertise to produce and sell their equipment and services in many different parts of the world. This is illustrated by the fact that IBM has already been appointed one of the initial suppliers of equipment for the proposed UK national EFTPOS service.

It will not be an easy task, however, to supply new equipment in line with the specifications and installation dates laid down by banks, retailers, and other organizations. Problems often arise with new technological developments, as has already been shown in countries such as Singapore, where initial EFT installations did not work entirely satisfactorily. Computer manufacturers also have the problem that they are not usually responsible for telecommunications networks, which are sometimes unable to handle an unexpectedly high volume of transactions. In the UK, IBM and British Telecom are working together in the overall provision of services for the proposed EFTPOS scheme, and this, it is hoped, will resolve most of the major installation problems.

Security and reliability of EFT systems have already been considered in previous chapters. EFT suppliers must be very much aware that one or two disastrous experiences with fraud or breakdown could destroy confidence and set back developments for several years. Nevertheless, it is extremely doubtful whether these problems will be completely avoided in the UK and other developed countries, and pessimists are already predicting large-scale payment breakdowns and fraudulent transactions at some time in the early years of EFTPOS operation.

Software problems are also likely to arise. Costs are often underestimated, with the amount spent on programming new developments frequently exceeding the costs of the associated hardware. Programming procedures are also becoming more complex, and this may mean that more programmers will have to be recruited in a market where good personnel are in very short supply. Heavy reliance on computer personnel can, of course, be dangerous, as several UK government departments have found out recently when pay disputes led to disruptive action.

In many small and medium-sized companies it will be difficult or impossible to obtain the necessary equipment and expertise because of financial constraints and shortages of skilled personnel. Computer bureaux are therefore likely to benefit as more businesses install EFT systems. This has already become very clear in the provision of computer-input material for BACS. The bureaux are also suffering from shortages of qualified personnel, although the larger organizations are generally capable of training their own staff.

Computer and telecommunications suppliers are therefore likely to experience considerable demands for EFT equipment over the next decade. Nobody has any idea, however, as to the likely scale of demand, or whether domestic businesses will be given any preference over international suppliers. In the UK it must be hoped that the private sector responds to these challenges, as it seems unlikely that the government will be prepared to provide substantial financial support for the research and development required for these processes.

PREPARATION FOR CHANGE

Business payers and payees have for many years been accustomed to a situation in which cash and paper-based systems have been the major forms of payment. This situation is changing very rapidly, and substantial savings are now available for organizations prepared to use electronic systems.

Business payments have for many years been dominated by the cheque system. In recent years there has, however, been a small but increasing awareness of the costs attached to cheque preparation, despatch and bank services. Electronic payment systems have the potential to reduce most of these costs. Some payers feel, however, that the cost savings could be wiped out as a result of interest lost through earlier payment, although the importance of this matter naturally declines as interest rates fall. Unfortunately, very few organizations have carried out a detailed study of costs and benefits, and this must be one of the priorities attached to the introduction of electronic systems.

Payers must also become fully familiar with the range of services provided by BACS. Numerous publications and visual aids are now available regarding the operation of the BACS system; these should be readily obtainable through all major bank branches. Highly sophisticated computer equipment is no longer essential, as most efficient computer bureaux will produce input material. Payers may be hesitant about paying large bills in this form, in which case cheques could still be used for payments over £1,000 or other appropriate amount.

A detailed examination of the costs of different payment methods usually shows that cash and cheque payments cost at least two to three times as much as electronic payments. The BACS settlement system should therefore be seriously considered by all business payers, except for those who do not have a sufficient volume of activity to justify its use. Most salaries are now paid by electronic transfer, but little movement has taken place on purchase ledger accounts. More wage payments should be made in this form, especially now that telecommunications processes can be used for BACS input purposes. Numerous other smaller payment applications should also be considered, e.g. expenses, pensions, interest, dividends, etc. There is considerable potential, therefore, for many more business and government payments to be made by electronic transfer, although there will inevitably be resistance by some private individuals, such as recipients of wages and government benefits, to this method of payment.

Business payers should also become familiar with the CHAPS and SWIFT services for urgent payments in respect of domestic and international transactions. In the larger organization these may be combined with corporate card management systems which can provide valuable information on worldwide cash balances, exchange rates and other relevant data. In the past, many urgent payments have had to be arranged by telephone or telex, and this has often been a time-consuming and expensive process. The newer electronic systems should provide a quicker and more efficient service.

In those situations where receipts are dominated by cheque settlements, careful consideration should be given to the practicability of introducing direct debits through the BACS system. Incentives may have to be offered by less powerful organizations for settlement in this form, but benefits could still be very significant. More opportunities may be available if businesses are dealing with private individuals. The potential savings in this area have in the past been badly neglected by central and local government, nationalized industries, professional bodies, charities, credit and hire purchase companies, building societies and many other similar organizations.

Retailers have, of course, found it difficult to move away from cash transactions. In the future it will be essential that research is carried out to ascertain the costs involved in cash receipts, storage, security, transport, insurance, bank charges, etc. These costs will not necessarily be proportionately reduced if cash receipts fall by, say 10 per cent, but there should be an awareness of the costs attached to different methods of payment so that a proper assessment can be made of alternative settlement practices.

EFTPOS and home banking cannot, of course, be properly costed at present as national systems have not yet been introduced, but retail directors and accountants should already be studying the potential costs and benefits. The scale of usage will in the long term be an essential component of these calculations, as there may be little point in installing EFTPOS systems if only 1 per cent of customers use this facility. Large retailers should therefore be carrying out some consumer research to establish probable consumer reactions to automated debit and credit card transactions.

At the very least, therefore, business payers and payees should be acquiring reasonable knowledge of current EFT payment systems together with an awareness of probable future developments. This should ideally be combined with information regarding current costs for paper-based and electronic systems including a full appreciation of bank charges for all types of payments. Armed with this information, directors, accountants and treasurers should be well prepared for the changes to come.

SUMMARY AND CONCLUSIONS

The payment systems of most developed countries will by the end of the current century still be dominated by cash transactions, especially for small retail payments. There will, however, have been a substantial movement towards electronic transfers, which in the UK could make up between 10 and 15 per cent of all payments and considerably more than 50 per cent of non-cash payments. Electronic payment services will be provided by several organizations, although BACS facilities will be extremely popular, especially for credit transfers arranged by business and government organizations, and direct debits paid by private individuals. The CHAPS and SWIFT systems will also be extensively used, mainly for large and medium-sized payments which have to be made at short notice.

The EFTPOS and home banking developments of the late 1980s and early 1990s should by the end of the 1990s be getting established and it should be possible to make a much more detailed assessment of retailer and consumer reactions. The number of credit card transactions will probably be at least 100 per cent greater than 1986 figures, with a large part of the accounting data being processed by electronic communication methods. On the other hand, consumer reactions to debit cards and home banking may not be as favourable as the banks and other interested parties hoped, although there seems little doubt that a significant minority of the population will welcome these developments. It remains to be seen, however, whether there will be enough debit card usage to justify the substantial capital costs that will need to be incurred if a national system is introduced.

The cashless society will therefore be a long way off by the end of the 1990s, and the banks may by then have some regrets about the widespread availability of ATM and rapid cash tills with continuous cash withdrawal facilities. There will, however, be a 'less-cash' society, as increasing use is made of electronic payment facilities. Business organizations and private individuals must therefore prepare for a decade of rapid change, as there is little doubt that cash and paper-based systems will become increasingly expensive as we move into an era of electronic money.

Index

Access credit card 43, 46, 47, 52, 53, 55, 56, 57, 58, 62, 171
American Express credit card 43, 45, 46, 50
Anglia Building Society 164–5
Association for Payment Clearing Services (APACS) 18, 32
Australia 140, 162
automated clearing houses (ACHs) 72–3
automated teller machines (ATMs) 15, 138–48, 207, 210, 213, 227
Automobile Association 91

bank charges 26–9, 40, 78, 83, 106
bank clearing 18–19
Bank of England 13, 22
Bank of Scotland 142, 182, 188–9
Barclaycard 43, 45, 46, 48, 52, 56, 57, 58, 61, 63, 171
Barclays Bank 14, 27, 29, 61, 141, 142, 163, 171, 190, 200
Belgium 32, 160–1
bills of exchange 2
British Telecom 80, 166, 178
building society payments 17, 96, 97, 98–100, 101

Canada 2, 140, 160, 184
cash
  dispensing machines 14–15, 138–48,
  payments 1, 4, 5, 8–10, 12
  user viewpoints 10–14
central government payments 104, 128–37

Chemical Bank 181, 185, 201
cheque
  guarantee card 29–31
  payments 1, 2, 4, 5, 9, 12, 17–33
  truncation 32
  users 24–6
Citibank 44, 144, 201, 202
Clearing House Automated Payments System (CHAPS) 23, 65, 68, 69, 79–82, 196, 198, 225, 227
Clydesdale Bank 154, 163–4
consumer interests 55, 146, 156, 157, 204–6
Co-operative Bank 28, 46, 142
credit cards 3, 4, 5, 12, 43–64, 168–80
credit clearing 36–8
credit transfers 4, 9, 34–42, 77

Debenhams 9, 44
Denmark 161, 183
Department of Health & Social Security (DHSS) 136
Diners Club credit card 43, 45, 46, 50
direct debit agreements 2, 77, 88–103

electronic cash management services 194–203
electronic funds transfers at the point-of-sale (EFTPOS) 63, 149–67, 207, 208, 215, 222, 226
electronic funds transfer systems (EFT) 1, 5, 6, 66–8
employment implications 212–14
encryption techniques 199, 211

Eurocheque card 3, 31, 140

Finland 186
France 2, 6, 113, 140, 154, 160, 175, 184, 186, 213
fraud 30, 58–61, 81, 147–8, 209–12, 215

general clearing 19–22
Germany 2, 3, 113, 140, 161, 176, 186, 213, 218
government benefits 128–37
government involvement 13, 14, 215–16

Halifax Building Society 142, 147
hardware problems 223–4
home and office banking 70, 181–92
Hong Kong 140, 162

Inter-Bank Research Organization (IBRO) 9, 134
Italy 2, 176, 213

Japan 2, 140, 161–2, 176, 181, 184, 186

laser cards 178
laser scanning 149
legal implications 114–15, 206–9
life assurance payments 95, 96, 98–100, 101
Lloyds Bank 29, 46, 75, 124, 141, 142, 147, 190, 200
local government payments 96–7, 104, 128

magnetic stripe cards 169–72
Marks and Spencer 44, 62, 124
Mastercard 46, 51, 154, 176
memory cards 63, 70, 172–7
Midland Bank 27, 46, 141, 142, 165, 171, 184, 187–8, 200
Monopolies and Mergers Commission 48, 49, 52, 57, 58

National Federation of Sub-Postmasters 132, 133
National Girobank 4, 27, 35, 46, 68, 72, 82–4, 121, 129, 142, 147

National Westminster Bank 27, 31, 36, 46, 141, 142, 165, 200
Netherlands 2, 3, 184
New Zealand 140, 162
Norway 161, 171
Nottingham Building Society 182, 187

Office of Fair Trading (OFT) 206, 209

personal identification number (PIN) 139, 151, 159, 170, 172, 207
petrol cards 45
point-of-sale transactions 149–67
postal orders 2, 4
Prestel 183–4, 187, 188
purchase ledger payments 104–11

Retail Consortium 152
Royal Bank of Scotland 142

Singapore 140, 162
Smiths Industries 107
social security payments 129–31, 135
Society for Worldwide Interbank Financial Telecommunication (SWIFT) 84–5, 196, 198, 225, 227
software problems 223–4
Spain 2, 140, 161
standing orders 35, 77, 98–100
store cards 44
Sweden 2
Switzerland 2, 161

Tesco Stores 62
Thailand 162
town clearing 22–3
trades unions 5, 6, 120, 213
transaction telephones 59, 60, 160, 169, 170
travel and entertainment cards 44
travellers cheques 3
Truck Acts 114–15
Trustcard 46, 52
Trustee Savings Bank 142, 147

United States of America (USA) 2, 3, 6, 113, 139, 152, 159–60, 170–1, 176, 181, 184, 193, 219 utility billing 97

viewdata systems 182, 183, 188

Visa credit card 46, 51, 154

Wages and salaries payments 112–27